Don't Run Naked Through The Office

Your GUIDE TO SURVIVING IN ANY WORKPLACE ENVIRONMENT

written by

Fred Stawitz

StoryMakers, Inc.

First published in 2014 by

STORYMAKERS, INC.
P.O. Box 91338
Houston, Texas 77291-1338
www.storymakersinc.com

From a Declaration of Principles Jointly Adopted by a Committee of the American Bar Association and a Committee of Publishers and Associations

ISBN: 978-0-9888079-0-7

Printed in the United States of America

Dedicated to
the millions of people who are
frustrated with their jobs and feel
hopeless to do anything about it.

May this book provide the guidance
they need to take control of their
careers and create a happy,
prosperous future for
themselves and
their families.

Table of Contents

Acknowledgements

Let me thank my family for their steadfast interest and support in helping bring this book into being. They represent the foundations upon which all of my accomplishments are built. My wife Dolores Colunga-Stawitz provided comments, suggestions, encouragement, and a lengthy string of relevant articles which she printed and lovingly laid upon my desk for my review. She also shared personal experiences which reinforce several of the concepts presented in these pages. Let me also recognize the selfless commitment of our dogs and cats who tirelessly took turns napping on the floor, the desk or my lap in quiet support of my labors at the keyboard. I remain confident that they placed their furry little bodies in front of the door in an effort to thwart any attempt at escape that I might have contemplated before each writing session produced something of substance.

I confidently believe that you would not be reading these words if not for the support of many friends and colleagues who gave of their valuable time to read and reread these pages in an effort to identify and suggest thoughtful improvements. I gratefully acknowledge the contributions of Kelley Hicks, Derek Davidson, Amy Livingston, Felicia Mendygral, Katie Stroud, Jacinta Sole, Jessica High, Ariella Furman, Kiara Craft, Veronica Kirkland, Jeffrey Kolb, Mary Jane Black, Milind Pataskar, Janie Munoz, Ruda Chimhanda, Ross Buckner, Donie Nelson, Patt Healy, Debbie Richards, and the wonderful lady who suggested during a chance conversation as we both waited in line for an employment event that an expert job recruiter and I might benefit from meeting each other. Who would have known how right she was. I trust that even those who are not listed here but provided guidance and support know how much I honor and appreciate them.

I would also like to recognize two professionals who guided me in the right direction even before the idea of writing a book twinkled in my brain. Judy Juneau, my colleague in arms at the Topeka Public Schools Alternative Education Program, fastidiously reviewed my fifteen-page, single-spaced essay application for NASA's Teacher In Space Program. In helping me to rewrite the lengthy application, she patiently showed me how to recognize good grammar from bad. While my application to be the first teacher in space did not succeed, her kind tutelage did guide me toward developing the ability to edit my own material. Cheryl Halpern, my business communications instructor at Washburn University, educated me in the importance of considering the audience who would consume the words I was committing to paper. While tolerating my eccentric sense of humor that often accompanied me to class, she steadfastly reinforced attention to how well the message of my writing was being conveyed. I offer my sincere appreciation to these two fine individuals for their contribution to my literary development.

Some of the stories contained in this book were provided by an expert job recruiter and consultant with 25 years of experience in placing top candidates. He has interviewed thousands of individuals and has heard every reason why people leave their jobs. He kindly contributed a number of these stories to this book. While I would like to thank all of you who experienced these tales of woe personally, let it suffice to say that you know who you are. But you can be assured that your collective experiences have helped influenced the direction this work has taken.

While it is easy to recall the few individuals I encountered during my career with superior management skills, I struggle to find a way to acknowledge the contribution of the many bosses who demonstrated ineffective ways to manage people. Thanks may not be an entirely appropriate way to recognize their contribution to this book.

Although most of the bosses that I have seen up close and personal during the past several decades may not be the cream of this distasteful crop, they were sufficiently rich in their misguided pursuits to fester in my memory until the idea of writing about them surfaced in my consciousness. While subordinated to their authority, I relished nothing more than to escape the punitive non-supportive environments they fostered.

Now, however, I must acknowledge that they, too, were part of the compendium of life experiences that have led me to where I am today. Were it not for them, I may have not had this opportunity to share with you the wisdom I have gleaned from my close encounters with them. I wish them all well and hope they will someday see a more benevolent path forward.

And I hope for you, the reader, that the words you are about to read will assist you in dealing with such bosses and guide you in creating a successful path through each of the four types of workplace environments you may encounter during your career.

CHAPTER 1

Taking Charge of Your Professional Life

If you are unsatisfied with your job, you are not alone. However, you may be running through the office naked if you don't know how to leverage some control and how to protect yourself from unscrupulous bosses. With this book, we will provide you the guidance you need to take control of your career.

Engagement

The Gallup Management Journal's semi-annual "Employee Engagement Index" reveals in their most recent survey that only 29 percent of employees 18 or older in the United States are actively engaged in their jobs, 54 percent are not engaged, and 17 percent are actively disengaged. Given the increased stresses placed on the workplace by a dysfunctional economy and the increased threat of unemployment, many workers may have simply adjusted to the reality that having any job is better than the alternative. If workplace happiness and engagement in your job equate, and we believe that they do, this means that you have slightly over a one-in-four chance of being happy with your current situation. While better than your odds of returning from Las Vegas a millionaire, these odds are still not desirable indeed.

We boldly suggest that the "Employee Engagement Index" categories map closely with the four workplace environments that we will introduce within these pages.

This means that approximately:

- 15 percent of employees work in Antagonistic Environments
- 55 percent of employees work in Contentious or Benign Environments
- 30 percent of employees work in Supportive Environments

It would seem reasonable that the characteristics which foster employee engagement have some tangible relationship with a Supportive Environment while those characteristics that foster non-engagement bear a connection to the non-supportive environments.

The Gallup Organization estimates that the 17 percent of employees who are actively disengaged from their jobs costs the United States economy from $300 to $350 billion a year with these figures holding fairly steady since 2002. This is why it is difficult to understand how corporate executives can justify fostering or even tolerating non-supportive environments in which the ability to retain experienced workers is severely compromised. The truth is that no one has asked them to justify this. Certainly, if the shareholders were to demand a study of such practices, many corporate executives might receive a personal introduction to the concept of outsourcing once the study's results were revealed.

Regardless of the reason that causes some bosses to cling to working environments that stifle productivity, what does all this mean for you? We review these issues here because it is important for you to understand the current climate as this is where your career rises or falls. We also want you to realize that the pervasiveness of non-supportive environments simply means that changing jobs is not likely to solve your problem.

What You Will Learn

The good news is that this book will place at your disposal a set of tools to help tilt the playing field in your favor. We will explain the benefits of a Supportive Environment, the failings of a non-supportive environment, and teach you to accurately categorize your workplace environment as Supportive, Benign, Contentious or Antagonistic. You will learn why it is important to pace your activities in a non-supportive environment as you will not receive the level of support you need to sustain true peak performance. You will also learn that your best means of being successful in a non-supportive environment is to fill the support gap that inherently exists in that type of environment by drawing aggressively upon every resource at your disposal.

Additionally, you will become familiar with many of the techniques that a boss in a non-supportive environment may employ against you. Equally important, you will find out how to avoid falling victim to them. This may sound like combat and to some degree it is. Know that your boss may fight dirty. You must fight smart. Your boss may use tricks, deceit, and lies. You must rely on truth. Your boss may be obnoxiously stubborn. You must be persistent. There are no guarantees of success in this conflagration for it is not a battle from which you or your boss can emerge victorious by defeating the adversary. Even if your boss succeeds in expelling you from the organization, she has not won. She has only succeeded in alienating everyone who saw you as a valued colleague and an asset to the organization. She is destined to face an unending string of adversaries since that is what her behavior produces.

In a non-supportive environment, your boss is fighting for control since realistically she lost it when she chose not to foster a Supportive Environment. You, however, are fighting for the opportunity to be a productive member of the organization. Whose struggle is easier to justify?

Even so, you face an ongoing battle to succeed and you must be prepared to fight the good fight every day with nothing more than your skills, your intellect, and your Workplace Survival Plan which pulls together all the resources you have at your disposal.

Your Source of Motivation

But what are you really fighting for? A job? A paycheck? A successful career? More likely you are fighting for what a job, a paycheck, and a successful career would bring to you and your family. You are fighting for whatever it is that motivates you to keep showing up at work every working day in spite of the challenges your working environment places upon you.

It is essential for you to clearly identify what motivates you to keep up the fight. This is the engine that will drive you to sustain a high level of performance and a positive relationship with your workplace environment regardless of what occurs around you. It is the fuel that powers you through the frustration in your quest for success.

Different people have different views of success. You must determine how you define success. Attributes which people commonly affiliate with success in the workplace include:

- Happiness
- Self-satisfaction
- Financial security
- Quality of life

You may have already asked yourself some or all of the following questions: Am I happy with the job I have now? Do I leave work each day with a sense of satisfaction for what I have accomplished? Has my job provided me and my family a sense of financial security and made a positive contribution to our quality of life? Your answers to these questions provide an overall indication of your satisfaction with your workplace experience but we ask that you take it a step further. Are happiness and self-satisfaction your primary drivers? If so, ask yourself what makes me happy? What drives my self-satisfaction? If financial security is most important to you, ask yourself these questions: Do I want a hefty salary? How much wealth do I have to accumulate to consider myself successful? How will I know when I have achieved financial security? Both the questions and the answers must come from you.

Knowing what really motivates you is valuable knowledge to have as it puts the power of evaluating your success in your hands. Your sense of success is, and should be, entirely independent of the company and your manager. It is a determination you make based on whatever criteria you deem to be important. You set your goals, you determine your measures of success, and you evaluate the results but it does not end there. Success is a moving target and any individual assessment of it is merely a snapshot. Your idea of success may very well evolve as your career develops.

Valid Sources of Feedback

What is important in any assessment of your of success is that you utilize valid sources of feedback. The ranting of a boss who would just as soon fire you as sneeze, the opining of one who perpetuates failure at your expense and that of shareholders, or even the musings of a boss who has never seen you in action are not valid sources of feedback. Any assessment of your performance provided by your boss in a non-supportive environment should always be considered suspect. While your boss and other detractors may not provide valid feedback regarding your performance as they often represent a tainted view of your efforts, it is still useful to give their views some consideration. It is up to you to sort out what is valid criticism from the garbage. The danger lies in giving the garbage more weight than it deserves.

In a Supportive Environment, you can take any feedback you receive from your manager to the bank. Frequently, it will be couched in terms of constructive suggestions that are intended to help you improve. You can learn a lot about yourself from a manager who partners with you in your professional development. Still it is up to you to determine what course of action will keep you on your path to success.

Other valid sources of feedback include friends and co-workers whose opinions you value even though their observations may be slightly biased in your favor. All positive or all negative feedback is not as helpful as a balance between doing well and room for improvement. Your friends and supporters are less likely to exaggerate negative feedback. However, it is important to determine whether they are providing you an overly rosy picture. While they may skew their comments in a positive direction, they will more often than not refrain from giving you bad news as opposed to lying about it.

By contrast, we have seen bosses in non-supportive environments not only embellish but flat out fabricate negative comments. In the final analysis, you must judge for yourself whether your boss or your detractors have any valid points at all. We would recommend putting more weight on the comments you receive from your supporters as they have shown to have your best interests at heart.

Ultimately, you must consider and weigh all feedback you receive to generate an accurate, objective assessment of your success. You must judge for yourself how close or distant you are from your goals and whether you are moving in the right direction. It is, admittedly, challenging to reflect objectively on your own activities, accomplishments, and expectations, particularly in the heat of a non-supportive environment but you are best positioned to make the call.

If you feel that you are achieving success in your current situation then you have no reason to alter significantly what you are doing unless you see room for improvement. If success has proven to be an elusive commodity, then you may want to consider some type of change.

Risks of Flight

You must be aware that there are risks associated with leaving your current job. In addition to the time and effort it takes to find a new job while at the same time losing an important source of income. The fact is you may not be in a position to quit. Plus, you have no guarantee that your next job will be in a better environment. We can infer from the Gallup Management Journal's survey that you may be equally disappointed with your next workplace environment. The plain fact is that most jobs are to be found in non-supportive environments where turnover is bound to be high. You could ask the hiring manager before accepting an offer but how many of them are going to answer honestly: No, I'm sorry we don't believe in Supportive Environments and have no desire to change just for you.

I cannot tell you the number of clients who confided in me how extremely bad their bosses were only to realize, once they had found a new job, that the new boss was even worse. Some people are subconsciously attracted to a non-supportive environment in the same manner that other people are attracted to abusive relationships. As sad as it may seem, that is the type of environment where they feel most comfortable and, therefore, the one to which they gravitate.

Plus, what guarantee do you have that the hiring manager in a Supportive Environment will recognize you as a good candidate for her team. Ask yourself. Do I have any experience working in a Supportive Environment? Can I take responsibility and run with it? Could I actually function in a truly Supportive Environment or am I too accustomed to the myriad of distractions present in a non-supportive environment? Be honest with yourself. In a Supportive Environment, the focus is on productive work, not looking busy or jumping through hoops contrived by your boss.

Unless you face a serious issue of ethics, integrity or legal concerns or you have the next step in your career ladder within easy reach, we do not recommend approaching the decision to leave your current job without giving it serious consideration. Employees who are dissatisfied at work often believe that no one that can do their jobs as well as they do. I should just quit and see how much the company will miss me when I'm gone is a common but misguided refrain.

Just the other day, a colleague related the following story to me. He said that a man, who was fed up with the antics of his boss had left the company about a year before. It was a knee-jerk reaction that he now regrets. Having invited his friends and former colleagues out to lunch, he was offering his advice sadly based on personal experience.

The man reveals to all in attendance that there is a way to tell how much the company will miss you when you leave. This could be a useful thing to know, I thought to myself as my colleague began the following story. A few skeptics speak up. They doubt that such a method exists. The man confidently explains that this is one of those tried and true methods passed down from generation to generation and furthermore he had never known it to fail. Everyone draws quiet in anticipation.

"Get a coffee cup and fill it with water," he tells one of the younger hands. "It works best if it's full."

The young man quickly sets a cup of water in front of the man.

"Be careful not to bump the cup or create any kind of waves on the surface of the water," the man explains as he pauses momentarily to look at the young man, "Then carefully stick your index finger in the water if you've been on the job for less than five years. If you've got ten years or more put two fingers in the water."

The young man carefully sinks his index finger into the glass.

"Wait for a moment till the surface of the water settles, then, and this part is really important," he pauses briefly to make sure he has everyone's attention. "Quickly pull your finger out of the water."

The young man jerks his finger up and away from the glass of water. Confused he comments, "What's that supposed to do?"

"You missed it?" the man queries the young man. "OK, do it again only this time I'll time how long it takes for the water to fill in where your finger was 'cause that will let you know how long the company will miss you when you leave."

The young man blushes with embarrassment knowing the joke is on him.

You may think the company cannot do without you. Think again. Whether the company cannot do without you is not even up for consideration. The point is they will do without you. Only your true friends will genuinely miss you when you leave. A boss in a non-supportive environment will view your departure as freedom from the pain you caused in her backside. That is why your resignation should never be about what will hurt or cause remorse amongst those you leave behind. If you choose this path, a resignation should always be tempered with what is in your best interest and should happen on a schedule that suits your needs.

Change Depends on You

If you are unsatisfied with your current job situation, then you have some choices to make. Do you focus your efforts on changing your manager, the environment or yourself? We suggest focusing on you. Not because you are at fault but rather because you represent the individual over which you have the most influence.

The change of which we speak involves releasing the untapped capabilities and vast reserves of creativity that each of us have in a way that helps us fortify ourselves against the destructive effects of working in a non-supportive environment. In a Supportive Environment, such a release simply serves to augment your level of success. In any of the non-supportive environments which we have discussed, it may be essential to your survival.

We will provide you with an effective set of tools to use to enhance your role as a professional but how and whether you use them is up to you. Motivational speaker Jim Rohn suggests in one of his articles circulated by the DailyInBox.com, "The major key to your better future is YOU." The Beatles expressed a similar sentiment in their song Hey Jude written by Paul McCartney. "The movement you need is on your shoulders." Saturn General Manager Jill A. Lajdziak in a recent letter to customers explained that although the parent company General Motors was teetering on the edge of bankruptcy and may spin off the Saturn brand, "Difficult times sometimes yield the most innovative solutions, and those who are willing to take on the challenge will emerge victorious." **The fact is that little in your life will change for the better without you becoming an active participant in making it happen.**

We will also walk you through the process of developing an effective Workplace Survival Plan. Our hope is that your Workplace Survival Plan will work so well for you that it inspires your co-workers to develop their own plans to aid in their survival. You can assist them yourself or direct them to our work. Through your collective efforts to support each other, you may find that the scope and impact of your individual efforts are multiplied until you and your co-workers surround your entire workgroup with a Supportive Environment. Your success might inspire workers in other parts of the company to establish Workplace Survival Plans of their own. Eventually, a difference in the level of performance where Supportive Environments exist will be obvious to anyone paying attention. The executive team might even realize that implementing an enterprise-wide Supportive Environment is actually in the best interest of not only the company but them as well.

As you read these pages, please carry with you the idea that if you strive to be the type of employee that you would want to manage or the type of manager that you would like to have manage you, then you are better positioned to welcome success. And as more and more employees, confident in the effectiveness of their Workplace Survival Plans, take this approach, the number of companies fostering Supportive Environments will increase as will the number of productive employees.

The bottom line for why you should develop and implement your Workplace Survival Plan and do everything in your power to promote your continued presence and success in the workplace is something many business leaders frequently tout as a corporate value but far too often fail to act upon. Some executives state it differently but it generally goes like this: Our most important corporate assets are our people. **Even though many of the bosses that you encounter during your career may not act like they value that asset, you must if for no other reason than the fact that you are that asset and if you do not see value in yourself, no one else will either.**

CHAPTER 2

Seeking a Path to Success

Cal Jones, Senior Account Exec

6:00 AM. Monday morning. The alarm rings. Cal Jones bolts out of bed. He's primed and ready for work, not because he is anxious for another week at Axiom Business Services but rather because he has had enough of his boss, Arthur Breedlove.

Breedlove took over as the director of Major Accounts earlier this year and ever since he has been gunning for Cal, the most senior account exec in the department. Cal made a decision last Friday that he had had enough. It did not matter that he was only five years from retirement or that there would be no golden parachute to soften his departure from Axiom. At best, there was a free lunch at the local watering hole with a bunch of his buddies and a gold-plated retirement watch probably made in China, and waiting for that was not enough to sell out his self-respect to Breedlove for another five years.

Marge, his wife of 30 years, wondered why Cal had skipped breakfast and forgotten to pack his lunch as he blew out the front door. She did not know that he wanted to be on the road before she had time to ask any questions. Weaving through traffic on I-75, he reached downtown Atlanta in record time and screeched to a stop in the Axiom parking lot right next to Breedlove's SUV.

As Cal stormed in through the same revolving door he had entered every workday for the past fifteen years and turned down the hallway, he could see Breedlove rummaging through the papers on his desk. Breedlove, who was in Cal's office, did not expect Cal to show up this early and was obviously looking for some way to sabotage yet another one of his accounts. Cal shoved his office door back on its hinges and slammed his portfolio down on the desk in front of the skinny man. Breedlove, deep in thought, nearly jumped out of his skin.

"Honey, wake up!" Marge said, gently shaking Cal. Her concerned voice ripped him out of his office and tossed him back in his bed. "It's 6:30, Honey. You overslept. You're going to be late for work if you don't hurry." Cal glanced at the clock on the night stand. He expelled a deep sigh then pushed himself out of bed.

Cal Jones, like millions of workers in America's aging workforce, has tolerated all types of bosses, some good but most lacking even basic managerial skills. People become bosses through a number of different paths, not the least of which being their ability to outlast or out-maneuver more qualified colleagues. Rarely do they ascend to management because of their stellar ability to manage and motivate people.

Now that Cal is within reach of retirement, the stress of dealing with incompetence, misguided motivations, and unadulterated spite, weigh heavily upon his mind. At a time in his life when he should to be able to capitalize on his experience to perform his job with ease and grace, his energy is sapped by having to deal with issues that have little or nothing to do with the mission of the company or increasing shareholder value. Instead, he has joined millions of people in offices, factories, and showrooms across the country, whose attention is diverted by the need to watch their backs.

Jennifer Lakes, Production Supervisor

Twelve hundred miles away, Jennifer Lakes scrapes the ice off her car windows. She can see her breath in the crisp morning air as the sun crests the foothills on the outskirts of Colorado Springs. Jennifer has worked her way up from a "gofer," fresh out of trade school, to a production supervisor at Elskerson Controls. She has doubts that her new boss values her contribution to the company.

Bren Voltek, the owner's nephew, was brought in two years ago to fill the Director of Production position Jennifer thought was rightfully hers after her old boss was suddenly killed in a motorcycle accident. She cannot put her finger on it but something about Voltek bothers her. It seems the harder she tries to please him, the more strained their relationship becomes. She hopes that going in early for a while might help the situation but the ice that formed overnight on her car windows is unusually thick and it is taking her an extra fifteen minutes to clear it off. By the time she finally arrives at work. She is five minutes late and Voltek is waiting.

"Long weekend?" Voltek snipes then quickly glances at his watch to punctuate the question, as Jennifer passes him on her way to the production floor. She knows it is better not to say anything when he is in this kind of mood. She just hopes that none of the equipment breaks down this week, so her team can meet their production quota after nearly a month of shortfalls.

In the middle of what could be a long and rewarding career, Jennifer Lakes knows her job inside and out. Lots of workers are in her position. They have paid their dues and they know how to get the job done. If given the right conditions, they could be stellar performers who lead and motivate others to excellence but poor equipment and lack of support thwart even their best efforts. As if that were not enough, their bosses view them as competition and place additional obstacles in their way or withhold meaningful assistance.

Mario Molina, New Hire

Mario Molina straightens his tie then flashes a big smile and his employee badge as he passes the guard station before stepping into the elevator for a short ride to his office on the 16th floor. As he completes logging onto his computer, a reminder notice flashes on his screen telling him that this is his one month anniversary at Aztec Aerospace in Downey, California. Not that anybody else will notice but it is an important milestone for Mario. He was recruited right out of grad school and this is the first time he has had an office with a view.

He has tried hard to make a good first impression by dressing for success and striving to be a valuable member of the engineering design team but that is the problem; he is not sure where he fits on the team. Everyone else seems to know exactly what to do and he does not want to get the reputation of always asking for direction but that is exactly what he needs.

Sally Beaujolais, the project lead, was supposed to sit down with him after he got settled to let him know what was expected of him and to help him set his goals but so far it has not happened. After each weekly tag up with a team of twenty-five engineers, she rushes off to another meeting offering Mario a quick suggestion, "Catch me at my desk if you have an issue." He tried that for the first two weeks but she was never at her desk.

The third week, Mario even went to the secretary to get on Beaujolais's calendar but last Friday when he stepped into her office for their meeting, she brushed past him, with an armload of papers, saying, "I'm sorry, we're going to have to reschedule."

As Mario walked back to this office, he reflected on what the Human Resources rep told him during the new employee orientation session. She wanted him to be aware that he was getting into a very competitive environment where everyone was viewed as a professional and all employees were expected to pull their own weight. "At the end of the year," she explained, "your bonus, any raise, and your value to Aztec will be determined

14

by how well you have met or exceeded your goals." She seemed to imply that any employee, who did not meet his goals, did not stay around for very long.

Mario Molina wants to make a good impression as do most new college graduates joining the workforce for the first time. Unfortunately, school provides them with the skills and knowledge required of their discipline but little or no preparation for the actual challenges of the workplace. Most institutions of higher learning fail to offer instruction on the fine art of navigating through the battlefield of office politics. Pushed out of the academic nest, new grads not only have to learn to fly but feed and defend themselves in a workplace where, at times, dogs eat other dogs. This situation is compounded by the fact that even the best managers concede that entry level employees rarely walk through the door with a basic understanding of what working for a living is really all about.

Addressing Your Situation

Here we have three frustrated employees, in different stages of their careers in different industries located in three different parts of the country, working for three different bosses. Of course, our three fictional characters – Cal, Jennifer, and Mario – represent the millions of workers who face similar workplace challenges every day. Whether they realize it, their careers have hit a brick wall. The fact that you are reading about them may indicate that you are in a similar situation and are on or are seeking a path to success in your professional life. We commend you for taking the initiative. Let us provide reassurance that you have come to the right place; we will not disappoint you.

Whether you are a line employee or a technical specialist, a factory worker or a truck driver, a ditch digger or an accountant, we believe that before you finish reading these pages, you will lean back, nod your head, and say: *Finally, someone understands exactly what I have to put up with every day at work.* We think that you will recognize and be able to relate to at least one of the workplace environments that we will introduce and discuss. Rest assured that by seeking out this book, you have already taken the first step toward improving your situation. We will provide you the knowledge and tools you need to work more effectively and to leverage more control over your particular situation.

If you, as a project lead, supervisor, manager, director or executive, are responsible for the performance of others, we think you may recognize, in the pages ahead, many of the misguided behaviors employed by some individuals in positions of authority. Such behaviors are not conducive to an efficient, productive work environment. We provide this perspective, first, so that employees learn to recognize and either avoid or deal effectively with individuals exhibiting these behaviors and, second, with the hope that all parties will work to create a more supportive and productive environment.

Implications of Problems at Work

Suffering under an unrelenting barrage of comments that minimize your feelings of self-worth over time takes a toll regardless of how strongly you view yourself as an individual. It is especially troubling if that barrage comes from the individual who signs your paycheck. Now I do not want to get entangled in a psychobabble discussion of the problems associated with the myriad of factors that may influence your self-perception but on the other hand I have spent a good part of my career counseling people who experienced a loss of self-worth in conjunction with work-related problems. It is not unreasonable to assume that your self-esteem could be impacted, for better or worse, by feedback you receive at work. When that feedback, whether justified or not, is consistently negative it takes a toll and, unfortunately, it can spill over into other aspects of your life.

Steve Crabtree with the Gallup Organization reports that "it's now tougher than ever for employees to leave their work problems at the door when they head home, and vice versa." In an article published in *Life & Work Connections* by the University of Arizona, Crabtree cautions that "employees who are not engaged in their roles [at work] are more likely to register discontent with their lives in general and their personal lives in particular." The stresses associated with frustration at work can and have resulted in illness, divorce, physical abuse, and even murder. You do not want to go down this road.

Jerry Krueger and Emily Killham, also of the Gallup Organization, explain why this is an important concern from the company's perspective in an article published in the *Gallup Management Journal*. "Other research on happiness in the workplace suggests that worker well-being plays a major role in organizational performance." Still other research indicates that productivity leads to happiness. What seems to be more certain is that happiness and productivity co-exist well and are of benefit to the organization. The *Journal of Occupational and Environmental Medicine* would seem to concur in reporting that "healthcare expenditures are nearly 50% greater for workers who report high stress levels." Krueger and Killham contend, "Organizations that understand the connections between worker stress and health and well-being can help their employees manage stress and find balance in their work and personal lives. When they do, productivity and engagement improve." But what if you work at one of those companies that do not effectively address these issues? Millions of workers clock-in at such businesses every day. It is certainly not easy to face the constant barrage of abuses present in non-supportive environments.

Old Guard

Consider Cal Jones, who we introduced earlier. He is a veteran salesman with fifteen years of experience for Axiom Business Services in Atlanta, Georgia. He is the most senior account executive in the department and is only five years away from retirement. From Cal's perspective, his boss Arthur Breedlove is "gunning" for him. Cal is concerned about losing his job so close to retirement. At his age, he thinks, and rightly so, that it may be difficult to find another position of equal status and compensation.

Cal also has the idea that some young "brainiac" executive might see it as an effective cost cutting measure if Breedlove can find a less seasoned individual to fill Cal's capable shoes. Of course, Cal may be replaced by some neophyte who cannot bring to the table the same experience and reasoned action that Cal now provides. That, however, may not stop the "brainiac," who may ignore the long term interests of the company for a short term boost to the bottom line. Although, it is illegal for the "brainiac" or Breedlove to discriminate against Cal because of his age, Breedlove may be able to set Cal up for failure so he can be dismissed for *cause* avoiding the necessity of offering him a severance package.

Replacing older, more experienced employees is a quick and easy way to cut costs. This approach ignores the loss of corporate knowledge embodied in the senior worker and does not give due consideration to the hit workforce morale takes when a respected employee is dismissed for what may be seen by his co-workers as a rather petty reason. If the employee is dismissed and not replaced then additional resentment may develop due to the remaining employees having to pick up the slack. Even if the departing employee is replaced, the new, usually younger person often drags down the productivity of those around him as he struggles in a non-supportive environment to get up to speed. The allegiance of colleagues of the employee who was "retired" may exacerbate the situation as they might be reluctant to assist in the development of their colleague's replacement. All of these factors have a potentially negative impact on organizational productivity.

How middle or lower management approaches such issues often depends on the behaviors of those at the top. "I think most CEOs on an intellectual level would agree that people are their most important asset," asserts Daniel Weinfurter, CEO of the Chicago-based Capital H Group, in a featured interview published in *The Houston Chronicle.* "The actual behavior, though, varies widely. To really gauge a CEOs belief that people matter, you have to look at what they do in more difficult times."

We have all seen news headlines announcing the layoff of anywhere from a handful of workers up to 20,000 or more at a time. We would suggest that leaders who choose to lay off thousands of workers at a time were caught asleep at the wheel or were blissfully unaware of changing market conditions. Rather than making small adjustments to adapt, they waited too long to act and had to opt for a slash and burn policy to try and regain fiscal control.

Other corporate executives might even close an entire department or facility and lay off all of its employees to rid themselves of one or more *pesky* individuals. According to the Retail, Wholesale and Department Store Union, Wal-Mart did just that when two hundred "workers voted to join UFCW [United Food and Commercial Workers] Canada Local 503." Rather than concede any territory to the union, Wal-Mart executives closed the entire facility.

Such actions are inherently at conflict with the often echoed refrain that *people are our most important asset.* Valuing workers as more than mere assets flows down to the managers at the operational level from the actions of the bosses at the top. Their actions reveal their true attitudes regardless of how much lip service they lend to the idea. This, however, is of little consolation to Cal and those of you who might be confronted with losing your jobs as a result of decisions made in the executive suites.

When slash and burn policies impact entire organizations, there is little you can do about it. However, when such decisions are implemented at the local level and your boss has you in his sights, you do have some steps you can take to reduce your vulnerability. Remember the old mantra from the seventies attributed to Colin Sautar? *Just because you're paranoid doesn't mean they're not out to get you!* A few tablespoons of prevention can go a long way to sustain your position when the hungry-eyed wolves gather near your desk. Rest assured that we will delve deeply into this issue in subsequent chapters.

Middle Ranks

Jennifer Lakes who works for Elskerson Controls in Colorado Springs, Colorado, as a production supervisor came up through the ranks and feels she was overlooked when a replacement for her old boss was needed. From Jennifer's perspective, her new boss Bren Voltek may not have been there long enough to fully appreciate her value to the company. She hopes that as long as she can maintain the productivity level on the production floor that it is just a matter of time before he will notice her contribution.

This is a common misconception in the workplace. Some bosses are simply oblivious to the individual contributions of their employees. Other bosses purposely ignore the hard work of their subordinates, thinking that to acknowledge such contributions places them in a weakened position. And others view experienced workers as competition. Either way, the result generates a *why-bother* mentality amongst employees who arrive at the conclusion: *The boss just doesn't care whether I put forth extra effort or not, so why bother!*

This kind of attitude can have a decidedly negative impact on your productivity as well as your morale. Left unchecked, it can easily spread to other areas of the organization. You would be well-advised to shed such an attitude as quickly as possible. Maintaining a positive attitude and an acceptable level of productivity, even in the face of adversity, sustains your value to the organization and, therefore, your reason for being on the job. We will shed more light on this and other ways to increase your value to the organization in the pages ahead.

New Recruits

Mario Molina, our aerospace engineer fresh out of grad school, has just finished his first month with Aztec Aerospace. From Mario's perspective, his boss Sally

Beaujolais appears nice enough but she never seems to have enough time to give him the guidance he needs to be successful in this competitive environment. He is afraid of getting stuck with a reputation as the weak link in the team and not being able to overcome it or worse yet, being passed over, demoted, laid off or fired for not having met his goals at the end of the year.

Young, inexperienced employees can easily flounder if not provided the guidance and support they need to be successful. Unofficial mentoring by employees who no longer have the will to excel in an environment that does not respect excellence can easily taint a novice employee making it all the more difficult to establish in them a healthy sense of self-motivation.

One of the questions each employee must ask himself, especially if he is a new hire, is: *Can I make it here?* This question addresses more than simply considering whether the environment is supportive or non-supportive. Even supportive environments can be fast-paced, relatively unstructured, and require a good measure of self-confidence and stubborn tenacity to get the job done.

Your first clue to the type of workplace environment surfaces during the interview process which serves both the company and the candidate. The interview process provides the hiring manager a means to assess whether the respective candidate is likely to succeed in the position for which he has applied. There is nothing wrong with the candidate assessing what the company has to offer him in the negative and moving on to a more conducive environment or other opportunities. The candidate, however, bears some responsibility for being able to do the work once he assumes the position. At this point, the question shifts. *Can I make it here?* is replaced by *What do I need to do to be successful here?* This question is as important for new hires as it is for veteran employees. As the challenges of your workplace change in response to market forces, changing personnel, and other influences, you must have the ability to continue to adapt.

Each candidate for employment makes some representation during the application and interview process of his capability to do the job for which he is being considered. Should he then be selected and hired, it is somewhat disingenuous for him to scapegoat management for failing to provide for his needs unless those needs were addressed during the interview or the workplace environment changed significantly. Training is frequently mentioned as the need in question. We note that Mario has not taken this path yet.

In considering candidates for employment, my firm makes it clear that this is a fast-paced, competitive environment with rapidly changing priorities centered on our clients' needs. While management attempts to be supportive, we let candidates know up front that they better be equal to the challenge as no one is going to hold their hands and point the way. That may sound harsh but that is the way it is and if candidates are not up to the challenge, they need not apply here. All this to say that just because there may be *bad* bosses in the workplace, employees are not absolved of the responsibility to show some initiative by assessing the environment and making a concerted effort to be productive.

When I first moved to Houston, I began work as a temp at NASA's prime space shuttle contractor. I was young and hungry for work which translated into an aggressive desire to succeed. I quickly learned that each paycheck depended upon representing my value to the managers, all five of them, whose signatures were required on my employment voucher each week. If I didn't get their signatures on the voucher by Friday, I would not have a job the following Monday morning. Through observation, I determined that the prevailing philosophy in this environment was: *If you can figure out what your job is and make yourself useful, you can continue to work here.* No one had to tell me what to do. I made it part of my job to figure out what needed to be done then do it. Within a month I was hired fulltime. I stayed with the company for ten years. But that is just me. I have always been stubbornly persistent when faced with challenges. Not everybody is built that way.

Beginning Your Journey

We do believe, however, that everybody has untapped potential upon which to draw in challenging times if sufficiently motivated to do so. Our goal is to inspire those of you with the desire and will to take charge of your situations to begin that journey today. If you are in management, we will offer you a look at how certain behaviors are perceived by your employees and guide you toward creating a more supportive environment where true peak performance is possible. If you are one of the *troops*, we will help you learn to recognize the peculiarities of different workplace environments and show you how to leverage more control over the environment in which you currently work. In the pages ahead, we will share with you the life-altering workplace lessons we have learned sometimes through thoughtful contemplation but more often through painful personal experience.

Sometimes we will speak to those of you who serve in positions of authority as supervisors, managers, directors, or executives. Regardless of your position of authority, you and the viability of your careers are also impacted by the workplace environment. But most of the time our words will be directed to those of you rank and file employees who are seeking a path to success because if you are not performing at your best, everyone suffers. This includes customers, co-workers, management, shareholders, your family, and you. This is not to say that you are the source of the problem. Quite to the contrary! **Regardless of the source of the problem, you can always be the source of the solution at least as it applies to strengthening your ability to deal with the challenges presented to you within the environment in which you work.**

CHAPTER 3

Deciding to Stay and Prevail

Arthur Breedlove, Cal's boss, took over as Director of Major Accounts earlier this year. What challenges did he face when he took on that role? Did he replace a director who had retired or moved on to a more lucrative position? Was he brought in to bolster sagging sales? Did Human Resources need a place to warehouse him till there was a solid reason to lay him off or fire him? Suppose Breedlove had discovered that upper management wants to cut Cal from the payroll before he takes retirement and becomes a long term liability to the company. Therefore, Breedlove is pressuring Cal to perform in order to help him preserve his job. Suddenly, Breedlove does not seem like such a bad guy. This, in fact, is nothing more than speculation but it does serve to demonstrate how our perception of the boss can be altered by taking a few steps in his shoes. At this point, all we know is that Cal's level of frustration has reached the boiling point.

Jennifer's boss Bren Voltek came to his position of leadership upon the unfortunate death of his predecessor. Some may question his background since he was the owner's nephew. But Voltek has held his position for two years, so that issue carries less weight. Nepotism is typically regarded as a bad thing but it does not necessarily qualify Voltek as a *bad* boss nor does it presage his success or failure in this role. Obviously, there is some friction between Jennifer and Voltek and we can make some assumptions as to its source but this, too, would only be speculation. We simply do not have enough information to accurately judge whether Voltek is a *good* boss or a *bad* boss. We do not have a complete picture, only a brief snapshot of him.

In regard to Sally Beaujolais, Mario's boss, we do not know how long she has been a project lead. We get the impression that she is extremely busy with numerous interests vying for her attention and multiple issues that she has to address at any given time. Also, it seems that she has maintained a respectful and professional demeanor with a new employee who seeks some of her time even though she has not been able to accede to his requests.

Bosses versus Managers

What is clear is that Cal, Jennifer, and Mario each face a different challenge with a different kind of boss in a different work environment. Some readers may jump to the conclusion that what Cal, Jennifer, and Mario have in common is a *bad* boss. It is human nature to want to place a label on behaviors even if we may not have sufficient knowledge of the situation to make an objective, informed determination of whether the behavior is actually *good* or *bad*. This is a natural, instinctual function that helps us survive. We are attracted to good food, good climates, and good bosses. Anything prefaced by the adjective *bad*, for most people, is to be avoided, especially bad bosses. Until we know whether something is *good* or *bad* we may not know how to respond to it. But in the cases of Breedlove, Voltek, and Beaujolais, let us forestall a rush to judgment.

First, we want to distinguish between the words *boss* and *manager*. *Webster's New Universal Unabridged Dictionary* offers an intriguing definition of *boss*: "A protuberance or roundish excrescence on the body or on some organ of an animal or plant." OK, admittedly, we recite the botanical/zoological definition here. Actually, we use the word *boss* more in the sense of how it was used to describe William Marcy Tweed, commonly known as *Boss Tweed*, the corrupt ruler of the Tammany Hall political machine in New York City during the mid-1800s, or Thomas Joseph Pendergast better known as *Boss Tom* by his Kansas City constituents during the Roaring Twenties. It should be noted that both *Boss Tweed* and *Boss Tom* were convicted for their criminal behavior and both served time in prison. This is not to say that every boss will end up behind bars. That might be too much for employees who have endured interminable abuses in the workplace to hope for and quite simply is not the case.

We use the word **boss** here to indicate someone who employs a less than desirable approach to leadership in the workplace. This would be someone in a position of authority who contributes to a non-supportive workplace environment. On the other hand, we use the word **manager** to emphasize the more desirable role of leadership used by an authority figure to create and maintain a supportive workplace environment.

Please note that we alternate between the use of *he* and *she* pronouns in referring to bosses and managers, so as not to give the impression that one gender prevails over the other in terms of good or bad management styles. In this chapter, we begin with the use of *he*. In the next chapter, we use *she* and so on. We do, however, retain unaltered any references to gender employed by the authors of quoted passages.

During my career as a recruiter, I have reviewed thousands of resumes and have met face-to-face with hundreds of individuals who identified themselves as having some level of management experience. As a result, I have noticed a trend. Many of these individuals listed having responsibility *for hiring, firing, and enforcing company policies.* I would categorize these individuals as *bosses*. They present rigid, condescending, and potentially confrontational personalities and see management's role in terms of crowd control.

Other individuals I interviewed described their duties as *building teams, supporting professional development, and enabling employees to achieve their goals.* I would categorize these individuals as *managers*. They displayed respect for their employees and appeared to have focused a majority of their energy toward creating the circumstances and support structures that allow people to be productive.

Both individuals had the same job title, but conveyed two radically different points of view on how to deal with employees. I will leave it to you to formulate an opinion on which of these two types of individuals you would prefer to have sign your paycheck.

Whether you report to a *boss* or a *manager*, let us clearly state that you still have the responsibility to perform your job to the best of your ability. Many employees who encounter problems in the workplace find it far too easy to identify management as the source of irritation and shift responsibility for the problems to their superiors. This does nothing other than postpone your ability to find a solution to the undesirable situation in which you find yourself.

As a recruiter with twenty years of experience, I know for a fact that not all bosses are *bad* and for every *bad* boss there is at least one *bad* employee. Having said that, I also know that there are some very good managers out there. Unfortunately, they seem to be outnumbered by some astoundingly *bad* bosses. Nearly everyone you talk to has a story about a *bad* boss for whom he or she has worked. Some are mean, conniving, manipulative exploiters who for some reason or other happen to have been promoted to positions of leadership. Others might have a more subtle modus operandi. At the church social or the local softball game, they might appear to be the nicest people you would want to know. But once they step foot in the workplace, they revert to their role as sharp-toothed carnivores hungry for meat.

In the past two decades, I have interviewed an average of three candidates every day. You can image the stories I have heard. It is, however, like pulling teeth to get past the superficial exit interview response: *I got a better opportunity.*

Sure, I say, *but you wouldn't have gotten a better offer if you hadn't been in the market!* After some probing, the truth spills out.

Unfortunately many of the stories that I hear about *bad* bosses are told with heartfelt trepidation in the present tense. These are stories that upper management never hears because during the exit interview the true facts are rarely revealed since most people are cautioned against burning bridges on their way out. What *they* know could hurt you. A bad exit interview can close the door to ever working at that company again or taint a reference needed for a new employer. Sharing bad information about your former employer with a new employer is also not recommended since it makes the new employer wonder, *who was really at fault?*

28

No good can come from a negative exchange during the exit interview. While people are less apt to share a bad work experience with their employer, they are much less reticent to share that story with a career counselor or recruiter and believe me I have heard lots of sad stories.

While I know that there are two sides to every story, some of the tales I hear leave me dumbfounded to believe that people would actually do such things. Sometimes, I feel as though I should wipe off the bar and serve another drink. Often, I know where the stories are headed simply because I know where the individuals worked. Every recruiter who has been in business for more than a couple years knows which companies produce such stories. Former employees consistently confirm how bad the management at those companies really is. I put those places on my *companies-to-be-avoided* list.

Much of the popular literature on the subject of *bad* bosses only helps employees identify, name, and categorize the specific type of behavior that makes a boss bad. These books do little more than let employees vent about *bad* bosses, *nasty* bosses, *dumb* bosses, and *idiot* bosses as well as bosses raised by vicious carnivores and, of course, the bosses from *hell*. One author describes *bad* bosses with titles such as "The Carrot Dangler" and "The Violator." Another author uses terms such as "Critically Clueless" and "Scatterboss." Some authors are psychologists and a few are therapists for dysfunctional organizations while others serve as organizational leadership consultants. Regardless of their backgrounds, most popular authors on the subject of *bad* bosses have approached the subject in a similar manner, one that demonizes the boss while posturing the embattled employee in the untenable position of having to figure out how to deal with a whole host of psychotic behaviors.

And what if the corporate leaders come to their senses, at least partially, and replace the *bad* boss with someone new? One day you are working for "Ms. Carrot Dangler" and the next day "Mr. Violator" signs your timecard. That is right; they replaced the *bad* boss with a *worse* boss because the corporate executives themselves have not changed. Their ability to select bosses is not any different than when they tapped "Ms. Carrot Dangler" to run your organization.

Bottom line? Sometimes, *the devil I know is better than the new devil I may have to face tomorrow*. And just when you got the protective asbestos skivvies and heavy flak jacket to fit, the new boss bumps you off the deep end with a whole new set of aberrant behaviors for which you are ill-prepared. How frustrating would it be to find yourself sinking under the weight of the armor that protected you against "Ms. Carrot Dangler" but does nothing against "Mr. Violator?" The point is, changing bosses in and of itself may not lead to a better situation.

It Just Doesn't Matter

In one publication, the author focuses on the idea that you need to figure out what it is you do to provoke your boss implying that you are always the problem. The truth is you may not have to do anything to receive the wrath of your boss. Nathanael Fast, in an article posted on the Harvard Business Review Blog Network, indicates that the findings of recent studies conducted with Serena Chen, a psychologist at UC Berkeley, reveal "it was the simultaneous pairing of power with feelings of inadequacy that led people to lash out [in the workplace]. In our studies, the power holders who felt personally incompetent became aggressive, not because they were power hungry or had domineering personalities but because they were trying to overcome ego threat. Put simply, bullying is a cheap way to nurse a wounded ego."

In any case, whenever there is conflict, except for cases of schizophrenia, there are two parties involved and each party usually contributes something to the conflict. We will show you how to make certain you are not part of the problem while providing you the means to protect yourself and increase your control over situations where there is a high potential for conflict between you and your boss. We aim to help you be the solution.

By now, you may be thinking that we have made a concerted effort to reinforce the idea that *bad* bosses do exist while in nearly the same breath hinting at the idea that this does not make much difference. It is true. We confess. *Bad* bosses do exist and there is not much you can do to change this glaring fact of life. We simply believe that it is a waste of time and effort to try to figure out why a *bad* boss is bad.

Here is a case in point. For years a good friend of mine relayed to me stories of working for the *boss-from-hell*. This boss, my friend told me, would rant and rave about the most insignificant things that were being done, usually upon his request. But, of course, the boss never remembered making such requests. The workplace was always in turmoil and when it was not, my friend and his co-workers were simply enjoying the calm before the next storm. This went on for years until my friend moved on with his career to a job in the space program. Recently, however, he sent me an email to let me know that the *boss-from-hell* had died of complications related to Alzheimer's disease. When this boss had ranted on about not remembering having made the requests his employees attributed to him, he was not kidding; *he truly did not remember!*

Rare are the occasions that you are lucky enough to find out the real reason behind your boss's erratic behavior but even knowing the real reason does will not alter the facts. You are stuck working with this individual, at least for now, and you had best learn how to survive in that environment until you can avail yourself of other options.

Let it suffice to say that unless you are a trained psychologist, analyzing your boss is a useless pursuit. Who could have guessed that the *boss-from-hell* under which my friend suffered had Alzheimer's disease? It is easier to simply pick a reason, whether correct or not, and be satisfied that this is the actual explanation for why your boss behaves the way he does. For example, your boss behaves badly because he was beaten and abused by his step-father when he got out of reform school. As a child, your boss gnawed the lead paint off the door frame when his parents locked him in the closet and now he is slightly insane. Your boss was fired from his last three jobs for standing up for his employees and now thinks that *nice bosses finish last!* Pick one. Trust us. It does not much matter which one you pick as long as it makes you feel better.

In most situations, going so far as to classify a boss as *bad* is most often a non-productive path to follow. While it may give you some consolation, what does it change?

Nothing! Revealing what you perceive as your boss's inadequacies to your boss or to a higher level of management is usually a career limiting remedy and not one that we would casually advise.

Stephen M. Pollan and Mark Levine, authors of *Lifescripts*, tend to agree. "If you've tried to speak to your immediate superior about her behavior and have gotten nowhere, the only solution is to make an end run and speak with her supervisor. Of course, this is one of the most dangerous political maneuvers you can make in an office environment." They advise going over your boss's head "only if you believe your future at the firm is at stake."

Select this path and the best case scenario is often *mutually assured destruction*, commonly known as MAD. This is the approach that kept the superpowers – USA and USSR – from launching a nuclear strike against each other during the Cold War. What made this philosophy effective, in terms of geopolitical stabilization, was that both parties were equally powerful as well as able and theoretically willing to carry through with the threat of total annihilation of each other. Most boss-employee relationships skew power toward the boss. How many employees are able to bring their boss down at will? End of story. In such a situation, the best you can hope for is that your boss's career rushes down the same drain at the same time or soon after your career takes that long dark ride.

We strongly recommend that if you plan on engaging your boss in an interoffice battle that you make certain that you can win that battle. Otherwise, prepay the burial plot where your career will reside as you seek another job.

Communicating the boss's failings to co-workers may garner support and empathy from peers but what can they do about it? While there is usually safety in numbers, the question here is: How many employees does it take to unscrew your boss from the seat of power? This is a more appropriate question to ask: *How many of my co-workers would be willing to trash their careers in support of my battle with the boss?* Most likely, fellow employees are stuck in the same seemingly impotent position as you and, unless their own professional survival is directly threatened, they may be less than enthusiastic about taking on the boss in what most of them might see as a suicide mission.

At best, such a scenario makes for a hilarious episode of a sitcom. You know the one where a group of employees works themselves into a frenzy in the lunchroom with grievances and complaints about the boss. Then suddenly, one brave soul jumps to his feet and proclaims, "We should go tell him what we really think!"

"That's right!" shouts someone else.

"Let's do it!" a voice echoes from the back.

And so, off they march across the factory floor into the office hallways, led by the brave soul.

Cut to the boss who is quietly working at his desk. Suddenly, the brave soul bursts into the boss's office and defiantly confronts the boss.

"We're not going to take it anymore!"

The boss looks up from his work with a puzzled expression, "We who?"

The camera pans to show only the brave soul standing before the boss. A close-up reveals that all but familiar uh-oh expression oozing across the brave soul's face as he looks around to find his co-conspirators nowhere in sight.

Cut to two workers who helped inflame the insurrection as they sheepishly slink back to their workstations. One glances at the other and says, "What do you think the boss is going to do to him?"

His co-conspirator shrugs.

Then back to the office for one final shot of the boss filling with rage as he rises slowly from his desk to tower over the now timid soul standing alone in the boss's shadow.

Source of the Problem

While you may see your boss as the problem, your boss can just as easily declare you as the problem. Who has the larger podium from which to raise this issue? Unless you are a union member or have an ironclad employment contract, any disagreement with your boss could leave you standing alone against the power of the corporation. Do not proceed under the mistaken assumption that anyone in Human Resources will come to your aid.

"HR is not there to help employees anymore," states former human resource executive Cynthia Shapiro, author of the book *Corporate Confidential: 50 Secrets Your Company Doesn't Want You To Know.* "HR is there to support management. Anything you say can and will be used against you if need be – no matter how sympathetic and helpful the person you talk to may seem." You may find that preserving the legitimacy of a management decision, whether right or wrong, may be one of those interests. At the risk of repeating ourselves, have a couple of lucrative job offers in your pocket before strolling into your bosses' office with confrontation on your mind.

Bosses, as well as the rest of us, are comprised of personalities shaped by past experiences, more specifically, the type of management under which they learned the ropes. If, as is often the case, the culture which recognized and promoted them is dysfunctional, then it would not be unusual for the boss's behavior to reflect the dysfunctional quality of the environment. Regardless of whether it is fair or just, it may be that they are in the position they are in precisely because they have learned to survive in such an environment.

Enron, conjures a clear image of an environment where integrity and ethics took a back seat to personal and financial gains. Enron might have risen and faded quietly had it not been for Sherron Watkins, Vice President of Corporate Development, who surfaced her concerns to CEO Kenneth L. Lay. While she is not considered a whistleblower, in the strict sense of the term, because she did not go public with her information about the company's state of affairs, she did confront senior management with problems that drew the wrath of CFO Andrew S. Fastow. Watkins contends in *Forbes Magazine* that Fastow wanted her fired after she sounded the alarm.

How many Enron employees do you think it would have taken to change Ken Lay's behavior or that of his replacement Jeffrey K. Skilling? How many of them could have acted individually to alter the Enron culture of corruption? Sherron Watkins was a vice president and she succumbed to early retirement. She was only able to enact the MAD solution in her suicidal confrontation with Enron management aided by media exposure and a team of federal prosecutors. By comparison, most Enron employees were simply ants running around on a hot sidewalk, trying to avoid being crushed by upper management who scurried about in search of fat golden parachutes as the corporate walls crumbled around them. It should be safe to say that those of lesser accomplishment than Sherron Watkins who dared question the behavior of Enron's management would have been easily crushed under the Italian leather sole of Ken Lay's shoe.

We note that while both Ken Lay and Jeffrey Skilling were convicted of fraud and conspiracy in federal district court, only Jeffrey Skilling was sentenced to prison. Ken Lay died of a heart attack before his sentencing hearing; therefore, his indictment and conviction were dismissed by U.S. District Judge Simeon T. Lake III.

Common Dilemma

Let us return now to our three fictional bosses Breedlove, Voltek, and Beaujolais who were created, based on our experience, to represent many of the bosses you may encounter during your career. What can we learn from them that might offer additional insight into their working relationships with subordinates Cal, Jennifer, and Mario?

Breedlove confronted Cal when he arrived at work, albeit late. "Where's your monthly sales report?" he fumed. "It should have been on my desk last Friday!"
"You said that you wouldn't have time to review it till this afternoon."

"That doesn't mean you can turn it in late!" Breedlove punched back. "I don't care how long you've been here, your excuses aren't going to cut it with me," he spewed. "You can't afford any screw-ups," Breedlove muttered under his breath as he stomped out of Cal's office in a huff.

Cal fished through the papers on his desk, grabbed the monthly sales report, then hurried after the skinny man with the report in hand. He had tried to give it to Breedlove last week when he saw him in the hallway outside his office but Breedlove would not accept it. Now, Cal felt like he had been purposely set up.

That provides us a little more information about Cal and Breedlove's troubled relationship. You might even conclude from this exchange that Breedlove seems hostile toward Cal. Is Breedlove justified in being upset? How should Cal respond to this situation?

Hard at work on the production floor, Jennifer is busily checking on each of her machine operators. She knows them all to be dedicated professionals, most of whom have nearly as much experience as she does. She is pleased to see that production is off to a good start for a Monday.

But the problem has never been the operators; it has always been the machines. They are old and prone to break down at the most inopportune time and Jennifer has yet to convince management to upgrade. She has explained to Voltek numerous times how much it would save the company, in the long run, to upgrade but he seems committed to the status quo. She does not even know if he has passed her cost-saving calculations up the line. It seems he is tired of hearing about the issue.

Just then Voltek pops through the door with hard hat and earplugs already in place. His eyes scan the room, going from machine to machine until he spies Jennifer and makes a beeline for her. "I reviewed your numbers on upgrading," Voltek yells above the grind of the machines. "Can you break that out by machine?"

"Sure!" The shock was as clearly evident in Jennifer's eyes as it was in the tone of her voice. She wanted to follow up with a question, something like, "Why now, when I submitted my calculations four months ago," but Voltek was already headed back to his office and confronting him with that issue may not have been a wise move. She was just happy that he had finally taken an interest in her suggestion.

For months, Jennifer's boss has acted like he could care less about the upgrade Jennifer suggested. Then one day, out of the blue, he wants to see more detail. Maybe he has finally recognized the value of her suggestion. Should Jennifer believe that Voltek will now act upon her suggestion? What do you think Voltek will do with the additional information Jennifer provides him?

Mario spends most of his Monday helping other members of the project team with reports and making copies. He tells his fiancée, when he talks to her on the phone at lunch, "I must be the highest paid copy machine operator on the planet."

"Why don't you ask some of the other team members what you should really be doing and see what they recommend," she suggests. "Or just find something that needs to be done and do it."

"That's what I'm trying to do, Baby. I'm just concerned that they'll think I can't carry my weight," Mario counters.

"Isn't there someone there that you can trust enough to ask?"

"I don't know. I've got to get back. I'll see you this evening," he says. After he hangs up he realizes that he had been a little too curt and he had better stop for flowers on the way home.

The Aztec environment is obviously not structured around supervisors who micro-manage work. While Mario has taken some positive steps to contribute, the steps he has not taken place him at risk of being positioned as an assistant to other members of the team rather than as a contributing peer. Was his fiancée on the right tract with her advice? What would you do if you were Mario?

Obviously, Cal, Jennifer, and Mario are in tough situations with no easy answers. While individually they each face a different challenge, what they have in common is dissatisfaction with their job situations. Do they stay and tolerate a bad situation or do they cut their losses and seek greener pastures elsewhere? If they stay, is there any way for them to prevail over the challenges presented by their environments?

This is a common dilemma shared by millions of people. When confronted with adverse conditions what do you do? Do you immediately begin looking for an out? Statistics indicate that your chances of finding a better workplace situation are dim. But if you decide to stay and fight, will this simply prolong an already bad situation? Probably.

Stay and Prevail

We recommend that your first option should be deciding to stay and prevail over a challenging workplace environment. The distinction is *fight* versus *prevail*. Fighting the environment provokes additional conflict and is a useless pursuit. But can you really prevail without fighting? We say, *yes*, if you have the right tools, and this book will provide you with those tools. In fact, this book is all about fully investigating how to leverage increased control over your workplace environment without provoking conflict. This means that you increase your chances of improving your working conditions without losing the tenure or seniority you have accrued in your current position. It also means that you are better able to depart on your own schedule and terms should you decide at some point that that course of action is in your best interest.

During my career as a recruiter, I have conducted thousands of probing interviews with employees seeking to make a job change. The vast majority of them ultimately reported that their desire to change jobs was inspired by the undesirable characteristics of the workplace environment created through default or intention by management. As a result, I have come to believe that the workplace environment is the most important factor relating to job satisfaction.

Most Important Question

Whether you work in the front office, on the shop floor or bury trash in a landfill, job satisfaction can be measured in similar ways. Things like respect, compensation, job security, challenges, recognition, and stress are some of the factors that often rank high on the job satisfaction scale. We could also look at things like hazards to health and wellbeing, the nature of the work, the distance of your commute or how your job contributes to or detracts from the overall quality of your life. The list is nearly endless but ultimately only one thing is important. **The single most important factor is how you answer when someone asks:** *Do you like your job?* If you answer, *yes*, without a moment's hesitation, all the individual factors that contribute to job satisfaction pale by comparison. If you hesitate, or answer in the negative, then something in your workplace environment is not pleasing to you and a review of the factors that characterize your workplace becomes more salient.

Many of my clients initially insist that the change they seek is all about money. From my experience in deciphering the influence of "hot buttons" associated with employee satisfaction, salary consistently ranks near the bottom. When clients insist that money is the driver for changing jobs, I frequently toss out an incredibly bad job that pays top dollar. In all cases, the client looks at me like I am crazy for even suggesting such a position. It does not take them long to realize it is not so much about the money as the job itself.

According to Jacqueline S. Martin, former CEO of the United Way of Texas Gulf Coast, "The No. 1 reason people leave their jobs is that they do not feel valued and appreciated. You can throw money [at them] all you want to, but if people do not feel valued and appreciated, then they won't stay or they won't do good work." If, because of your actions, your employees are spending more time looking for a way out than looking for ways to improve productivity, then you both have a problem.

For this very reason, most recruiters raise a skeptical eyebrow when a position pays excessively above market rates. It is almost always an indicator that there is something askew below the surface and the only way the employer can keep people from bailing out is to throw money at them. Guess what? It only works in the short term. Money alone is not enough of an incentive to keep people coming to work in an environment that drains every ounce of motivation. Such a position will be plagued by an abnormally high turnover rate.

High Cost of Turnover

An article in *Talent Management Magazine,* penned by David Austin, President and COO of Contextware, addresses the costly nature of excessive employee turnover. "This is an expensive problem that affects every industry – the Saratoga Institute [specialists in quantitative measurement of human capital and a subsidiary of Spherion Corporation] estimates the cost of turnover is anywhere between half and three times a person's salary." That equates to a 30 percent fee tacked onto the current cost of labor. This statistic stands in your favor. It is in your best interest and that of the company for you to continue serving in your current position rather than quit in hopes of finding a better job elsewhere.

Issues surrounding conditions that promote high turnover in the workplace have received increased public attention recently. "A bill in New Jersey would give an individual the right to seek as much as $25,000 in damages if an employer created 'an abusive work environment.' Similar measures are pending in New York State, Vermont and Washington State," reports Molly Selvin of *The Los Angeles Times.* While similar legislation has been introduced in several states, we have not found that any of these bills have actually become law. Even so, claimants have been successful in winning sizable civil judgments against bosses who created a hostile or abusive work environment often in conjunction with discrimination.

Notice that the focus in Selvin's article is on the "work environment" rather than on the boss. This is an important distinction. As we have previously stated, we believe the focus should be on the workplace environment rather than the boss because what type of boss you have is only one component of your workplace environment. Even though, your boss is an extremely influential component of your workplace environment, it is important to understand that your satisfaction with your workplace environment is really what underlies how you answer the question: *Do I like my job?* Therefore, it is to your benefit to gain a solid understanding of the environment in which you work.

Impact of the Workplace Environment

Your workplace environment is an amalgamation of factors that when simplified, can be thought of in the same manner as the events staged in the coliseums of olden times where gladiators went to do battle. In the coliseum, battles rage because the goal of each combatant is to survive while the rules of the game demand the death of one party or the other. In the workplace, the environment is ripe for battle when the goals of the three key combatants – employee, manager, and company – are out of alignment. This misalignment often results in a tremendous amount of energy being expended fighting each other over personal agendas as opposed to working productively toward a common goal.

Consider this. The ***company*** has bought and paid for, or at least rents space specifically to provide for your daily pleasure. Not likely. Rather their investment in providing you a place to work is generally considered to be for the purpose of building a product or performing a service that earns money for the owners or stockholders. If this can be accomplished without providing you a place to sit or stand for eight hours each day, then so be it.

The company influences your workplace environment, for better or worse, through what is commonly referred to as the corporate culture. Corporate executives can design and implement a particular corporate culture or by default let the culture be defined by random influences.

Some of the best companies from an employee perspective are known for their employee-friendly cultures which are often rooted in a social conscience and a sense of humor. None has risen to the heights of the reputation enjoyed by Ben & Jerry's Ice Cream as documented by Milton Moskowitz, coauthor of *The 101 Best Companies to Work for in America* written about self-made ice cream moguls Ben Cohen and Jerry Greenfield.

At the other end of the spectrum, there is the less employee-friendly culture fostered by James Halpin, who during his reign as CEO of CompUSA was known for pitting employees against each other as enemies. Halpin is quoted by Stanford organizational behavior professor Robert Sutton in Academy of Management's *Executive* magazine as suggesting that employees ask themselves, "What did I do today to put myself above my co-workers? If you can't come up with anything, you wasted a day."

It should be relatively clear from these two examples that the company culture can have a huge impact on the working environment and the players in the corporate coliseum.

The ***manager***, another key player in the workplace, is intended to be an on-the-scene representative of the company. But as a unique individual in his own right, the manager invariably influences the workplace environment with his own set of hopes and fears.

Then we have you, the ***employee***, with your goals and ambitions inspired by a whole different set of hopes and fears. You know best what drives your pursuits in the workplace but, in general, employees tend to seek a means to attain a sense of self-fulfillment and a measure of financial security. As such, many of your personal goals may actually be similar in nature to those of your manager.

When the goals of the company, the manager, and you align in frictionless harmony, life in the workplace is beautiful. Most people know, however, that this almost never happens. On any given workday, at least one party must submit to the will of another or the potential for battle ensues. Most often, the employee demurs to the superior power of the manager and the manager subjugates himself to the company.

Have you ever seen that pesky little phrase in most job descriptions which indicates that you should perform all the duties listed plus whatever else your supervisor asks you to do? And if such a phrase, or one similar to it, is missing from your actual job description, should you actually have one, then rest assured there is a company policy, written or unwritten, that demands your subordination to the dictates of management. This means that your goals and your point-of-view play second fiddle to those of the company and your manager. That certainly does not prevent clashes but it does clearly establish on which end of the food chain your career dangles.

Clearly, the workplace environment is a complex entanglement of relationships. At a minimum, it is comprised of your relationship with your boss, your boss's relationship with the company, your relationship with the company as well as the company's relationship with you, and its relationship with your boss, not to mention, your boss's relationship with you and on and on. If all this seems rather confusing, ask yourself: *Is my relationship with the boss the same as the boss's relationship with me?* Well, is it? Would your boss describe your relationship with him in the same terms that you describe your relationship with him? Probably not! And we have yet to consider all the influences of your co-workers and the people that influence their lives. When everyone is thrown into the mix, it all boils down to lots of people and personalities, topped off with all the intricacies of how humans interact. No wonder so many people hang up a metaphorical *do not disturb* sign by hiding out with jazz great Dave Koz, international songstress Celine Dion, Latin sensation Luis Miguel or rapper Fifty Cent under a pair of noise-reduction headphones.

Once you decide to stay and prevail, rather than embroil yourself in all this complexity and worry about why your boss is the way he is or why the corporate culture is hostile to teamwork, we suggest that you focus your attention on where you can make a difference. The secret of your success is to recognize what your workplace environment holds in store for you then prepare yourself to survive to produce another day regardless of the challenges with which you may be confronted.

Think about it this way. Knowing why the weather report calls for storms with gale force winds does not change the fact that if you go out unprepared in such inclement weather, you will likely get drenched by the rain, pounded by the winds, and fried by the lightning. A weather report does, however, allow you the opportunity to prepare yourself should you choose or need to venture out in such inclement weather. Rather than worry about why it is raining the wise individual concerns himself with what preparations are necessary to deal with the rain.

Every workplace is as unpredictable and varied as the weather whose complex patterns have only the Chaos Theory for explanation. And yet, we have all learned to deal with the pleasantries and dangers of the weather by following four simple rules:

- If you live in a stormy climate, have a safe place to take shelter.
- If you endure frequent rains, keep your raincoat and galoshes handy.
- If the wind is your constant neighbor, hang onto something solid.
- If the sun brightens and warms your days, enjoy yourself.

While at times the workplace may also seem to be governed by the Chaos Theory, it, too, can be distilled down into a simple and useful set of rules that govern how to survive in the different environments which you might reasonably encounter, regardless of where you work. In the pages ahead, we will help you learn to recognize the characteristics of the different workplace environments you may encounter and the hazards each of them present. We will also guide you in developing the means to protect yourself and your productivity when *stormy weather* hits your workplace.

CHAPTER 4

Identifying Your Workplace Environment

It is important to focus less on the characteristics, bad behaviors, personality, or lack of management skills of your boss and pay more attention to what it takes to be successful in the environment in which you find yourself. Doing this requires some knowledge of the kinds of forces, both internal and external to the company, that influence your work environment.

The complex mix of forces that influence your workplace environment may appear just as chaotic as those that shape the weather patterns which sometimes wreak havoc as they travel across the surface of the earth. However, unlike the weather, some of the forces that shape your workplace environment reside within your ability to control while others are entirely beyond your control. It is important for you to know which ones are within your control.

Key Players

Let us consider the following key players in workplace environment:

- **Company**
- **Manager**
- **You**

We could include your co-workers and customers on this list but that would unnecessarily complicate matters. The fact is that the company, your manager, and you are the players whose actions and behaviors influence your workplace environment the most. The simple reason is conflict. The potential for conflict exists in the workplace because these key players each have goals and expectations which may not always be in perfect alignment.

Conflict is expelled from your work environment only when the goals and expectations of these three key players are fully aligned. In other words, when there is a win-win-win situation. Ever heard of that? Win-win situations are challenging enough to create with only two parties tugging on the rope. Given the different perspectives of the people with whom you share your workspace, what must happen for the goals of your company, your manager, and you to miraculously align?

Suppose the company wants to reduce expenses but your manager needs to staff a new position requiring specialized skills and you want to increase your overtime work to pay for a much needed vacation.

Ask yourself: Which of these three parties has the most power to influence or prevent change in your workplace? The immediate answer might seem to be that the company has total control over the workplace but is that really the case? Actually, there are elements in your workplace that are within your ability to control if not change. You simply have to know what they are.

If you are dissatisfied with your situation, you have two options. You can quit your job and depart for an entirely new environment, or you can adjust your actions, behaviors, or expectations to be more in sync with the demands of the other key players in the environment in which you work. Some would even say that there is a third option. You could try to change the environment in which you work but as we have mentioned previously, the chances of success in such an endeavor are questionable. The point is that each of us by our mere presence can have an influence, however large or small, on our workplace environment.

There are, however, other forces at work here that are not within our control. Suppose that you worked at Radio Shack, in 2006, when they departed from traditional protocol in announcing a layoff. Instead of calling workers together for a face-to-face announcement, Radio Shack management sent nearly 400 employees in the company's Fort Worth, Texas, headquarters an email that according to *The Houston Chronicle* stated, "The work force reduction notification is currently in progress. Unfortunately your position is one that has been eliminated." The targeted employees then had "30 minutes to collect their thoughts, make phone calls, and say goodbye to employees before they went to meet with senior leaders." While this seems like a rather crude way to deal with such a sensitive subject, this is the path Radio Shack executives decided to take. It is doubtful that any of the employees or even any of the line managers were involved in formulating this decision.

What if the Board of Directors of Axiom Business Services decides tomorrow to lay off its entire sales force in favor of a "sales-by-phone" call center in Mumbai, India? Cal Jones may disagree with that plan but there is not much he can do about it.

When Cal Jones began his career at Axiom Business Services nearly fifteen years ago, worker expectations were different. His father, Charlie Jones, was nearing retirement age. Charlie only had a high school education but was persistent enough to land a good paying job at a large automotive plant where he bought into a workplace promise that was common at the time—"if you put your shoulder to the wheel and keep your nose clean, you can work here until you retire." It was a good deal but Charlie was not a gambling man, so he joined the local union as added insurance that the company would keep their part of the bargain. And, so they did as did hundreds of other businesses and as a result, millions of Americans dedicated their working lives to a single company and the middle class prospered.

By the time Charlie retired, he had saved enough to live out his retirement years in comfort and still have a little tucked away to help Cal start his family. Now, Cal was eagerly looking forward to his retirement but something had changed. Since his father,

47

God rest his soul, retired, the number of jobs trickling off to Mexico, China, India or Southeast Asia had become a torrent and legislation hostile to unions had taken its toll on good-paying union jobs. The security that Cal's father had found in the workplace had all but evaporated.

In an effort to compete in the global marketplace, companies restructured. Some flattened their organizational hierarchy effectively eliminating much of middle management. Large corporations gobbled up competitors, consolidated jobs, and slashed what they considered to be excess manpower from the payroll. Massive layoffs topped the headlines devastating communities whose fortunes were tied to the "local" factory.

As Robert Allen Zimmerman, better known as the folksinger Bob Dylan, warned years earlier that "the times they are a changing." And, so they did and continue to change right in front of Cal's eyes.

Cal had given Axiom what he considered the best years of his working life. Now that he was nearing the time in his life where the company had promised to pay off with a comfortable retirement for him and his family, things had changed and Cal was not very happy about it.

Rumors that Axiom was ripe for a buyout flourished and the idea that a layoff was imminent seemed to surface every few months. The old bargain, "if you put your shoulder to the wheel and keep your nose clean, you can work here until you retire," was out the window as well and pensions were on the chopping block.

As much as Cal wanted to shield his wife Marge from the turmoil at work, he could not keep it to himself any longer. "The way things are going with Breedlove if a layoff actually materializes, who do you think will be the first to go?" Marge wanted to think that the new boss would consider other factors, but she knew Cal was right.

When the goals of the company, your manager, and you do not align in a natural confluence, a win-win-win situation is created only if someone is willing to bend. So as we look more closely at what type of forces influence the key workplace players in formulating their goals, let us not forego consideration of how resistant to change you, your manager, or the company might be.

Company

The company, an abstract entity authorized by the state, is embodied in the executive officers and a board of directors who are responsible to the owners or shareholders who hold stock in the company and expect a return on their investments. Companies come in a variety of sizes, from the small mom-and-pop shops on the corner down the street to the giants like General Motors, Wal-Mart, Exxon Mobil, and Ford to name a few of the largest corporations in the world. These behemoths have sales in the billions and exceed the gross domestic product of many countries.

Many influences drive the decisions corporate leaders make and can mean life or death for the company in an increasingly competitive global marketplace. These issues filter down into the workplace environment depending upon how the executives deal with the stresses these issues propagate. Many of the more notable influences that weigh upon the minds of executives have to do with the costs of doing business and include:

- **Credit**
- **Energy**
- **Health Care**
- **Labor**
- **Aging Workforce**
- **Regulatory Compliance**
- **Public Relations**

Credit: Issues surrounding the cost of borrowing money may not enter into the consciousness of most people. However, access to credit has long been a major concern for business executives who need ready sources of capital to acquire equipment, expand operations, or meet payroll.

The Chicago Federal Reserve Bank provides a simple explanation for what drives the cost of credit. "The general level of interest rates is determined by the interaction of the supply and demand for credit." Supply is created when people save money and banks have a ready supply of money to loan to borrowers. Demand for credit is created when people or businesses want to borrow money. Several factors influence this equation, such as expected inflation, economic conditions, Federal Reserve actions, and governmental fiscal policy.

When the Fed tightens access to money by increasing interest rates, businesses feel the pinch through an increased cost of borrowing. An increase of a quarter of a point means that banks will be charged a quarter of a percentage point more for money they borrow from the Federal Reserve, a cost they pass on to customers who borrow from them. "The level of interest rates influences people's behavior," according to information provided by the Chicago Federal Reserve Bank, "by affecting economic decisions that determine the well-being of the nation: how much people are willing to save, and how much businesses are willing to invest."

This is how it is supposed to work. However, in times of crisis, key players in the financial system may be constrained by fear or excessive caution regarding an uncertain future. In the fall of 2008, access to credit dried up. CNN International reported that global markets were reeling "after a historic day on Wall Street that saw [leading U.S. investment bank Lehman Brothers and brokerage firm Merrill Lynch] become the latest victims of the credit crunch."

According to CNN International, "Both Lehmans and Merrill have been caught with huge exposures to unsecured mortgages, the bad debts at the heart of the so-called credit crunch that has devalued the U.S. housing market and sent financial shockwaves worldwide." With doubts rippling through the financial community as to which major institution might be the next to fall, formerly reliable sources of credit have dried up thus precipitating uncertainty in the business community about who may be swept away in the next domino sequence of failures.

Experts say the stage for this crisis was set on October 22, 1999, when Congress voted to repeal the Glass-Steagall Act of 1933. *Frontline*, a respected investigative program aired on PBS, broached this issue in a segment entitled "The Long Demise of Glass-Steagall." *Frontline* reported that "following the Great Crash of 1929, one of every five banks in America fails. Many people, especially politicians, see market speculation engaged in by banks during the 1920s as a cause of the crash." As a result, "individual investors were seriously hurt by banks whose overriding interest was promoting stocks of interest and benefit to the banks, rather than to individual investors." Businesses that relied on the banks for sources of capital also suffered.

In 1933, Congress erected a *wall* between banks and investment firms with passage of the Glass-Steagall Act which prevented banks from pursuing risky speculative investments, and created the Federal Deposit Insurance Corporation (FDIC) to insure bank deposits thus cementing consumer confidence in the stability of banks. But in 1986 cracks began to appear when the Federal Reserve Board reinterpreted the Glass-Steagall Act with its decision that "banks can have *up to 5 percent* of gross revenues from investment banking business," reports *Frontline*. This action by the Federal Reserve Board overruled objections of Fed Chairman Paul Volcker who expressed "his fear that lenders will recklessly lower loan standards in pursuit of lucrative securities offerings and market bad loans to the public." Sound familiar? Subsequent incremental actions by the Fed precipitated complete removal of the *wall* between banks and investment firms by Congress with repeal of the Glass-Steagall Act in 1999.

As a result of the collapse of financial markets in 2008, the stock market, one measure of the financial health of the business community, took a nose dive "with the Dow and S&P 500 falling to 12-year lows after mammoth insurance company American International Group's huge quarterly loss added to worries about the financial sector and the economy," reported CNN Money on March 2, 2009.

Restarting the economy and rebuilding consumer confidence are significant challenges given the current economic climate. Even though Congress poured nearly a trillion dollars of taxpayer money into a constipated economy, financial markets continue on a rollercoaster ride. Nearly half a decade after the collapse of the housing market, investor fears have yet to be calmed, business growth remains constrained by sluggish credit markets, and full recovery looms titillating over the horizon.

Energy: The cost of energy impacts everything that moves in the business world. According to the Energy Information Administration which provides official energy statistics from the U.S. government, the price of crude oil on the world market hovered around $25.72 in May of 2003. Military action in Iraq commenced in March of that year. In 2004, oil prices began a steady climb reaching $115.11 on May 9, 2008.

"Worries that world oil demand will outstrip global supplies intensified on [May 22, 2008], sending ripples through the global economy as oil prices leaped above $135, a new record high," reported Graham Bowley and David Jolly in *The International Harold Tribune*. That was the situation until the U.S. economy plunged toward recession in the latter half of 2008 and the price of oil plummeted to unexpected lows.

The popular television news magazine *60 Minutes* covered the issue of wild swings in oil prices in a segment entitled "Did Speculation Fuel Oil Price Swings?" The moderator opened with the following comment about oil prices. "In a year's time, a commodity that was theoretically priced according to supply and demand doubled from $69 a barrel to nearly $150, and then in a period of three months, crashed along with the stock market."

Oil company representatives have traditionally blamed price fluctuations on the forces of supply and demand, and the lack of new processing facilities due to over-regulation. However, Petroleum Marketers Association President Dan Gilligan offered a different rationale to *60 Minutes* reporter Steve Kroft, "Approximately 60 to 70 percent of the oil contracts in the futures markets are now held by speculative entities. Not by companies that need oil." These are investors looking for market fluctuations in order to capitalize on their investments, not users of oil products such as airlines and oil companies that have traditionally driven demand for petroleum products Gilligan explains. "All [investors] do is buy the paper, and hope that they can sell it for more than they paid for it. Before they have to take delivery."

Michael W. Masters, Managing Member and Portfolio Manager for Masters Capital Management, who also appeared on the *60 Minutes* program, offered in testimony before the U.S. Senate Subcommittee on Energy his explanation for excessive oil price fluctuations. "When Index Speculators pour large amounts of money into the commodities markets and buy large amounts of futures contracts, prices go up. When they pull large amounts of money out prices go down. These large financial players have become the primary source of the dramatic and damaging volatility seen in oil prices," Masters told members the Subcommittee. The players to whom Masters refers are "the big Wall Street investment banks like Morgan Stanley, Goldman Sachs, Barclays, and J.P. Morgan." These are the same large investment firms whose names have been closely associated with the sub-prime mortgage meltdown blamed for the near collapse of the U.S. financial system.

While market fluctuations due to supply and demand may present a significant challenge to executives trying to position their companies to deal with them, such fluctuations are often cyclical and somewhat predictable. However, when energy price fluctuations are amplified by excessive speculation, the results can appear unexpectedly like a rogue wave on an otherwise calm ocean and sweep through the business community with devastating results.

"The 2009 [*International Energy Outlook*] report [released by the Energy Information Administration of the U.S. Department of Energy] highlights Asia's insatiable demand for energy and suggests that China is moving ever closer to the point where it will overtake the Unites States as the world's number one energy consumer," writes Professor Michael T. Klare, author of "Rising Powers, Shrinking Plant: The New Geopolitics of Energy" and "Blood and Oil" in an article he posted on TomDispatch.com, "Clearly, a new era of cutthroat energy consumption is upon us." Add to that continued speculation that the *peak oil* milestone has been reached or is fast approaching and concerns over energy costs are unlikely to diminish anytime soon.

Health Care: Concerns over the skyrocketing costs of health care have added to the burdens weighing on the minds of business leaders. "The reform of the country's health care system is not only essential for ensuring people have access to high quality health care, it is also increasingly important for the country's economic well-being. The inefficiency of the health care system is imposing an ever-greater strain on the economy," writes Dean Baker, co-director of the Center for Economic and Policy Research in a *TruthOut* editorial in 2008. What affects the American economy often cascades down to companies doing business within the current economic climate. "The United States already pays more than twice as much per person for health care," Baker continues, as compared with the average cost in other wealthy nations. This is one explanation for the competitive nature of foreign labor markets.

"Workers are concerned with maintaining or expanding their coverage, while employers seek relief from the relentless cost of inflation that has made health benefits the fastest-rising component of employee compensation," explains Joel C. Cantor, Nancy L. Barrand, Randolph A. Desonia, and Alan B. Cohen of The Robert Wood Johnson Foundation and Jeffrey C. Merrill, a professor at the Columbia School of Public Health, in a *DataWatch* article entitled "Business Leaders' Views on American Health Care." "Ninety-one percent of the top executives surveyed [by The Gallup Organization in 1990 on behalf of The Robert Wood Johnson Foundation] expressed the view that fundamental changes or complete rebuilding of the [health care] system is needed." Executives who once shied away from any alternative to employer-sponsored health insurance are now beginning to line up in support of other less costly options.

Sensing that change was in the works following the election of Barack Obama, big pharmaceutical and health insurance companies recruited an army of lobbyists to descend on Congress in opposition to any plan that would cut into the astronomical profits they have enjoyed in spite of the economic recession which has devastated so many other enterprises. Those supporting a government-operated, single-payer health insurance option similar to Medicare marshaled a grassroots response. On March 23, 2010, President Obama signed into law, The Affordable Care Act which rolls out comprehensive health insurance reforms with the most significant changes occurring in 2014. What impact this has on health care costs and the economy remains to be seen.

Labor: As a commodity, labor is frequently valued in terms of supply and demand. That means the larger the pool of available workers, the lower the price. In the early 1900s, Henry Ford instituted balance in this equation with the idea that workers at Ford plants should be able to afford the cars they manufactured. History records often bloody battles between union organizers and those corporate bosses who lacked Ford's sense of balance. While unionization has represented a significant concern of executives challenged with managing the cost of labor, increased globalization of the economy seems to have matched if not overtaken that concern.

With continued expansion of the global marketplace, more and more businesses feel the pinch of shifting global economic conditions. This truth was aptly stated in an editorial in the *American Progress* in 2008. "Our economy is inextricably linked to the global economy. Globalization encompasses not only the accelerated movement of capital and goods and services across international boundaries, but also the less reflected-upon movement of labor across international borders."

Rivers follow a downhill course, especially when swollen by flood waters, unless checked by dikes and levees. Wages follow a similar downhill path unless balanced by equitable and enforceable labor agreements, especially when there is an abundant source of cheap labor. Cheap, because in some industries foreign workers toil under horrendous conditions without the protections of government regulations and are paid a mere fraction of what an American worker would earn doing the same job.

Globalization and the Poor, a report on sweatshops issued by The Independent Institute in 2004, indicates apparel workers in El Salvador take home $1.38 per hour for their efforts. At that rate, workers earn $2,760 per year. How can companies paying the prevailing wages in America compete with that? The plain unvarnished fact is they cannot which is why most clothing products are now produced overseas.

Other countries with newly emerging economies such as India provide highly skilled workers willing to develop software, man international call centers, and provide medical services for wages and benefits that undercut compensation expected by American workers. Under prevailing conditions, executives who want their companies to remain competitive in the global marketplace often have no choice but to reduce the wages of domestic workers or ship jobs to foreign production centers.

According to The Office of The U.S. Trade Representative in 2011, the United States had "free trade agreements" with 17 countries with three more pending Congressional approval. International trade agreements such as the General Agreement on Trade and Tariffs (GATT), the North American Free Trade Agreement (NAFTA), and the Central American Free Trade Agreement (CAFTA) which were sold with the idea that they would increase commerce while helping improve conditions and wages for workers in third world countries have not entirely lived up to that hype. They have, however, resulted in a temptingly available supply of cheap foreign labor for corporate executives desperate to cut production costs in an increasingly competitive global marketplace.

Aging Workforce: An aging workforce inserts additional dynamics into the workplace in terms of the massive number of pending retirements in the coming decade. Executives must develop plans to replace critical skills while ensuring retirement programs are adequately funded. The problem is so acute that Senator Herb Kohl (D-Wisconsin) announced in a press release in 2005 that he had introduced the Older Worker Opportunity Act. "The bill is aimed at expanding opportunities for older Americans and baby boomers to work longer if they so choose" to "curb a major workforce drain as seventy-seven million people quickly approach retirement age." The bill was introduced again in 2007 and 2009 but has not reached the Senate floor for a vote.

An article in *The Houston Chronicle,* penned by Eun Kyung Kim, indicates that "the U.S. Office of Personnel Management estimates 60 percent of the federal workforce will be eligible to retire in the next decade, and about 40 percent of those workers are likely to do so. The office has launched a recruitment effort to stem what the agency's Director Linda Springer is calling the 'federal retirement tsunami.'" On a national scale with "the first of 78 million baby boomers turning 60 this year, the U.S. faces a shortfall in skilled workers that promises to accelerate as more employees move toward retirement." The prospect of such a massive flood of impending retirements challenges corporate executives to find sustainable solutions to funding retirement benefits and recruiting large numbers of skilled workers to replace the retirees.

Regulatory Compliance: Through laws, regulatory mandates, and audits, regulatory agencies charged with oversight of companies operating in various industries have varying degrees of influence over the operational environment of these companies. Even so, each regulatory mandate comes at a cost for business both in terms of compliance and possible fines for non-compliance. While the cost of regulatory compliance is generally seen as overhead, it can also be viewed by corporate executives in terms of cost avoidance. Avoiding an accident or incident means avoiding costly downtime, medical care, and possible litigation.

Various government agencies regulate and provide oversight authority for their associated industries. For example, the Securities and Exchange Commission (SEC) oversees Wall Street and investment markets. The Federal Aviation Administration (FAA) keeps a watchful eye on the aviation industry while the Federal Energy Regulatory Commission (FERC) monitors the power industry.

Government regulatory agencies serve to monitor and regulate the behavior of various industries while at the same time providing a buffer between companies operating in those industries and a concerned public. The Interstate Commerce Commission (ICC), the first regulatory agency established in America, was formed in 1893 to calm demands from enraged citizens to reign in the abuses of the large railroad monopolies formed in the wake of the American Civil War. According to the Community Environmental Legal Defense Fund, Richard Olney, the U.S. Attorney General at that time, reassured railroad executives that the ICC "satisfied the popular clamor for a government supervision of the railroads, at the same time that the supervision is almost entirely nominal. Further, the older such a commission gets to be, the more inclined it will be to take the business and railroad side of things. It thus becomes a sort of barrier between the railroad corporations and the people and a sort of protection against hasty and crude legislation hostile to railroad interests."

Despite the duplicitous motivations expressed by U.S. Attorney General Richard Olney with the establishment of the ICC, regulatory agencies do, at times, vigorously serve the public interest through rigorous enforcement of laws and regulatory mandates. On other occasions, they may complacently tolerate lack of compliance.

"BP's massive oil spill [following an explosion on the oil rig Deepwater Horizon owned by British Petroleum and operated by Transocean] has brought to light the lax oversight of offshore drilling by federal regulators, who have routinely allowed oil companies to engage in risky deep water drilling operations with waivers from environmental review and wholly inadequate emergency response plans. The result is the worst manmade environmental disaster in the nation's history," stated the Southern Environmental Law Center in summarizing a law suit they have filed against the Minerals Management Service (now known as the Bureau of Ocean Energy Management, Regulation, and Enforcement).

Corporate leaders carefully monitor which way this pendulum swings as it invariably has a direct impact on workplace environments with real costs that appear on corporate balance sheets.

Public Relations: And finally, there is the cost of corporate turmoil which has associated costs in terms of declining stock prices, goodwill, employee morale, and customer loyalty. Whether it is CEOs behaving badly, stockholders fighting for control, questions of product safety, or employee malfeasance, all can have a negative effect on the bottom line and, therefore, must be of concern to company leaders.

When issues surface in the public eye as has been the case with the arrest of Rupert Murdoch's News of the World former editor Rebekah Brooks in conjunction with the phone hacking scandal in the United Kingdom, the criminal investigation of Goldman Sachs Group by the Manhattan District Attorney's Office for alleged securities fraud in association with the credit crisis, Halliburton's questionable performance in feeding American troops serving in Iraq, the exorbitant $400 million severance package given Exxon-Mobil's departing CEO Lee R. Raymond in 2005, and Royal Dutch Shell's alleged association with paramilitary death squads in Nigeria, shareholders may voice concerns and dissatisfaction at an annual shareholder's meeting or customers may be swayed to shift their allegiance to a rival brand.

The marketplace is full of unknowns and these unknowns create stresses that can weigh heavily upon corporate executives whose tenure may rest precariously upon whether their decisions result in an increase of shareholder value. The fact is that the decisions corporate executives make, in response to the various influences they encounter, have an impact on you and your workplace environment. Some decisions may make your job easier while other decisions may eliminate your job altogether. These and a whole host of other factors influence changes to the corporate agenda and help shape the conditions you encounter when you step foot in the door.

Newton's first law of motion states that a body in motion will continue in motion unless acted upon by an outside force. The larger the body, the more force it takes to change its direction. For this reason, large companies are at least as hard to steer as a large ocean liner. Once the lookouts on the RMS Titanic spotted the iceberg on that dark North Atlantic night in 1912, it was too late for the captain, even with all the ship's controls at his disposal, to alter the path of that ill-fated vessel. More than 1500 souls perished as a result.

While many chief executives are well compensated for their efforts to steer the corporate ship on a path that profits shareholders, not all executives are up to the task. Changing the path of a large corporation to coincide with or in anticipation of changes in the marketplace or worker concerns is no easy job. CEOs may be hampered by a burdensome decision-making process, an inherent fear of change, or the challenge of communicating intentions through a communication-challenged organization. Often details of the new course must seep deep into the organization for the change to take hold. This takes time, and it takes persistence. Not all executives have the luxury of both.

When considering the question of change, especially in terms of large organizations, I reflect upon the wisdom Evelyn Ganzglass, Director of Workforce Development for the Center of Law and Social Policy, once shared with me: *Think of organizational change in glacial terms.*

Manager

Managers are the on-site representatives of the company. What motivates them are some of the same things that motivate anyone to keep showing up at work such as a sense of accomplishment or a paycheck. A personal agenda drives some managers. Others are pushed by the desire to do what is necessary to keep their jobs. Still others seek a sense of accomplishment in serving those individuals who report to them.

However, managers find themselves in the unenviable position of having their performance scrutinized from above as well as below. They are confronted with many of the same challenges of the company plus issues of resources, budget, worker productivity plus they often have to fend off peers out to lay claim to their turf. At the same time, they must keep upper management content, keep their subordinates motivated and productive, serve the needs of both internal and external customers, and do it all with limited resources and shrinking budgets.

Some of the key factors that weigh upon the manager and may influence behavior include the following:

- **Resources**
- **Talent**
- **Production Quotas**
- **Expectations of Quality**
- **Management Skills**
- **Personal Issues**

Resources: The availability of resources often determines the success or failure of a manager. Resources can mean equipment, supplies, information or personnel but usually in terms of getting the job done, an adequate supply of qualified personnel is the key. When the company fails to recruit or retain a sufficient number of skilled and motivated workers, the result is often that a small group of top talent is overburdened while everyone else is grossly underutilized. This leads to early burnout of the manager's most valuable employees. Having the best resumes, the top talent also has the easiest time finding a new job which exacerbates the situation for those left behind and simply encourages further departures.

Lean budgets can impact the availability of critical equipment and supplies. Communications can affect access to essential information. Budget and hiring practices can limit the availability of human resources. While managers may be free to request additional resources, they are not always in a position to demand them; therefore, the resources realistically necessary to do the job may not always be forthcoming.

Talent: Hiring Practices have a significant influence over a manager's ability to manage. Some organizations hire only the "best" and the "brightest," or so they say, while other organizations may serve as a collection point for the dregs, poor performers, troublemakers, and old timers waiting out the clock until retirement. How and why employees are assigned to an organization and the skills, knowledge, and abilities or lack of them are all important influences weighing on the manager.

In the 1960s, NASA launched the Mercury, Gemini, and Apollo missions which landed several men on the moon and returned them safely to Earth, a goal set by President John Fitzgerald Kennedy. Money flowed as America's best and brightest were assembled in a common national goal. In the 1990s, NASA budgets were slashed. As veterans with extensive experience retired, they were replaced by aerospace engineers fresh out of college. The culture of America's manned-space program had shifted from a financially flush "gung-ho" test pilot atmosphere to a more timid *if-there's-an-accident-I-hope-I'm-not-the-one-that-caused-it* sentiment of novice engineers doing the best they could to operate what was thought to be the most complex machine on the planet with an ever shrinking budget.

I worked in this environment and could feel the tension build before each shuttle flight and relax by flight phases as we watched the mission unfold on monitors hung from hallway ceilings in our building. Once the vehicle reached orbit, the Ascent Flight Design Group would relax their tightly clenched fists. Members of the Orbit Design Group remained on edge until the de-orbit burn. Only after *wheel stop* following touchdown at either Vandenberg Air Force Base in the high desert of California or on a runway alongside alligator infested canals at the Kennedy Space Center on Florida's east coast did members of the Descent Flight Design group breathe a sigh of relief. You can imagine the pressure this placed on the Shuttle Flight Design managers who had little or no control over the recruitment process due to budget constraints imposed upon them from above.

Production Quotas: Production quotas can be realistic and possible to achieve or unrealistic and impossible to achieve. When they are realistic and based on historical data, they can be useful tools to sustain or guide incremental increases in production over time. When they are unrealistic, they can be deadly.

"Cintas Corp. sets unrealistic production quotas for laundry workers that cause dangerous conditions and it led to the death of one worker in March 2007, according to a motion filed in a lawsuit against the company," reports Kevin Osborne on CityBeat.com. "The U.S. Occupational Safety and Health Administration (OSHA) fined Cintas $2.78 million" for the incident. The amount was reduced to $2.76 million in a settlement reached with the U.S. Justice Department."

A natural tension exists between production quotas and safety. Unless properly managed production quotas can easily drive employees to take risks they would not otherwise consider. Companies that favor production over safety are gambling with the health and wellbeing of their employees.

Managers who face unrealistic production quotas or productivity targets are caught in a lose-lose situation. They lose if they don't achieve the prescribed quotas or targets. If they drive their workers to achieve the impossible, what they gain in the short term risks the destruction of employee morale when it becomes apparent that upper management now expects a level of performance which is unsustainable in the long term.

Expectations of Quality: The level of quality expected by customers can have a significant effect on the manager. Potential exists for quality to drop at every step in a process for which the manager may be responsible but over which she may have little control. The culture set by upper management in conjunction with the expectations of the customer base can drive a quality rich or quality starved environment regardless of actions taken by the manager. High production quotas buttressed with high expectations of quality promotes the tendency to cut corners if the resources necessary to meet production targets are not readily available.

Some customers have demanding requirements and little tolerance for error without risking catastrophic results similar to those experienced with the loss of the space shuttle Challenger in 1986. Such disasters leave scars on an industry for years, if not decades. In the case of Challenger, Morton-Thiokol management questioned the judgment of engineers who recognized that a launch on that frigid January morning was outside the experience window for operation of the solid rocket booster joint seals and therefore, was extremely risky. Driven by pressure from NASA to avoid astronomical costs associated with launch delays, management overruled the engineers. As it turns out, the engineers were justified in their fear of the unknown.

Six Sigma is, as defined by iSixSigma LLC, "a disciplined, data-driven approach and methodology for eliminating defects in any process – from manufacturing to transactional and from product to service." Motorola and Allied Signal were among the first to implement Six Sigma methodologies with General Electric following in 1995. While these companies reported significant savings, such an approach is not implemented without a significant investment of capital and resources.

When capital and resources are insufficient to achieve management's demand for quality, the manager may be left hanging. Unfortunately, the quest for excellence sometimes results in a paralytic philosophy that dictates it is safer to do nothing than to risk doing something which might turn out to be wrong.

Management Skills: Management skills are essential to a manager's ability to be successful. Many of these skills are not ones that most people come by naturally. When circumstances conspire and people suddenly find themselves in an official position of leadership, the skills that made them successful in their professional areas may not be sufficient to make them successful as managers.

"Skills that once seemed optional—creating strategic advantage, promoting global perspective, leveraging individual and cultural diversity, to name a few—have become as important as the core management skills of, for example, building relationships or establishing plans," Susan H. Gebelein, Lisa A. Stevens, Carol J. Skube, David G. Lee, Brian L. Davis, and Lowel W. Hellervik authors of the 2000 edition of the *Successful Manager's Handbook*. "Other managerial skills that were basically nonexistent sixteen years ago such as managing technology have become requirements for survival in today's business world."

Managing people requires a different set of skills then those required to program a computer. Engineers who can solve complex equations may be challenged to resolve conflict between subordinates. Accountants who can audit billion-dollar transactions may not have the skills to create customer loyalty. Computer programmers who can design complex software solutions may have difficulty inspiring team synergy.

The *Successful Manager's Handbook* documents a useful, although lengthy repertoire of skills for a manager to master. Those managers who are missing essential skills may find themselves challenged to address all the situations that might arise under their watch. Authors of the *Successful Manager's Handbook* view the road to becoming an effective manager as a journey and offer the following relevant advice for those pursuing a management path, "a basic plan or roadmap can help guide you to achieve your personal and career goals. The plan you choose will depend on your desired destination." We will visit this idea as it applies to your desire to find success in the workplace in more detail later.

Personal Issues: Personal issues do not always park themselves at the door when the work day begins. Managers are not immune to the trials and tribulations of everyday life in a modern society. Since we address these issues in more detail in terms of forces that influence you, we will not labor you with that discussion here.

Regardless of the challenges your manager may face or the influences that may exacerbate those challenges, she holds the potential for having a tremendous influence over the environment in which you work. She can shield you from negative as well as positive external forces. She can levy near dictatorial control over your work activities or go missing in action. She can make the workplace a fun, challenging place to be or turn it into a living hell even on Saturdays. The point is that, for better or worse, your manager wields a great amount of power to shape the workplace environment and is herself influenced by a variety of forces. Unfortunately, some managers become so mired in responding to the forces that weigh upon their decisions that they are not fully present when it comes to creating the workplace culture. This either enhances or complicates your ability to perform and their ability to manage.

You

And then, there is *you*, the employee, with all of the needs, expectations, goals, strengths, and human frailties that we all share. Do you have financial troubles? A second mortgage? Overbearing tax burdens? Are you living off credit cards? Do family problems intrude on your thoughts when you are at work? Were you recently granted bail on charges of threatening to throttle the police officer who gave you a speeding ticket? Did you fail the GED? Are you really qualified to do your job? All of us bring to work with us a certain amount of baggage. Take an introspective moment to review which of the following forces may significantly influence your decisions and behavior in the workplace:

- **Professional Skills**
- **Job Security**
- **Job Satisfaction**
- **Personal Issues**

Professional Skills: Each profession has its own set of skills. Some are transportable from other professions while some are not. It would be impossible to itemize here all of the professions that encompass human activity, let alone to provide a list of the skills necessary to perform successfully in even a few them.

The skill requirements of some professions change rapidly, especially those driven by advances in science or technology. Regardless of how fast your industry embraces the future, it is important for you to evaluate whether you possess all the skills you need to meet the requirements of your job and to perform at your very best.

Any lack of an essential skill may cause your performance to suffer as well as your confidence and the confidence your peers have in your ability to perform. Therefore, we will suffice to say that unless you have reached the masters level in your chosen field, there is more that you can do to improve how well you perform your job. If continuing to enhance your skill base is not a concern to you, it probably should be; otherwise, you will find it difficult to advance your career.

Job Security: Job security is a serious issue for many people. Losing your job may impact your self-esteem, leave you without health insurance, or put undue stress on your family relationships. For people who live paycheck-to-paycheck, losing their job can quickly place them at risk of slipping below the poverty line. How real of a possibility is that for you?

The White House announced early in 2009 that 598,000 names had been added to the unemployment rolls in January alone, this news coming on the heels of economic turmoil caused by the collapse of the sub-prime mortgage bubble in 2008. In March 2009, CNN reported that the "U.S. unemployment rate jump[ed] to 8.1%," up significantly from 5.0% reported by the United States Bureau of Labor Statistics in May of 2008. In July of 2011 it had trended up to 9.1%. With the economy hovering on recession, job growth figures show little likelihood that the unemployment rate will drop significantly anytime soon.

In states that have adopted the so-called *at will* laws, job security is a questionable concept at best since employees can be terminated *without cause*. According to Ronald B. Standler, author of "*History of At-Will Employment Law in the USA*," the principle of *at will* employment first surfaced in the legal treatise *Master and Servant* published by Horace C. Wood in 1877. "The rule is that an employee can quit at any time and an employer can fire an employee at any time and for any [lawful] reason," states Ross Runkel, founder of LawMemo and Professor of Law Emeritus at Willamette University College of Law. "Because this is a contract rule, the employer and employee are free to change it by agreement. But if their agreement is silent on the question, then the employee can be discharged without warning, without a hearing, and without a reason."

Sure, you have the right to quit but your *at will* departure would certainly have less impact on the company than your *at will* termination by the company would have on you. In these volatile economic times, this leaves whether you have a job tomorrow almost entirely in the hands of the company unless you have a contract which specifically addresses the conditions under which you can be terminated. Most people do not have such a contract with their employer.

Union members, however, have some recourse against arbitrary termination due to their membership in the bargaining unit which negotiated a work contract with the company. This might explain why the business lobby vehemently opposes efforts by employees to unionize? "Most of the time, employees who want to form a union are threatened and intimidated by their employers. And all too often, if they don't heed the warnings, they're fired, even though that's illegal," reveals former Secretary of Labor Robert B. Reich in a piece he penned for *The Los Angeles Times* in January of 2009. "We tried to penalize employers that broke the law, but the fines are minuscule. Too many employers consider them a cost of doing business." David R. Francis writes in an article for *The Christian Science Monitor* that the United States is the only industrialized nation to have a "'union avoidance' industry of any size engaged in helping management resist unionization, undermine union strength, or unload existing unions."

Business leaders often rationalize attempts to emasculate unions as an effort to drive down the cost of labor to be more competitive in the global marketplace. How valid is that claim? True, "corporate profits have doubled since 2001," states Kaplan, "while real wages have flatlined [sic]." However, CNN Money.com reveals, "In 2004, the ratio of the average CEO pay to the average pay of a production (i.e., non-management) worker was 431-to-1, up from 301-to-1 in 2003, according to 'Executive Excess,'" an annual report released by United for a Fair Economy and the Institute for Policy Studies. This means that if you earned $30,000 last year, the average CEO took home nearly $13 million, up from $9 million the year before. That equates to a 44% raise. You may be wondering: Why has the cost of *executive labor* skyrocketed while worker pay has stagnated? Good question!

Performance is often cited as the reason for astronomical executive salaries but CNN Money.com counters that assertion. "Between 1991 and 2004, the stock of the previous year's most highly paid CEO underperformed the S&P 500 half the time, in some instances by a stunning amount. The most glaring example was Computer Associates. In 1999, the company paid its CEO $655 million as part of his share of a $1.1 billion stock bonus for the company's three top officers. In 2000, the stock plummeted 72 percent, while the S&P 500 fell 10 percent." Regardless of any rationale to the contrary, the result of the growing disparity between worker and CEO compensation has created an upward redistribution of wealth.

We simply want to underscore the point that there is an ongoing battle between organized labor and management over control of the workplace and distribution of corporate profits. In general, organized labor represents the interests of workers while the business lobby represents corporate interests. The long-standing bias toward business appeared to be swinging back toward labor with President Barack H. Obama's appointment of former California Representative Hilda Solis, a longtime proponent of labor, as the new Secretary of Labor. However, overreaching attacks on unionized public workers initiated by Wisconsin Governor Scott Walker, with the support of the so-called "Tea Party" movement believed to be funded by the oil billionaires David and Charles Koch may have done more to galvanize public sentiment in favor of defending the collective bargaining power unions bring to the workplace than any single appointment by President Obama.

Still organizing a union is one of the most risky pursuits a worker can undertake. It is, however, less risky to join a union where one already exists. Even so, the simple fact is that there is safety in numbers. When workers organize under a union banner, they are more able to negotiate for better working conditions, a bigger cut of corporate profits, and increased job security. Besides that, ask yourself: *Who else will stand with me against the power of the corporation when confronted with issues that may threaten my job?*

Job Satisfaction: An important factor relating to your success at work is job satisfaction. Unfortunately, job satisfaction amongst American workers is declining. "Rapid technological changes, rising productivity demands and changing employee expectations have all contributed to a decline in job satisfaction," says Lynn Franco, Director of the National Federation of Independent Business' The Conference Board, a business research organization which is best known for the Consumer Confidence Index and the Leading Economic Indicators. A survey commissioned by The Conference Board found that "employees are least satisfied with their companies' bonus plans, promotion policies, health plans, and pensions."

Pay disparity between men and women performing the same job can easily impact job satisfaction. Women may be marching in April on *Equal Pay Day* but they are certainly not celebrating. The National Committee on Pay Equity (NCPE) "organizes the national observance of Equal Pay Day to raise awareness of unfair pay [practices] in America," states the NCPE web site. "Tuesday is symbolic of the point into the new week that a woman must work in order to earn the wages paid a man in the previous week."

Concerns over pay disparity will certainly not be assuaged by Hanah Cho writing in *The South Florida Sun-Sentinel*. "Ten years after graduation, the pay gap gets worse with women earning 69 percent of what men earn, according to a new study by the American Association of University Women Educational Foundation." Earlier in her article, she had mentioned that one year out of college, "women earn 20 percent less than their male counterparts."

If you are a minority female, "you have the highest levels of disparities in income in comparison to men." This is according to Linda Chavez-Thompson, executive vice president of the AFL-CIO, and Gabriela Lemus, executive director of the Labor Council for Latin American Advancement, writing in *The Chicago Sun-Times*. In their article entitled "Erosion of Unions Hurts Women, Particularly Latinas," Chavez-Thompson and Lemus write, "Women are struggling. As a result, their families are also facing challenges. Women are the foundation for family decisions and unfortunately, more and more, they carry the primary responsibility and are the sole decision-makers in their children's welfare." Even so, surveys indicate that it is not just women who have expressed dissatisfaction with their jobs. This unrest in the workplace is a cross-gender issue that is impacting millions of workers.

In addition to not being appropriately paid for what you do, the Mayo Foundation for Medical Education and Research offers other reasons why you may not be completely satisfied with your job:

- Conflict between co-workers
- Conflict with your supervisor
- Not having the necessary equipment or resources to succeed
- Lack of opportunities for promotion
- Fear of losing your job through downsizing or outsourcing
- Having little or no say in decisions that affect you

Dissatisfaction with your job brings with it issues that can certainly affect your motivation and productivity.

Personal Issues: As with managers or, for that matter, anyone, personal issues do not always stay at home when the work day begins. Any issue that causes you concern in your personal life has the opportunity of invading your thoughts at work. Such distractions can impair your ability to concentrate. This can negatively affect productivity or can have a serious impact on your personal safety and the safety of those around you.

One of the largest personal issues relates to home ownership. Reporting for MSNBC in 2007, Alex Johnson writes about the mortgage crisis. "The national surge in mortgage defaults is claiming more victims than just the thousands of [sub-prime] borrowers facing the prospect of losing their homes." Other reports put the number of homeowners at risk of defaulting on sub-prime loans in the millions. "Social service agencies say homeless rates are on the rise not only as families lose their own homes to foreclosures but also as renters are evicted after their landlords default." This situation has worsened as the economy teeters on the edge of recession.

The rising cost of living is another issue. Bob Herbert reports in *The New York Times*, "More than 90 million Americans, close to a third of the entire population, are struggling to make ends meet on incomes that are less than twice the official poverty line." You may not be one of those 90 million struggling to make ends meet but even so, such numbers cannot help but prompt concerns that you could be next.

Citing statistics from the Center on Budget and Policy Priorities, Antonia Juhasz, author of *The Bush Agenda: Invading the World, One Economy at a Time,* states, "In 2004, while seventy-six more Americans became billionaires, poverty increased (both the number of poor people and their percentage of the population), real median earnings of fulltime workers fell, median household income fell, fewer people had health insurance, and more people were living in poverty even though they had jobs."

The ability to pay for quality health care is another issue weighing heavily on the minds of many people. Sally Kohn, a principal in the Campaign for Community Values, writes for Common Dreams that "47 million Americans lack health coverage and 79 million more have significant health care debt." Currently, if you lose your job, you loose your health care insurance or the rates you pay go through the roof. This places you at risk of joining the unfortunate millions mentioned by Kohn.

Other personal issues could be prompted by marital problems, conflict with the neighbors, you name it. If it is a problem in your personal life, there is a chance that it could become a problem in your professional life. Such issues are not only a potential source of performance problems, they are also viewed by ethics professionals as indicators of your potential for unethical or illegal behavior on the job.

Prevailing Environment

Of the entire cast of characters that influence your workplace environment, you and your manager share the starring roles. While the company may be the 800-pound gorilla in the building, that gorilla, figuratively speaking, hangs out a safe distance away in the executive suites on the top floor. Your manager is the 400-pound gorilla next door. The relationship you have with your manager is possibly the greatest determinant of the kind of environment you will inhabit during your working hours.

Most of us do not know what influences actually drive management decisions. We may not know what turbulent conditions our manager has recently experienced. We see only the actions she takes in our presence and we can only guess at what might motivate those actions. Therefore, we are left to speculate in an area which could easily lead us to a wrong conclusion. This could, then, cause us to behave in a way that might make a troubled situation worse.

As previously mentioned, the workplace environment is rife with the potential for conflict. Just as diplomacy is often the best route to harmony among nations, some level of give-and-take is necessary in the workplace to achieve peaceful co-existence. When conflict exists, it is beneficial if all parties practice a little tolerance but how likely is that where you work? It all depends. Who has the most bargaining power? From greatest to least, here is how you rank on the bargaining power scale with the other parties that influence your workplace environment.

1. **Company** – most bargaining power
2. **Manager** – more than you; less than the company
3. **You** – least bargaining power

As you probably suspected, you are on the bottom. The company sits at the top with the manager in the middle. It is a simple matter of who has the authority to hire and fire. Obviously, you do not have authority to fire the company executives or even your manager. That does not mean that under certain conditions you do not have the power to bring them down. Remember the concept of Mutually Assured Destruction? You are also on the bottom in terms of being able to coerce change or sustain the status quo. That does not mean that you cannot suggest or inspire these things but in terms of demanding that others align with your personal agenda, you have the least power.

Even so, the manager does not hold complete power over you and if you approach your relationship with your manager from that point-of-view, you are greatly minimizing your level of influence. The majority of your leverage lies in you being able to manage yourself or being able to walk away from the job if necessary. Oh, you are not able to walk away from your job with any sense of financial security? That is what being on the bottom means.

Your best option in terms of successfully operating within the prevailing environment is for you to be able to manage yourself.

Resistance to Change

Based on our experience and research on the topic, we would suggest that each and every one of the parties, who levy some type of influence over your workplace environment, is inherently resistant to change. Many people labor tirelessly over the idea that the boss will change her behavior. The fact is that she might be just as reluctant to change as you are. Everyone desires change when it is to their benefit but the idea of change carries with it some risk that the new environment may not be better than the previous one. If you do not have a clear view of what the post-change workplace will be like and you are uncertain of those who encourage you to trust them when they tell you that everything will be alright, you may be reticent to take that leap into the unknown. But sometimes you don't have a real choice.

You can labor in a futile effort to try to control all of the parties who levy influence in shaping your workplace environment, or you can focus your efforts in a more productive direction, on yourself. Which is easier? Trying to control whether it will rain tomorrow or having a raincoat available in case it does rain? We hope you are beginning to see that having a raincoat close at hand is the more effective approach to keeping dry when rain is a distinct possibility.

Workplace Environment

Every workplace environment provides limitations, challenges, and opportunities. These things do not always come with flashing lights and labels. It is your job to recognize and confront the limitations and challenges while taking advantage of the opportunities. Even in the seemingly darkest of situations, opportunities may await you just around the corner. Meteorologists know that amidst the whirling winds of a Category 5 hurricane, there is a tranquil eye with clear skies where serenity rules. Imagine how nice it would be to avoid all the devastation and turmoil by moving deftly with the eye of the hurricane until the storm dissipates.

The term *workplace environment*, as we use it throughout these pages, entails all the people and influences that shape the conditions in which you work. It also characterizes the relationship you have with your manager and reveals the motivational level of your manager to be supportive of your efforts to achieve peak performance. You might be fulltime, part time, or a contract employee. You might be exempt from overtime regulations or non-exempt. You might go to an air conditioned office five days a week, work outside in the heat and cold or login from home. You might work in a production line or go door-to-door to deliver the mail. You might serve drinks 30,000 feet above the surface of the earth or breathe heliox, a special mixture of compressed helium and oxygen, as you weld components of a drilling rig at the bottom of the sea. The individual who oversees you may micro-manage work or delegate it. All of these things, and more, could comprise your workplace environment. The environment in which you work is defined by all the factors that impact your ability to perform your job productively.

As we suggested earlier, the weather conditions that one might expect to encounter on any given day range from threatening to balmy and fall into just four categories. Similarly, the full range of workplace environments can be organized in the following four categories:

- **Antagonistic**
- **Contentious**
- **Benign**
- **Supportive**

Each of these workplace environments is defined in terms of the employee's point-of-view. This is an important distinction from other approaches that characterize the failings or frailties of a boss, as it relies specifically on what *you* experience in your workplace environment. This approach helps you avoid basing your judgments on speculation or gossip. You know for a fact what you have experienced personally and, as a result, you know exactly how you feel about your job, your manager, and your workplace. We will delve deeper into how to recognize and work as successfully as possible in each of these environments in subsequent chapters but, for now, let us begin with a snapshot description of each of these four environments.

In an Antagonistic Environment, you receive strong negative attention from your boss. This, to say the least, is a stormy environment with lots of career-killing potential. Your future on a day-to-day basis is not secure. And, while you may not be able to determine for a fact that your boss wants to fire you, transfer you, or by some other means terminate your employment in her organization, you certainly sense that it is a strong possibility. Cal Jones battles to survive in an Antagonistic Environment.

In a Contentious Environment, you receive non-supportive attention from your boss. This is similar to an antagonistic environment but dialed back several notches.

It rains on a regular basis and you may get wet unless you wear some sort of protective gear but the weather is not generally career-threatening. There is, however, a distinct lack of growth potential. There is plenty of opportunity for conflict and strong differences of opinions certainly can exist between you and your boss in this environment but the chances of the boss terminating you are much more remote than in an antagonistic environment. Jennifer Lakes confronts a Contentious Environment.

In a Benign Environment, you receive little or no attention from your boss. This means a lack of good attention as well as bad. It is windy and you may get jostled around by various influences unless you know where and when to seek shelter. This environment differs from an antagonistic or contentious environment in that the turbulence is often generated outside your organization and the boss is unwilling or unable to quell its effect on you and your co-workers. You are more or less on your own in dealing with whatever problems blow in the door. What you will generally experience in this environment is a vacuum of support. Also, it will be challenging to advance your career in this environment since your boss is unlikely to recognize or have any knowledge of your accomplishments or your value to the organization. Mario Molina languishes in a Benign Environment.

In a Supportive Environment, you receive supportive attention from your boss. This is a good place to be. A supportive environment means that your boss is there to help you overcome obstacles and to perform at your best. Your boss may even guide some challenges your way to aid in your professional development but she will not abandon you in times of crisis as long as you make an honest effort to do your best. However, this environment is not to be confused with a free ride. Your boss is not there to cover for you if you are unwilling or unable to put forth the effort that is required to get the job done. If that is the case, you will certainly face troubles in any workplace environment. Twila Fletcher, who we have yet to introduce, enjoys a Supportive Environment.

Antagonistic, **Contentious**, **Benign**, and *Supportive Environments* span the spectrum from an aggressively negative workspace to a pleasantly positive one. In the next few chapters, we will take a look at the characteristics of each environment to help you to recognize in what type of work environment you spend most of your waking hours. This is important knowledge to possess, as it is the first step to preparing a plan of action that will aid you in dealing with your specific workplace situation.

While many of the workplace environments may have similar characteristics, we will help you see the importance of recognizing trends that may be present. For instance, in the dry burning heat of the Mojave Desert it does rain, just not very often. Likewise, in a contentious workplace environment, there may be days when you and your manager have a cordial, friendly exchange. Your manager may even compliment you in public for work well done. Still, the underlying climate is contentious.

Additionally, we will help you learn how to interpret what your environment means for you in terms of challenges and opportunities. We will help you identify and avoid traps that unscrupulous bosses may use to trip you up. We will, then, guide you in preparing an effective plan of action to deal with your specific workplace situation. Finally, you will implement your plan of action and begin to experience the benefits of taking charge of your career, and your future, despite all of the uncontrollable influences that shape the activities going on around you. **The focus will remain on you and the power you have to control your own destiny.**

CHAPTER 5

Surviving in an Antagonistic Environment

An Antagonistic Environment is one in which you receive negative attention from your boss. But, an Antagonistic Environment can also be much more than that. It can be a stormy, potentially turbulent environment with lots of career-killing potential. Job security is non-existent and the sense that your boss wants to fire you, transfer you or by some other means terminate your current employment is an ever present perception.

According to Fair Measures, experts in the field of employment law, "firing an employee on the spot – or taking other fast (negative) action – will almost always be ruled illegal." That does not mean it cannot happen or will not happen. This simply means that if it happens to you, you may be able to successfully dispute the action in court. Winning in court does not guarantee that if you are reinstated, your working environment will be any better than before. Chances are very good that it will be decidedly worse.

An Antagonistic Environment can be a very damaging environment in which to work. It can have a profoundly deleterious influence on your motivation, productivity, and attitude toward the manager, the company, and your job. Unless confronted in an effective manner, an Antagonistic Environment may very well become a self-fulfilling prophecy of doom.

Surprisingly enough, an Antagonistic Environment may not actually be one in which your boss is overtly hostile or a battle of wills plays itself out in plain view of everyone. The battle may rumble under the surface for weeks or months with other employees oblivious to what is really happening. In group meetings, the boss may act politely, professionally, and even cordially toward you. In the presence of figures with higher authority, the boss may even seem supportive but, just as with icebergs, what goes on below the surface can be of extreme concern. One scrape below the waterline can sink a ship while dents and punctures above the water's surface may cause some unsightly damage but generally the vessel survives to sail another day.

Reversal of Roles

To better understand the conditions prevalent in an Antagonistic Environment, try reversing roles with your boss. Imagine that you are in charge and your boss works for you. The roles have changed but not the basic relationship. You have nothing good to say about him, and you have no compunction to rehabilitate him. You want him out of there but have no justifiable reason to fire him. So, let us have some fun. How many ways can you think of to make his workday a living hell in the hope that he will eventually get fed up and leave to find work elsewhere? Here are some of the things that we thought you might want to try.

You could create a generally hostile environment. This does not mean that you need to be mean to him all the time. Be nice once in a while to throw him off guard. Maybe he will start doubting his assessment of you and begin wondering whether he was just imaging that there is a problem. He might even begin to wonder whether he, not you, is really the source of the friction in your working relationship. What could be more perfect?

You could make unreasonable and confusing demands. Make your requests ambiguous enough that you keep him guessing what you actually want him to do. Give him assignments so that no matter what he does it will be wrong. Delegate the work but avoid giving him the authority and by all means do not give him the resources to actually get the job done. Do not get caught in the trap of providing him written instructions, so he can run to a colleague and ask: *Does this make sense to you?* He will use your instructions to find an ally. You want to isolate him. If he asks you for clarification, tell him that you do not understand why he is confused or tell him that you are too busy to show him how to do every little thing. If he is in your office, pick up the phone and stare at him until he gets the idea that this conversation is over and leaves.

Seek opportunities to criticize his performance. You can do this in public but then his peers have the opportunity to evaluate your assessment of his performance, and there is a chance that they may disagree with you. Walk sternly up to him while he is working with others around him and tell him you need to see him in your office right away, then turn and leave. Once he shows up in your office, tell him to close the door. Now rake him over the coals. Show him who is in charge. Question his performance, his judgment, the quality of his work. It is your word against his. Since all this goes on behind closed doors, it will make his co-workers wonder what he did wrong. If he tells them: *I don't know what I did wrong!* That's perfect! It will kick their imaginations into high gear. Plus, they won't know whether one of them might be the next one to wander into your sights.

Avoid addressing these issues directly in public. You can drop a few questions to him in front of his colleagues regarding why a project you gave him is not yet complete. If he has a valid answer, fine. If he does not, you have got him in front of his co-workers. Once a pattern of problems develops, his co-workers may start seeing him as incompetent and begin distancing themselves from him, not wanting to be associated with a poor performer. Once that happens, you are close to victory.

You could belittle any good ideas or accomplishments that he might have. Again, you must walk a fine line here. His co-workers cannot see you as rejecting good ideas that actually make sense. If he starts to suggest something that would place him in a favorable light, ignore it and quickly move on to something else. Put some distance between him and his good idea then assign someone else to implement it. If the idea succeeds, lavish that individual with praise for contributing to your organization. If he claims the idea was his, he looks bad for trying to take praise away from the co-worker you asked to implement the idea. For the most part, simply ignore his accomplishments or good work. Keep steadily focused on his missteps.

How you approach the problem of creating a hostile environment depends on whether you are targeting your wrath on one individual or an entire group. If you want an entire group to suffer, then you have only to preserve the sense of professionalism amongst your superiors. You can be much more proactive and overt in your efforts as long as you employ some means to prevent the group from aligning against you. Your success in antagonizing an entire group of employees to the point that they would rather quit then continue to work under such conditions depends on your ability to isolate them and minimize their credibility in the eyes of anyone with authority over you.

But alas, you are not the boss. You are the lowly employee who suffers through the misguided machinations of your boss. However, you should be starting to see more clearly some of the techniques that a boss in an Antagonistic Environment might employ to keep you and your co-workers in line. Be aware that there are infinitely many ways for your boss, whether consciously or not, to implement a strategy of antagonism.

Key Characteristics

Let us take a moment here to summarize some of the key characteristics of an Antagonistic Environment to help you contrast and compare it with your current environment. In an Antagonistic Environment, the manager:

- **Views you as the enemy**
- **Makes unreasonable and confusing demands**
- **Sets you up for failure**
- **Provides strong negative attention**
- **Criticizes your performance**
- **Minimizes accomplishments**

The preceding list is certainly not all inclusive. Rather, it is merely a summary of the key behaviors that a boss in an Antagonistic Environment might exhibit.

This boss dominates the environment as well as all meetings or conversations that take place in this environment. He only sees what he wants to see. Since his is the only point-of-view of importance, he has to make certain that his is the only voice that counts and may display righteous indignation and judgmental disgust at those who offer a different perspective. He is often egotistical, arrogant, and displays a sense of entitlement.

He sends mixed messages and understands that within confusion lies the opportunity for control. His mixed messages and the ambiguity of his communications keep people guessing and place him in the position as the sole arbitrator of the truth.

He forgets promises unless they are to his benefit. He will promise whatever he needs to promise to get what he wants then may conveniently forget to follow through on his side of the bargain. He dodges responsibility by tossing out a fast and loose excuse or by blaming others and accepting none of the blame himself.

He demonstrates little or no respect for anyone whose opinion differs from the law he has laid down and may attack them if it suits his agenda. He uses intimidation and threats as a tool to command a false sense of respect from the people who work for and around him. He may make snide remarks, use innuendoes, and yell at people as a means to maintain a sense of authority.

Whenever possible, he fosters a sense of shame and embarrassment in his subordinates. He is not above preying on the weaknesses and vulnerabilities of people around him in an effort to control them. He will use any information shared in confidence against someone who threatens his command.

He instills fear and self-doubt in those around him to create uncertainty and to deflect attention from his failings. All of his behaviors tend to alienate those around him. While his peers or subordinates may not be in a position to remove him, you might see them take steps to distance themselves from him.

It is not each individual action of your boss that determines the type of environment in which you work, but rather your boss's collective body of work. It is the trend exhibited by your boss's actions that helps define your environment. Sometimes that trend reveals itself straightaway. Other times, it may take weeks, months or years to become unavoidably clear.

Death Zone

Consider Cho Oyu, a peak in the Himalayan Mountains where the frontiers of Nepal and Tibet coalesce. Cho Oyu juts skyward to 26,906 feet above sea level. Most people would view this steep, craggy mountain as being a quite antagonistic, if not an overtly hostile environment. You can die within a few hours from high altitude cerebral edema (swelling of the brain) due to lack of oxygen. You can be buried by an avalanche. You can fall off a cliff or into a crevasse. You can freeze to death. You can starve. Certainly, people have succumbed to death on the high reaches of this mountain in a variety of ways. Does everyone that climbs the Cho Oyu die? Absolutely not! But, the harsh treatment that most of the climbers who approach the summit receive indicates that Cho Oyu presents a significant risk to life and limb.

The environment you encounter when challenging Cho Oyu trends toward risky due to its hostility to life. Due to the high number of deadly incidents that have occurred at this high altitude, the region above 25,000 feet has been dubbed the *Death Zone*. Reportedly, one out of every 36 climbers who reach the summit of Cho Oyu does not come back alive. Mount Everest presents a more hospitable record by claiming only one out of 54 climbers while K2, the second highest mountain in the world, is the deadliest taking the lives of one out of every seven who have enjoyed a view from its summit. Clearly, peaks which pierce *the Death Zone* offer climbers a dazzlingly spectacular view of the world while at the same time cloaking them in a deadly hostile environment.

The Death Zone is aptly named because of the high number of tragedies that have occurred there. It is this trend toward tragedy that justifies the name. Similarly, the type of environment in which you work is best categorized by looking at the trend set by your boss with his behavior.

Environment Defined by Trend

An Antagonistic Environment encompasses a full spectrum of management behaviors that can range from benevolent and seemingly supportive to outright hostile. If your boss has no need or desire to preserve the appearance of professionalism, he may descend into a fit of yelling and abusive language. He might be condescending, berating or belittling in an effort to leverage control. Additionally, he may resort to threats and intimidation. Such tactics might be more prevalent in businesses where the boss and the owner are one and the same person or in blue collar cultures where physical force is a component of job. The bottom line is that this behavior can occur anywhere and, whether subtle or overt, can contribute to de-motivation of the workforce and a reduction in productivity.

Cal Jones, our veteran salesman for Axiom Business Services in Atlanta, is the most senior and successful account executive in the department with fifteen years under his belt. He is only five years away from retirement but senses that the new Director of Major Accounts, Arthur Breedlove, is "gunning" for him.

A few days after Cal's run-in with Breedlove, he takes his time driving into the office. He knows he's already late for the Breedlove's Monday morning staff meeting. Frankly, he would rather miss the meeting altogether than walk in late and have to endure a public sermon on punctuality plus whatever else Breedlove has in store for him.

When Cal arrives at work, he goes directly to his office, flips on his computer, and pulls up his calendar. He notices that the message light on his phone is flashing. While he is almost certain he does not want to hear the message, there is a slight chance it is one of his clients calling. Reluctantly, he punches in his code and password then drops his finger on the playback key.

"Where the hell are you?" booms Breedlove's voice through the speaker. "Richardson has been calling me all morning. He was expecting a delivery on Friday and it still hasn't shown up! If you can't take care of your clients, damn it, I'll get someone in here who can!" The message ends abruptly.

Cal immediately punches an outside line and dials a number.

A pleasant voice on the other end answers.

"Good morning, Mr. Richardson's office."

"This is Cal Jones with Axiom. Mr. Richardson, please."

"One moment, please."

Cal pulls a folder out of his desk drawer and flips it open in front of him. His finger tracks down through a list of items on a shipping order.

"Cal, this is Richardson. How are you doing?"

"I'm fine. I hear you haven't received that shipment."

"Where'd you hear that?" Richardson inquires. "We got everything as planned on Friday afternoon. The event went off without a hitch. We couldn't have done it without you."

"That's great to hear," Cal responds.

"I called this morning to thank you for taking such good care of us but you weren't in, so I left a message with Breedlove."

"Well, glad everything worked out for you. Let me know when you need some help with your next event."

"Absolutely, and once again, thanks for your help. They're lucky to have you at Axiom."

Cal knows that he cannot trust his boss to do something as simple as accurately convey a message from a client. That is why he immediately called the client to gain a clearer picture of what really happened. Now when he encounters Breedlove, he has the facts on his side.

Breedlove's behavior is to be expected in an Antagonistic Environment. If this had been the only time that it happened, Cal should consider it in terms of any other negative behaviors and ask himself if he sees a trend developing? If there were no other negative behaviors then he can tuck it away as a warning sign. But since Breedlove has demonstrated a consistent pattern of negative behavior toward Cal, then Cal can be more certain in his assessment of Breedlove's desire to trip him up and, thereby, create a suitable reason to fire him. Rest assured that many of the traps and manipulation techniques that a boss in an Antagonistic Environment might employ are discussed in more detail in Chapter 13 and Appendix C.

A wise employee will always remember that in an Antagonistic Environment, your boss is not your friend, a member of your extended family, your confidante or a trusted member of the team. If you have seen the movie An Officer and A Gentleman, then you recall that Drill Sergeant Foley warns his new recruits, "I will use every means possible, fair and unfair, to trip you up." The difference is that Drill Sergeant Foley had the best interests of his employer, the United States Navy, at heart as well as some concern for the recruits. Your boss, in an Antagonistic Environment, is not concerned about the company and certainly does not have your best interests at heart. His concerns reside with how best to preserve or enhance his own status while advancing a personal agenda. You had better believe that he will use all means, fair and unfair, to trip you up.

Consider what happened to Michael Brown, Director of the Federal Emergency Management Agency (FEMA), following the devastation of New Orleans by Hurricane Katrina. Everyone remembers the infamous moment when people were still stranded on rooftops in the Big Easy and dead bodies floated in the streets. President George Walker Bush patted Brown on the back and proclaimed, "You're doing a heck of a job, Brownie." Not two weeks later, Brown was out of a job and the Secretary of Homeland Security Michael Chertoff was trashing him in the media for his poor performance. Now it may seem like Brown went from a Supportive Environment to an Antagonistic

Environment in the blink of an eye. Do not pass Benign or Contentious. Do not collect your next paycheck. Not true! Workplace environments do not deteriorate overnight. Neither do they improve that quickly. A Supportive Environment does not have insiders who because of circumstances suddenly fall out of favor with the boss. Brown was always in an Antagonistic Environment where he was useful as long as he served the immediate interests of his boss. Once he was no longer useful, he was unceremoniously discarded.

Brown fought back by showing tapes of a teleconference in which he fully briefed President Bush and Secretary Chertoff, before Katrina hit, about the impending dangers of this force of nature. Even so, who lost their job? Brown! And who continued collecting a taxpayer-funded paycheck? Bush and Chertoff! Public pressure and the need for the Bush Administration to deflect blame away from itself for the horrendous problems in New Orleans following Katrina led the Bush Administration to toss Brown under the bus. If not for the public outcry at the size and visibility of this catastrophe and the anemic government response, Brown may have very well weathered this storm.

Most workers are reluctant to think the worst of their bosses and we certainly do not recommend that anyone take such a position lightly. We do recommend, however, that even before preliminary evidence suggests that there might be reason to suspect you work in an Antagonistic Environment that you take precautions to protect yourself. Then, if or when sufficient evidence shows a clear trend supporting the idea that you do indeed work in an Antagonistic Environment, you are better prepared to deal with the situation.

Does this sound outrageous? Of course it does. Imagine the level of productivity that such an approach pushes out the door. If you were a shareholder in a company where productivity sapping Antagonistic Environments were widely tolerated by corporate executives, how long would you wait before dialing up your broker with an order to divest? **An environment where the behaviors of the boss clearly trend toward severe abuse is an Antagonistic Environment.**

Maintaining in a Contentious Environment

In a Contentious Environment, your boss is at odds with you in nearly every aspect of the job. She views you as an adversary and may provide misdirection and surreptitiously place obstacles in your path while trying to preserve the image of being helpful. This is a bad environment in which to work but not nearly as bad or career threatening as an Antagonistic Environment. One indicator that often proves useful in distinguishing a Contentious Environment from an Antagonistic Environment is the willingness of your co-workers to stand up to the boss when they know she is wrong. In a Contentious Environment, this may be a futile act. In an Antagonistic Environment, it could be risky.

A Contentious Environment is definitely self-destructive but only to a point since, like members of a dysfunctional family, you and your boss need each other. While the chance of getting fired in a Contentious Environment still exists, most likely it will not manifest itself unless you do something that offers your boss a solid reason for pursuing your dismissal because although she may treat you like an adversary, the fact is she needs you.

In a Contentious Environment, you will rarely do anything that pleases your boss no matter how hard you try. However, you are not there to please her. That may seem a reasonable assumption in any workplace but it is especially meaningful in a Contentious Environment where whatever you do will not be good enough. You lose if you excel because you make your boss and everyone who has bought into her mismanagement style look bad. You lose if you do not try hard enough because you have accepted a lower standard of performance. Clearly, a Contentious Environment is a lose-lose situation.

This is a rainy climate alternating between a gentle sprinkle and a downpour. You might as well be living in the tropical rain forests of Costa Rica. You should expect some kind of precipitation nearly every day. It may come first thing in the morning or later in the day when things have had time to heat up. Your only break is when you or your boss takes a vacation.

A wonderfully effective concept to help alleviate the damp nature of such an environment as this is a *rain coat*. Once you don your rain coat, the light showers simply bounce off and you are given some measure of shelter from the downpours.

You might theorize that in a Contentious Environment the boss views employees as an expendable resource to be exploited. Why? Because that is how she treats them. Regardless of any pleasant platitudes or references to family, team or bonds of friendship, you and your boss are not family. You are not in-laws. Most likely you are not even friends. Is this someone with whom you would choose to socialize outside of work? Of course, not! You and she are there to do a job but, as alluded to earlier, you should be aware that as absurd as it may seem, in your boss's eyes, that job may have very little to do with what is outlined on your job description. Here is why.

A Contentious Environment cannot long exist if there are no adversaries who have something over which to contend. This is why you will never succeed at pleasing your boss in a Contentious Environment. Your boss needs you to participate in an on-going, low-grade war. She does not want to destroy or eliminate you with the exception of periodic heated moments where mutual destruction seems like a viable option.

Mutually Assured Destruction

Consider the relationship that existed between the United States and the former Soviet Union. For several decades, thousands of extremely lethal nuclear warheads were pointed at each other. In an incident at the United Nations in 1960, Union of Soviet Socialists Republics Premier Nikita Sergeyevich Khrushchev, reportedly pounded his shoe on the desk at the General Assembly while proclaiming, "We will bury you!" While the true meaning of this statement is in dispute, we can surmise that it is probably not intended as a compliment.

Years later when the Soviet Union spiraled into collapse, "Soviet advisor Georgi Arbatov, in a quote mistakenly attributed to [Mikhail] Gorbechev, said: 'We are doing something terrible to you.' Asked what that was, Arbatov said, 'Deprive you of an enemy,'" reports Peter Eichenberger in *The Independent Weekly*.

Gorbechev knew that the feud between the superpowers could never be allowed to develop into open hostilities. Yet, he also understood that having an enemy served the interests of economies deeply rooted in military expenditures. Not surprisingly, the *peace dividend* promised to the American people by military leaders and politicians at the end of the Cold War was never realized. As communism and the former Soviet Union ceased to serve as a viable foe, the so-called Global War on Terror surfaced to continue America's extraordinary military expenditures.

Over the years, an acquaintance of mine, who works in a Contentious Environment, has kept me updated on the antics of her boss. She called me one afternoon to relay an interaction she had had with her boss earlier that day. I should explain that during the previous week the executives of her company had announced that a buyer for the company had finally been found. The company had been on the market for several years, so the news did not come as a big shock. The real surprise was that a buyer had actually been identified.

Earlier in the week, representatives of the soon-to-be owners came to town and spent several days in the office observing the operation and sharing their view of what the employees who would be retained could expect. They invited employees who desired to keep their jobs to submit resumes by email. Nerves were on edge as not one word had been offered as to how many of the existing employees would be retained or outsourced in the transition.

As the visitors were packing to head back home, my friend's boss circulated an invitation to her group inviting them to join her for lunch; it would be her treat. On the face, this seemed like a nice gesture: the boss taking her group to lunch to reinforce their sense of camaraderie during challenging times. Not! As the last few bites of lunch were consumed, the boss put her drink down, stood up, and immediately lit into a tirade.

"Why would you do this to me?" she blurted out in front of her employees as well as all of the other patrons enjoying lunch at the restaurant that day. "I worked harder than I've ever worked this quarter and I would have hoped that you would, too! But this has been one of the most problem-plagued year end closings I have ever experienced. I don't want to have to treat you like children but I will if I have to."

Everyone was in shock since the year end close had been just as problematic as in previous years.

"You may not know it but I'll be reviewing your resumes and making recommendations to the new owners which of you should stay," she continued. "From now on there will be no personal calls. And, I want your offices kept clean. I want invoices stacked in an orderly fashion so we can tell what they are. All we are doing is giving the new managers a bad impression of how we operate."

My friend had the foresight to disengage from this fiasco by thanking her irate hostess for the luncheon then politely excusing herself with the comment that she had to get back to work. On the short walk back to her office, my friend thought to herself: *She spends all day on her cell phone broadcasting her personal business in a loud voice up and down the hall. She has the messiest desk in the whole department and can't find anything. She is the last person on earth to talk about ethics and work habits. Who is she kidding?*

This boss was only kidding herself. Everyone recognized her behaviors as the ones she was railing against. This is not a good example of softening the bad news with a free meal. This is an example of a boss in a Contentious Environment nervously reacting to the scrutiny of new management. She was trying to deflect responsibility for her lack of leadership onto her subordinates while trying to sell the idea that she had favored status with the new owners.

Dysfunctional Family

A Contentious Environment is a lot like a dysfunctional family. Do you recognize in your workplace any of the following symptoms of family dysfunction as offered by Steven Farmer, author of *Adult Children of Abusive Parents*?

- Denial
- Inconsistency and unpredictability
- Lack of empathy toward family members
- Lack of clear boundaries
- Role reversals
- Mixed messages
- Extremes in conflict

In the field of family therapy, there are well-defined roles in a dysfunctional family where one parent is the *abuser* and another family member is the *enabler*. At the core of a dysfunctional family, is the *abuser*. This is a parent who is emotionally damaged and is usually the source of the family's problems. She might be an alcoholic, a drug-addict or otherwise emotionally damaged. The *abuser* cannot exist without the help of someone who enables her errant behavior.

The *enabler* is the person that picks up the pieces after a fight, fixes the hole in the wall or bails the abuser out of jail. This person is often the spouse of the *abuser*. Were it not for the efforts of the *enabler*, the failings of the *abuser* would be exposed to public ridicule.

From the neighbors' perspective, the dysfunctional family may have some issues but it is not that different than any other family on the block. On the inside, however, there is a constant battle to keep up the rouse in the face of never ending turmoil. Translated to a corporate environment, there are always fires to be put out. Sound familiar? Look for the *enabler* to be the individual constantly manning the firehouse.

In a Contentious Environment, the *abuser* might be your boss who abuses her authority over subordinates. The *enabler* could be an assistant, a ranking subordinate or your boss's boss. Needless to say, it is more difficult for the abusive boss to exist without an *enabler*. Be aware that anything you confide in the *enabler* may very well make an expedited trip to the ears of your boss.

The bottom line is that an abusive boss in a Contentious Environment thrives on conflict. She needs someone to engage with her in that conflict. If you are not prone to errors, she will do all in her power to help you make mistakes. If you are too efficient or too productive your boss may praise you in public but will do all in her power to rein you in because you serve as a threat.

Simply stated, your elevated level of performance serves a far different organization than the one she runs. As counter-intuitive as it may seem, efficiency and productivity are not priorities in this environment. Plainly stated, your boss needs someone to manage and if you can manage yourself then you do not fit into her view of the business world.

Often, your boss will switch positions on key issues without notice. This leaves you vulnerable to reprimand. She could shift directions based on re-direction from a client or higher ups without informing you. Meanwhile, you are merrily proceeding forward absent this tidbit of important information. When you present your results, the client is aghast and your boss hangs you out to dry. If you follow the original plan, you are wrong because the plan was changed and you are not in sync with the new plan. If you catch wind of the new plan and shift directions accordingly, she can hit you with this: *The new plan had not been fully approved. Who authorized you to go ahead with it?* Either you are to blame or you finger someone else as the problem and the witch hunt begins. In any case, it simply reinforces the idea that you require close oversight because you cannot stick to the plan or you are prone to following the instructions of a misguided peer. Once again, she has trapped you in a lose-lose situation.

In a similar tack to switching positions, your boss may offer misleading or ambiguous directives. This has the obvious potential for producing bad results. Misleading or ambiguous directives leave you guessing whether you have correctly understood your assignment. They also leave you vulnerable regardless of which path you chose to pursue. Along the way, you may discover inconsistencies or omissions in your assignment. When you surface them to your boss, you may hear: *Oh, yes, I was going to mention that!* An accompanying look of innocence tries to belay the idea that you would not have ever learned that little tidbit of information without discovering it for yourself. When crunch time arrives, you should entertain no expectation of support or comfort from your boss. She will do what is in her best interests which could leave you drowning in the mess that she will claim you created.

Regardless of the situation, your boss will fail to support you when confronted by negative forces, whether internal or external. Driven by what is best for her and those who have thoroughly and completely subjugated themselves to her, your boss will neither protect, nor defend you against complaints or questions from the client, upper management, or peers. She may go so far as to take credit for your successes even though they have occurred in spite of her best efforts to thwart them.

Key Characteristics

Here are some of the key characteristics of this environment to help you contrast and compare it with your current environment. In a Contentious Environment, the boss:

- **Views you as the problem**
- **Offers misleading or ambiguous directions**
- **Creates obstacles**
- **Provides non-supportive attention**
- **Seeks opportunities to criticize your performance**

The preceding list is certainly not all inclusive. Rather, it is merely a summary of the key behaviors that a boss in a Contentious Environment might exhibit.

This boss treats you as an expendable resource and will provide no shelter against undue negative influences. She is neither supportive nor overly punitive unless she feels threatened.

While highly hypocritical, she creates turmoil so she can be the one to fix the situation. She fails to provide support and accurate guidance in how to properly perform the work and ignores employee problems unless confronted with an issue which may impact her. Frequently, poor quality work is allowed to pass unless something could make her look bad.

She may be ill-informed but remains arrogant enough to bully her way through disagreements. She is prone to verbal tantrums and is not above using retribution and personal attacks to get what she wants. If that does not work, she acts cranky until she gets her way. She is quick to pull rank when necessary to counter dissention.

She employs cronyism to surround herself with yes-men and readily pits employees against each other. She snubs those who have figured out her game.

Young and inexperienced employees are particularly susceptible in this environment as they are often eager to make a good impression by jumping head-long into an assignment. They may lack the knowledge to know that the best way to make a good impression on the boss in this environment is to do something wrong. Do a good job and you threaten her tenuous sense of control. She may be quietly smiling but under her complimentary comments, she is seething. Do a bad job and she will happily rescue the situation but in the long run your career will suffer. In a Contentious Environment, there is no way to win. Even veteran employees must tread cautiously in this environment.

Late in the day, Bren Voltek sends Jennifer Lakes a note to stop by and see him on her way out. When she drops by his office at the end of the day, he tells her that he submitted her proposal to the Executive Committee for review.

"It's on their agenda. That's all I can do. The rest is up to them," he says with a shrug.

Jennifer thanks him and hurries out of his office. She's excited that the Executive Committee is actually reviewing her proposal.

On the way to her car, Jennifer encounters her friend Marcia who works as an assistant to the President. Marcia can't help but notice Jennifer's unusual level of excitement.

"What has you so excited, today?" Marcia asks.

Jennifer tells her about the proposal and how her boss put it on the agenda for the Executive Committee to review.

Marcia pulls Jennifer aside and looks around to make sure no one can hear them.

"I don't know what he's talking about. I prepare all the Executive Committee agendas and I haven't seen anything about a proposal for new machinery all year," she explains in a subdued voice.

A look of confusion spreads across Jennifer's face.

"But he said ..."

"Voltek was upstairs last week," Marcia continues, "but my boss called him in to have him explain why his group wasn't meeting production quotas. I overheard them talking and he didn't say anything about the machinery. He seemed to imply that it was the operators who were at fault."

Jennifer's confusion is quickly displaced by anger as she thanks her friend and hurries to her car.

If Jennifer had not run into her friend Marcia who provided her the real story about Voltek burying her proposal instead of submitting it to the Executive Committee for review, she might not have found out that Voltek lied to her. She might have gone for weeks thinking that he had picked up her cause and was trying to help her make a difference. He might have kept her hanging with reports that the Executive Committee was still studying the idea. Then in six months, he might have made up another story about how the Executive Committee passed on the idea, saying the timing was wrong, but that he would take another stab at it after concerns for budget overruns cooled. He could say anything he wanted as long as he thought Jennifer had no way to check his story. Good thing she had a friend in the President's office.

Contentious Environments Most Common

We believe that most American workers spend their time in Contentious Environments. That means that millions of people are engaged in some level of conflict with their bosses. Imagine the huge amount of human energy that is drained away from problem solving and more productive pursuits only to be wasted on inner-office warfare, not to mention how Contentious Environments contribute to a high and costly turnover rate.

"Turnover is not only costly in terms of replacement expense," states Eva Jenkins of VIP Innovations, a training and consulting company based in Washington,

D.C. "It's not productive, and it's demoralizing to other team members when they see good people leaving the organization." At times of low unemployment, even the loss of a marginal employee can be critical, since a suitable replacement may not exist in the local job market.

Andrea Coombes, writing for *MarketWatch*, quotes Dr. Gary Namie, a psychologist and senior consultant at The Work Doctor, in her article "Bully for You." "When the behavior perpetrates the boss's own agenda at the expense of the company's goals, you've got a boss who's going too far." Under these conditions, the only way to align yourself fully with your boss's interests in this environment is to abdicate your responsibility to perform the job, for which you were hired, to the best of your ability. Such an alignment may produce a short term improvement in your relationship with the boss but be aware that, ultimately, you will be the one who suffers.

Logical minds would think that intuitive corporate executives interested in growing shareholder value would go out of their way to eliminate any possibility of a counterproductive, inner-office conflict. **It is difficult to believe that the same corporate executives who have negotiated multimillion dollar compensation packages for themselves are not able to negotiate terms for a workplace where employees are encouraged and supported by management to be the best they can be.**

CHAPTER 7

Progressing in a Benign Environment

A Benign Environment is defined by a boss that is neither supportive, nor overly punitive, but rather allows the work environment to be unduly influenced by external forces. In this environment, the boss neither helps, nor hinders, your efforts to fulfill the intent of your employment with the company. He does not mentor, counsel, or guide your efforts to be productive. This is a boss that is missing in action and a sink-or-swim-by-your-own-devices type of environment. Either you seek out the resources you need to get the job done or you fail with no safety net to catch you.

Failure, in and of itself, in this environment does not necessarily lead to termination but it very well could. It all depends upon what culture of accountability exists in the company. If upper management expects good results and does not get them due to a failure on your part, certainly your boss will not explain that there may have been extenuating circumstances and attempt to intervene on your behalf. You are responsible for getting the work done and accountable for the outcome. However, a Benign Environment may be just as likely to exist where there is a general lack of accountability. If poor results go unnoticed, ultimately, no one may be held accountable. If someone important does take notice, watch out! You are on your own.

It is as if you are working out in the elements. You never know what could blow in with the wind. You must generate your own weather forecast. If you come to work expecting a sunny day and it rains, you get wet. If you forecast partly cloudy with a light southerly breeze and a storm blows up, hold onto your hat and everything else that you value. If lightning strikes and you are not safely sheltered, you could spend the rest of the day shell shocked.

Your boss does not run interference for you with outside influences that can impede your productivity. He does not guide needed resources in your direction. He does not ask if you have encountered any obstacles that he can help remove. In a sense, it is as though he is not there except to perform your annual performance review, if that process even exists. A performance review is particularly troublesome in this environment because your boss will not have an accurate view of your performance. He is not around to observe any good results you produce. Bad results, however, may very well develop legs and track him down.

Key Characteristics

Here are some of the key characteristics of this environment to help you contrast and compare it with your current environment. In a Benign Environment, the boss:

- **Ignores you unless confronted with a serious issue**
- **Provides little or no direction**
- **Gives no access to resources**
- **Allows you to be unduly influenced by external forces**
- **Is neither supportive, nor overly punitive**

A Benign Environment, at first glance, may seem like a nice place to wile away your workdays. Who would not want to work unfettered by the nagging eye of your boss? The main problem of this environment becomes self-evident at performance review time or when cuts have to be made. Having received no guidance on what is expected, you have no means to show that you met expectations. No goals were agreed upon between you and your boss; therefore, you have no way to indicate that you met your goals.

On Your Own

It is as though someone invited you to dinner then disappears once you arrive, leaving you to find the dining room, fix dinner, and serve yourself. While it may be obvious that a dinner guest and a new employee are not the same, the message is clear. You are left to your own devices to figure things out. Maybe your boss does not have the time. Maybe he does not have the interest. Either way, you are free to make your own successes and equally free to make your own mistakes. The price of not being micromanaged, or managed at all, is vulnerability. Mario Molina is about to learn this lesson.

Mario straightens his tie then flashes a big smile and his employee badge as he passes the guard station and steps into the elevator for a short ride to his office on the 16th floor. As he logs into his computer, a happy face message pops up from HR: "Congratulations on completing your first six months with Aztec!" As he closes the popup window, his eyes are drawn to a new email tagged urgent. He immediately opens it and reads about an all-employee meeting in 5 minutes on the second floor. He locks the computer and follows a stream of people to the elevators.

On the second floor, a crowd has already formed in the large hallway. The CEO and Vice President of HR stand at the front of the room. The CEO speaks first.

"Now I know this is short notice, so I'll get right to the point. NASA announced this morning that it is awarding the contract for the next generation Crew Emergency Rescue Vehicle to XRS. I wanted you to hear it from me, first, before it hits the news."

A groan rises from the crowd.

"We knew going into this that there was a chance we wouldn't get the contract but we gave it our best shot. The proposal team did an incredible job and we're very proud of them."

Applause mixes with whistles and shouts.

"I have to catch a plane in ten minutes, so I'll let Juan finish this announcement."

Juan Arrendondo, the Vice President of HR, takes the microphone as the CEO hurries to the elevator.

"I hate to be the bearer of bad news but as you may have guessed, since we didn't win this contract, there will have to be some cutbacks. Unfortunately, we're going to have to cut ten percent of the workforce. I have asked project leads to submit a list of candidates by Friday. The list will be reviewed by upper management and those employees who will be let go will be notified by the end of the month. That's all I have for you right now. Sorry to ruin your morning."

Mario takes a deep breath and releases an audible sigh as he ambles back to his office. He realizes he is in trouble. The chances of his name appearing on the layoff list are nearly as great as the chances of surviving a tumble over Niagara Falls in a rowboat.

The last time Mario offered comments at his boss's project meeting Beaujolais ignored his comment and asked, "Now who are you?"

Mario never surfaced on Sally Beaujolais's radar. Admittedly, her beam scanned the horizon with a weak signal but since he spent his time helping other engineers complete their work rather than defining his own worth, he risked being viewed as support staff when he was actually hired to do engineering work. Therefore, he was never able to focus her attention in his direction and register on her screen.

This is one of the dangers of a Benign Environment. If the group to which you are assigned is large enough, you might not be noticed by the boss. The risk is heightened when confronted with downsizing of the workforce. If the boss does not even know you are there then what chance is there that he will miss you when you leave?

In a Benign Environment, traps and manipulation techniques that the boss might employ are not issues for great concern. The boss will employ very few techniques in an effort to retain control over subordinates as retaining control is not a priority. Rather the boss creates distance from employees giving them free reign to do as they wish unless something bad happens. You have relatively free reign to do as you wish without fear of the boss wanting to micromanage your affairs. Likewise, you are relatively free to make as many mistakes as you wish up to the point that someone in authority notices. If you are self-motivated, you may strive to do a good job. If you lack motivation, you may be inspired to coast, at least, until there is a problem. Either way, don't count on backing from your boss. He will create a quick rationale for why he should not be held accountable for what happened. **The good news and the bad news of a Benign Environment rolled into one package:** *You are on your own!*

CHAPTER 8

Thriving in a Supportive Environment

A Supportive Environment is what every manager should want to create and where every employee should want to work. Why? Because a Supportive Environment supports the opportunity for you to be successful in the role for which you were hired. In a Supportive Environment, the manager partners with you to help you achieve peak productivity. Period!

When your manager tells you something, you can depend on it. Either she will hold true to her word or she will provide a reasonable explanation for why it was not possible. This differs from the other environments where you are more likely to hear a plethora of excuses or complaints.

In a Supportive Environment, your manager seeks to eliminate obstacles that may hinder your productivity while helping you to access the resources you need to safely and efficiently perform your assignments. Your manager also assists you in continuing to develop useful skills. She shields you from undue external influences. She serves as a buffer to run interference for you by intercepting and ameliorating external influences that might serve to disrupt your productivity. This is different than the manager in a Benign Environment who makes little or no effort to shield employees from such turbulence. In some ways, it is the difference between a mechanic having to rebuild an engine in an indoor heated garage as opposed to doing it in the driveway exposed to rain, wind, and other elements.

It is simply not possible, nor advisable, for your manager to shield you from all external forces. That would mean that you would never hear from customers about changes in specifications, from other departments about product delays or from upper management about budget cuts. It is essential for you to hear and incorporate all of this information into your work processes but there is a time and place for delivery of this information that best suits minimal disruption of the work process. Additionally, it is simply not necessary for you to consume every bit of information that external parties have to share.

Does this mean that everything operates smoothly? Of course, not! There is plenty of conflict in a Supportive Environment surrounding the challenges of solving problems but for the most part the conflict arises from the need to confront external forces. What is different between a Supportive Environment and non-supportive environments is that in a Supportive Environment the source of the conflict is relative to the challenge of doing business in a particular industry under prevailing economic conditions. By contrast, in non-supportive environments, the source of conflict is usually internal and focused more on personal or territorial issues. Most employees easily recognize the nonproductive nature of office politics. If you were the CEO, which challenges would you prefer your employees focus on, petty office squabbles or the challenges of succeeding in a competitive marketplace?

Conditions change and employees make mistakes in all environments. It is part of being human. In a Supportive Environment, your manager allows you to make honest mistakes. She understands that mistakes will be made and responds in a manner that makes sense given the concerns of all parties involved and the best interests of the organization.

Support for Honest Effort

There is a story circulating about how one CEO responded to an employee mistake that cost the company three million dollars. When called into the CEOs office, the employee entered with his head low and a typed resignation in hand. The CEO asked him to close the door and take a seat.

Several minutes passed until the CEO spoke.

"What do you have to say for yourself?"

The employee leaned forward and placed his resignation on the CEOs desk, "I'll have my office cleared out by close of business."

As the employee stood up to withdraw, the CEO calmly asked, "Did you learn anything?"

"I learned not to make that mistake again," he replied as he reached for the door.

"Then why would I fire you?" the CEO smiled. "I just spent three million dollars training you. Get back to work."

Mistakes happen in all environments as do errors in communications. Busy people sometimes forget things. Conditions change and everyone may not be apprised of the change in a timely manner. The key here is whether you have made an honest effort to perform at your best. Obviously, intentional mistakes, careless mistakes or mistakes based on poor judgment are not to be tolerated. But mistakes that occur as a result of an honest effort to do a good job should be considered part of the learning process. A manager in a Supportive Environment will see to it that you receive additional training, resources, or guidance as necessary to ensure that this mistake does not happen again.

This does not mean that employees in a Supportive Environment can shirk their duties and not be held accountable. This environment does not provide a pass for a poor performer. In fact, in this environment, people are more likely to be held accountable for how well they perform their duties. Issues related to poor performance are identified and corrected through a joint effort between you and your manager before they escalate into costly, insurmountable problems.

Good ideas are welcomed and rewarded by your manager in a Supportive Environment. Good ideas can help improve or streamline work processes, they can result in new products and services, or they can increase production. All of these things bring value to the organization.

Accomplishments are acknowledged in a Supportive Environment. Every employee benefits from a sense of feeling as though he has made a contribution to the success of the organization. When someone goes above and beyond what is anticipated or expected, that person is recognized and rewarded. Bosses in Contentious Environments may misuse recognition and reward as a means to spotlight cronies placed in positions of power or importance for their willingness to tow the manager's line.

Key Characteristics

Now let us summarize some of the key characteristics of this environment to help you contrast and compare it with your current environment. In a Supportive Environment, the manager:

- **Treats you with respect**
- **Values your contribution**
- **Provides supportive attention**
- **Shields you from undue external influences**
- **Rewards good ideas and accomplishments**
- **Partners in your development**

The preceding list is certainly not exhaustive. It is merely a summary of the key behaviors that a manager in a Supportive Environment might exhibit.

This manager demonstrates a sense of purpose. She knows what needs to be done to make the organization successful and works to make it happen without stepping on people. She understands how to guide alignment of the goals of all the parties involved in the process to maintain morale, motivation, and productivity. She sees the big picture yet understands how all of the key elements from which it is comprised come together. She delegates work to ensure that fulfillment of each objective serves to meet the overall goals of the organization.

She understands that communication is one of the most valuable tools at her command. She uses it effectively to communicate truthfully with employees knowing that there is a way to withhold confidential information without being misleading.

She knows that respect is a two-way street where she must respect herself and others before she can expect to gain their respect. Putting people at ease comes naturally to her. She treats her subordinates as colleagues. She chooses to bring out the best in people to inspire and encourage them to excel. She understands that she does not have all the answers and most likely does not know all the right questions to ask in every situation. Therefore, she welcomes other opinions, gives serious consideration to alternative suggestions, and shows a sincere interest in the ideas other people bring to the table.

She shares authority wisely while understanding that part of delegating work means sharing accountability. Still she holds ultimate responsibility for what you do on her behalf. As President Harry S. Truman once said, "The buck stops here!" On the occasion that a decision leads to a bad outcome, she takes responsibility for what happens and is accountable for her actions and the actions of those under her leadership. Overall, she demonstrates a thoughtfulness and wisdom relative to the responsibilities of her position.

Teamwork

Managers in a Supportive Environment will have well-functioning teams. Ken Blanchard, author of *The One Minute Manager*, offers the following list of supportive behaviors in his seminar "Building High Performing Teams:"

- Involve members in shaping and understanding the group's purpose and mission
- Practice active listening
- Encourage involvement in leadership, problem-solving, and decision-making
- Catch people doing something right
- Provide reassurance and support for task improvement
- Encourage the expression of difference in opinion and perspective
- Model confronting, challenging, and dealing with conflict
- Build supportive relationships

Not every manager in a Supportive Environment is going to exhibit all of the characteristics indicated above all of the time. Everyone, no matter how good their intentions, has a bad day once in a while. But overall, managers in a Supportive Environment will demonstrate these characteristics most of the time and certainly much more frequently than bosses in non-supportive workplace environments.

Likewise, bosses who revel in non-supportive environments may stray from their antagonistic, contentious or benign behaviors every once in a while. However, the trend set by their negative behaviors keeps them locked into an ineffective and counter-productive way of being. Verbally, they may claim these characteristics even though their actions clearly do not support that contention.

Even well-meaning bosses may try to convince employees that they are treated well and are highly valued. Eva Jenkins, a performance and productivity specialist, states that "in truly High Performance workplaces managers do not have to 'convince' employees that they are valued, the employees inherently know they are valued simply by the way the work is organized and performed." People inherently know when a team exists and they definitely know whether they are a member of the team.

Bottom Line: Respect

The primary challenge in a Supportive Environment is overcoming challenges presented to you in the normal course of business. Your manager, no matter how supportive, cannot filter out all obstacles nor should she. Part of your job is solving problems. It would be a miraculously unusual workplace if you never faced challenges or never had to solve problems. The distinction is that the challenges and problems should not be created by management. You and your manager are on the same team. Her job should be to help you solve the problems that exceed the scope of your ability to resolve.

Hopefully, you recall our discussion on alignment of goals. If so, you will remember that the best situation is when the goals of the company, the manager, and you are in perfect alignment. As we noted earlier, this rarely happens. In a Supportive Environment, your manager will hold an honest discussion with you regarding company goals, her goals as manager, and your goals. She will demonstrate an interest in helping you align your goals with the organizational goals and assist you in achieving your goals within the context of your role in the organization. She will do everything in her power to create an environment that inspires self-motivated employees and respects them for their efforts on behalf of the corporate cause.

Maybe it zipped past so fast in the last sentence that you missed it. The word is *respect*. **The key quality that drives every element of a Supportive Environment is respect.** If your manager treats you with respect, there are few limits to what you will do in return. You will volunteer to work late. She will not have to ask. You will take a troublesome problem home and return to work in the morning with a solution. You will look and act like you enjoy your job because you genuinely do. It is doubtful that a recruiter could entice you to go elsewhere without making an extremely lucrative offer. Even then, you might reject it if you did not believe that the new position offered you an environment that respected your contribution and was as supportive as the one you would have to leave behind.

Anyone who is forced by circumstances to move from a Supportive Environment to one of the non-supportive environments will immediately recognize the difference. This is a much harder and less desirable direction to move but sometimes because of circumstances out of your control it does happen. In such a case, your ability to recognize the new environment for what it is and be able to effectively prepare yourself to deal with it is a very important skill to possess.

Continuous Engagement

We have portrayed the Supportive Environment in very glowing and positive terms and believe we are accurate in doing so. Generally, employees know which managers in the company foster Supportive Environments. Sometimes, word even spreads outside the corporate walls. One of the many pluses enjoyed by managers in Supportive Environments is that they are generally better able to recruit anyone they want. Often, the only consideration is whether someone wants to do the kind of work that is being performed in that business unit.

Managers in a Supportive Environment work hard to create the circumstances that foster peak performance. They know that a few bad apples can radically disturb the chemistry of the group. Therefore, when they interview candidates, they are likely to spend as much time probing the candidate for shared common values as they do evaluating skills. They know that they can train the right candidate but changing a questionable attitude is much more difficult.

Once the new employee is in the door, managers who maintain a Supportive Environment make an effort to engage the new employee as quickly as possible and keep them continuously engaged throughout the term of their employment. Leadership Advantage, a Maryland-based executive coaching and organization development firm, provides advice on how to keep employees engaged in *"Power of Employee Engagement."* They suggest:

- A strong relationship with the manager
- Clear communication from the manager
- Clear path set for focusing on what the employee does best
- Strong relationships with co-workers
- Allow risk-taking and stretch for excellence.

It does not require too much of an imagination to see that when Leadership Advantage describes how to engage employees in the workplace it is really talking about creating a Supportive Environment.

Leadership Advantage further explains that "not-engaged employees tend to concentrate on tasks rather than the goals and outcomes they are expected to accomplish." This makes sense when you consider that employees who lack the boss's support may face a significant challenge in attempting to complete a difficult task. Simply performing an assignment, as directed by the boss, without regard for the outcome is less risky in a non-supportive environment. As we will discuss later, assuming responsibility is a much less job-threatening pursuit in a Supportive Environment than it is in a non-supportive environment. The safer route in a non-supportive environment is for employees to do exactly what the boss has instructed them to do. This leaves responsibility for the outcome in the boss's hands.

Gregory B. Calhoun, president and CEO of Calhoun Enterprises, the largest minority-owned business in Alabama, ascended from bagging groceries in the early 1970s to the boardroom. A feature article in *Business Alabama* magazine by staff writer

Jim Dunn quotes Calhoun's refreshing view of his employees, a perspective which seems to under gird his success. "They understand that there is an owner who started as a package clerk and who now owns his own business. Only in America could that happen, so they listen to me. I tell all my people that if you listen to me, I can carry you places that you probably could not get to yourself. And as you support me, I can get to places that I probably can't get to without you. So, we're a team." We think that Calhoun has a solid understanding of the mutual respect and support that goes into making a successful team.

You have already met Cal Jones, Jennifer Lakes, and Mario Molina. As you know, they work in non-supportive environments. Now meet someone who works in a Supportive Environment.

Twila Fletcher, Steam Press Operator

Twila Fletcher works for Carlyle Cleaners in Chicago, Illinois. She has arrived at work at 5:00 A.M. every weekday for the past seven years. This Monday morning is no different. Her manager, Billy Czarnecki, is busy arranging a new display at the front of the shop when Twila walks through the door. He has only been manager for a little over three years but during that time has made a world of difference.

"Good morning, Ms. Fletcher."

"Good morning to you, Billy," Twila replies. She's a bit surprised at his formality. "Is there something wrong?"

"I'll let you decide," he answers leaving the display. "Come back here. I want to show you something."

Uncertain what may have happened over the weekend, Twila follows Czarnecki through a dark hallway. As Twila steps into a dimly lit room filled with steam presses. Czarnecki flips a switch on the wall flooding the room with light.

"They did it!" Czarnecki exclaims pointing at brand new fans hanging from the ceiling above each steam press.

A smile explodes across Twila's face.

"I can't believe it!" she cries. "How did you convince them?"

"Not me. You! I simply told them what you told me about there not being any reason not to make a hot, demanding job like this as comfortable as possible. Since you organized all the press operators into a smooth functioning team, they'd be crazy not to listen to you," he said with a smile as he slowly shakes his head in admiration of her contribution.

Twila looks around for something.

"On the wall by the window," Czarnecki offers.

Twila flips the switch on for the fan above her press. The blades above her head start to twirl. While Twila enjoys the rush of air ruffling her hair, Czarnecki reaches behind some boxes on a shelf to retrieve a small package wrapped in colorful paper.

"Here." Czarnecki offers the gift to Twila.

"What's this?" she exclaims.

"I wanted you to have the first one."

"The first what?"

"Open it and find out."

Twila carefully pulls off the wrapping to expose a new iPod.

"You mean that we can ..."

"You can listen to music, the radio," he jumps in on her sentence. "You can listen to whatever you want to listen to while you're working."

Just then two women in their mid-twenties step into the room.

"What's going on?" one of the women asks.

"You won't believe it," Twila blurts out as she starts toward them then pauses and glances back at Czarnecki. "Thanks!"

Czarnecki acknowledges with a nod.

"You are simply not going to believe this!" Twila repeats as she joins the two women by the door.

"Let's get these machines warmed up, Ladies," Czarnecki suggests with an oversized smile.

That is how a Supportive Environment works. You and your manager operate as a team to eliminate obstacles and hindrances to productivity. Are there still challenges? Absolutely! Every workplace has its challenges. A Supportive Environment does not eliminate challenges. A significant difference between a Supportive Environment and a non-supportive environment is the source of the challenges. In a Supportive Environment, you are challenged by the work and external forces. You face questions such as: *How do I do this? How can I make that happen as easily as possible?* In non-supportive environments, challenges arise out of petty internal squabbles driven by personal agendas and bosses with control issues.

Most Productive Environment

Additionally, as Jim Clemmer, author and speaker, writes on HR.com, "Too many managers who aspire to lead and develop others haven't learned how to lead and develop themselves. They are trying to build organizations or provide services that are different than they are. These well-intentioned managers are trying to improve their teams or organizations without improving themselves."

A wise supervisor told me many years ago as I was beginning my rise through the ranks of the organization: ***Treat your people like you are preparing them to move on and they won't want to leave.*** Good advice for any manager interested in creating and sustaining a Supportive Environment.

Penelope Trunk received a "very good" rating from readers for her article "A Manager's Guide to Growing Happy Employees" which she posted on the Yahoo

Finance web site in 2007. "People aren't managers because they have a title. They're managers because they make people feel good about themselves and what they're doing," she states. "The best way to think about management is to treat everyone like an unpaid intern. Each day, your employees ask themselves, 'Am I getting enough out of this job to keep doing it?' And each day, you need to give them a reason to say, 'Yes!'"

"By creating an environment in which people are valued, developed and rewarded, organizations gain a significant competitive advantage and can begin to build a stronger, more loyal and more productive workforce," emphasized retention specialist Jeffrey M. Saltzman in his article "Corporate Culture: The Ultimate Competitive Advantage" published in *Talent Management Magazine.*

Our hope is that more bosses at all levels will come to realize that a Supportive Environment is the most productive sustainable environment that can be created. **Research clearly supports the idea that productive employees are happier and, therefore, more motivated which in turn makes them more productive.** This creates a win-win-win situation for you, your manager, and the company.

CHAPTER 9

Leveraging Control in Any Environment

Consider the question: *What will it take to survive in my workplace environment?* Survival in your workplace environment requires you to know which elements of your environment you can control and how to leverage that control.

Rules of the Environment

For a mariner tossed about in a storm at sea, a rudder and the means to power his ship can make all the difference in the world. No, a rudder and an engine will not calm the raging sea but it will give the mariner the means to turn his ship into the waves. Every old salt knows to confront the waves with the bow of his ship. Getting hit broadside by a massive wave can easily roll a vessel and send it plunging to a watery grave. Old sailors became old because they learned to avoid threats or knew what to do when confronted by them.

People have formulated a variety of rules that help us survive in the world in which we live. *Red sky in the morning, sailor take warning; red sky at night, sailor's delight. Feed a cold and starve a fever. Do not stand under a tree in a thunderstorm. Do not drink and drive. Buyer beware.* We have all heard such sayings which serve a useful purpose in our society by communicating information about how to increase our chances of surviving in a world fraught with dangers. The workplace is no different. Dangers abound there, too.

To survive in the workplace, it is useful to know the rules that can contribute to our survival. Many companies have gone to the trouble of documenting, in an employee handbook, many of the rules that management would like employees to follow. Everyone knows these rules as the company's policies and procedures. For purposes of clarity, *policies* indicate a position that management has taken on an issue while *procedures* indicate how work should be performed. There may be a policy that states that the company adheres to the Equal Employment Opportunity laws. There is probably a policy that addresses restrictions on the use of email and one that prohibits the use of obscene or vulgar language in the workplace. There may be a dress code policy. There could be a policy that indicates when and where it is acceptable to smoke even though the U.S. Surgeon General made it clear years ago that smoking is certainly dangerous to your health. There may be a procedure for hiring employees and one that governs terminations. Additionally, there could be both policies and procedures that ensure employees meet the requirements of regulatory agency mandates.

Companies establish policies and procedures to help ensure employees are aware of what types of behaviors will be tolerated. While policies and procedures are bent and broken every day, it should be clear to everyone that it is done at the employee's peril. The errant behaviors of the Enron personnel who bent and broke not only company policies and procedures but many federal laws finally caught up with them when criminal charges were filed. Some of them now receive their mail at a correctional facility.

We would never recommend circumventing any documented policy or procedure unless it is clearly contrary to the civil or criminal legal code. Well-written policies and procedures benefit both the company and employees by clearly spelling out expectations. They serve as a good tool for management to communicate expectations to employees and serve to benefit employees by providing clear guidance on which behaviors are acceptable and which ones are not. The policies and procedures that are clearly documented are not the problem. It is the ones which are not documented that hold the most problem causing potential.

When conservative columnist George Will was questioned by George Stephanopoulos, host of ABC's television news program *This Week*, regarding responsibility in run up to the financial crisis of 2008, he revealed some of the unwritten rules he thought the public should have known and heeded. "Don't play poker with a guy named Slim and don't take financial advice from a guy who is shouting at you." While the poker comment was obviously tongue-in-check, Will's reference to "a guy shouting at you" is squarely targeted at Jim Cramer, host of CNBC's financial advice program *Mad Money*, who was viewed as a credible source of financial information until skewered by Jon Stewart on the *Daily Show*. Stewart reminded Cramer that he advised viewers to buy Bear Stearns' stock weeks before it was bought out by J.P. Morgan Chase at a bargain basement price under the threat of bankruptcy. Stewart also suggested that Cramer had the experience and knowledge to be in a position to know and reveal the inadvisability of such a purchase. Cramer did not disagree.

Seems Will is reiterating the unwritten rule: *Buyer beware!* You are on your own in sorting out all the financial advice presented in the media when much of it, even if presented by experts in seemingly credible forums, may be intended to manipulate you to act against your best interests. In other words, if you don't know the unwritten rules of financial investing and run into a problem, it is your fault! And so it is in the workplace.

Every workplace environment has a set of rules that are not documented in a formal company policy or procedure and are rarely spoken. You may hear about them through the "grapevine" or learn about then the hard way through experience. Many of these rules have to do with what can and cannot be done given the type of environment in which you work. Knowing and abiding by the unwritten rules can be just as important as adhering to the ones that are well documented.

One such rule states that your boss may not be entirely straight forward about what he wants from you. Sometimes what your boss says he wants and what he really wants are miles apart. Obviously, this depends on your boss and the type of environment in which you work. Some employees learn this unwritten rule over time. What the boss says he wants, just like the documented policies and procedures at some companies, is for public consumption. What he really wants, just like the unwritten rules, is not for the public eye. The quicker you recognize this subtle distinction, the better off you will be.

Upon moving into a new environment, you can gain some clues about the prevailing environment from those around you. Company officials may unconsciously share some of the unwritten truths of their environment but, frankly, do not count on getting the full story. Few hiring managers and even fewer Human Resources professionals tell you the whole truth and nothing but the truth about their workplace environment. They read you the *prepared statement* but do not tell you what they really want from you or what the organization really needs. Often, you are left to figure it out on your own.

Every country-raised kid knows not to jump off the dock into the farm pond before knowing how shallow the water is. Youngsters who grow up outside the city often learn to investigate what dangers may lurk just beneath the surface. A friend of mine who was raised in the city and took a job as a cross-country trucker, stopped one hot afternoon for a swim in one of the cool lakes that lined a highway in Northern Florida. A local boy floated up in a boat and asked if my friend wanted to go for a ride. My friend, somewhat surprised by the offer, none-the-less climbed in the boat and off they went for a short trip to the other side of the lake where the local boy killed the engine allowing the boat to slowly drift near the shoreline. Without a word, he pointed to a row of alligators sunning themselves on the muddy bank. The boy took my friend back to the spot near his truck where he had been swimming and left him with a parting thought: *Not sure you want to swim here.*

My friend was lucky that someone took him into their confidence and showed him the dangers of the environment he had entered before he met with a disastrous end. Hopefully, you will find someone equally benevolent but do not rely on it. Ultimately, it is your responsibility to seek out as much information as you can about the environment in which you work before you jump in over your head.

Political Battles

When I began work in the space program, the hiring manager said she wanted me to develop a technical training program for her group of ninety aerospace engineers. While I am certain that she meant what she said when she voiced her desire for a technical training program, what she neglected to mention was that she was not speaking on behalf of her seven supervisors when she made that request.

A technical training program typically requires each supervisor or unit leader to give up a certain amount of control for the common good. I needed the supervisors to relinquish control over defining the range of activities that an engineer assigned to their group could perform. The supervisors had become accustomed to having ten to fifteen engineers at their beck and call to perform whatever tasks the supervisors determined needed to be done. This does not sound unreasonable until you take into account some of the special skills and knowledge needed to design a space shuttle mission. A technical training program identifies specific roles within each supervisory group and defines the training required for an engineer to perform the associated duties. The bottom line is safety. A technical training program helps to ensure that each engineer has the training needed to perform, in a proper and safe manner, all assigned tasks.

The benefit for the engineers is that they are not asked to perform tasks for which they are not qualified. The benefit for the supervisors is that they know who is properly qualified to perform which tasks. This means that when they assign an engineer to perform a task, there is a good chance that the task will be completed in a safe, timely, and proper fashion. This was not the situation when I arrived.

Actually, a well-designed training program is a win-win situation; however, some supervisors didn't initially view it that way. The supervisors knew that they could not overtly stop the development of a formal technical training program; however, nothing prevented them from quietly tossing one monkey wrench after another into the works to slow the process down. It was my job to remove the monkey wrenches as fast as I could while politely helping them to see the error of their ways.

From their point of view, much of the control that I was asking them to relinquish had been won as a result of some rather hard-fought internal battles. Therefore, it is understandable that they would be a bit reticent to relinquish what may have taken some of them years to achieve. Each of the seven supervisors publicly supported the idea of a technical training program in staff meetings and other public forums but in private they fought tooth and nail to retain every last bit of control. Normally, you would think that the manager would hold sway over what happens in the organization but as it turned out in this organization, managers would come and go every two years while supervisors were more or less permanent, the implications of which the supervisors knew and understood all too well. This little unwritten rule, which wasn't immediately apparent when I accepted the job, made the task of developing a technical training program for ninety aerospace engineers a couple notches more difficult than rolling an elephant up a hill sideways.

Therefore, we recommend that as a new or veteran employee, you should consider that part of your job is to gain a solid understanding of the environment in which you work as soon as possible. New employees may find that if they rush into the job that was described to them during the interview process, they will find themselves as the latest meal for a den of carnivorous veterans eager to devour any interloper who encroaches upon their territory.

Non-Supportive Environments

For the most part, non-supportive environments are the most problematic because by definition they lack the support mechanisms that help you succeed. They may also lack suitable boundaries and limitations to guide your behavior. Any infraction of the rules even though they may not be well-documented might invite severe repercussions from a boss in an Antagonistic Environment. In a Contentious Environment, the rules may be too ambiguous for accurate interpretation. Benign Environments may lack any meaningful oversight of the rules if any actually exist.

As much as well-documented rules may seem bothersome and are disparaged by some employees, they are an important factor in a well-functioning workplace and can provide you some means of protection. In a disagreement with your boss, you may have some standing if the policies and procedures are on your side. If the rules are too restrictive or too lax, they may not offer you the guidance needed to know what is expected. This leaves you vulnerable to a misguided boss who may concoct a new rule on the spot or interpret an ambiguous rule any way he likes. If the workplace rules are not well-documented and anything goes, you have little or no recourse if your boss determines that you have committed an infraction. Well-documented policies and procedures give you a measure of defense and thereby some control over your environment.

Areas of Control

In terms of control over the workplace environment, your manager and the corporate executives out rank you. If you are one of the tens of millions of workers who endure a non-supportive workplace environment, do not despair! You are not completely powerless. There are several areas in which you are able to leverage a significant amount of control. Your survival in a non-supportive environment may very well depend upon your taking charge of the following four elements of your environment:

- **Foundation** – establish a solid means to perform your best work
- **Image** – portray a professional image of yourself
- **Responsibility** – manage your acceptance of responsibility
- **Documentation** – keep a record of what you did, when you did it, and why

Foundation: Your *foundation* represents your ability and means to perform at your best. It includes your warehouse of skills, your network of professional contacts, and the resources at your disposal. These all support your ability to do your job well. Obviously, if you lack in any of these areas, the quality and quantity of your work may suffer. Therefore, the more solid and comprehensive your foundation, the more attention you can divert from figuring out how to get the job done, given the obstacles presented by the environment, and direct them to actually doing the job. The more gaps in your foundation, the more time you will need to spend shoring up the weak areas and the less able you will be to focus on doing the tasks at hand. As a result, your productivity certainly suffers.

Image: For the same reason that you check your reflection in the mirror before heading out the door in the morning, it is useful to ensure that you present the best possible *image* of yourself to your manager and your co-workers. This is a picture of how well you interface with your workplace environment. The less supportive the environment, the more important it is for you to avoid allowing your boss to find a hair out of place and the more important it is for you to be perceived by your peers as a competent, contributing member of the organization.

Responsibility: In any workplace, you have some control over accepting or deflecting *responsibility* for the outcome of any given task that you might be asked or directed to perform. The more supportive the environment, the more responsibility you can safely accept. The less supportive the environment, the more risk is involved in accepting responsibility; therefore, the more cautious you should be about accepting responsibility for a task for which you may not be able to drive the outcome.

Documentation: Just as a good manager documents the transgressions of miscreant employees to justify disciplinary actions, *documentation* can also work in your favor. In a non-supportive environment, you should document what you did, when you did it, and why you did it. This information can help you defend your actions, if you are called upon to do so. The less supportive the environment, the more often you may be called upon to defend your actions. Therefore, the greater is your need for an accurate record of what you did, when you did it, and why. Without such a defense, you can easily be hung out to dry by a malevolent boss. The more supportive the environment, the less need you have to document your actions.

It is very important to understand how each of the four workplace environments can impact your ability to focus effort toward productivity. As you know, in non-supportive environments your job is most at risk. This is particularly true of an Antagonistic Environment where your boss wants to terminate you and will employ every opportunity, fair or unfair, to do so.

Boss versus Company

Do not confuse the boss's skewed perspective with that of the company. It is useful to keep forefront in your mind the fact that you report to your boss but you work for the company. In all likelihood, the company wants you to be as productive as possible. There is every reason to assume that this is why you were hired. The fact that, in an Antagonistic Environment, your boss wants to terminate you is secondary and a goal that is most likely not aligned with company goals when you take into consideration all of the costs, which can be extensive, of finding a replacement and training someone to do what you already know how to do. This is especially true if you have been doing your job for any length of time and know how to do it well. It should be easy to see why it is in the company's best interest to create a Supportive Environment that respects the contribution you make to the organization.

Even so, in any confrontation with your boss, upper management and other figures of authority will likely align with your boss, not you. Therefore, to best serve the interests of the company for which you work as well as your own interest of self-preservation, you may need to divert a certain amount of attention away from being productive and direct that attention toward protecting and defending yourself in your current position.

Consider the work environment of a soldier whose commander orders him to: *Take that hill!* That soldier could not serve the interests of the Army for very long if he did not devote some effort to the job of staying alive while he pursues his assigned objective. The same is true of employees in non-supportive environments. You can not long serve the interests of your company, not to mention yourself and your family, if you lose your job.

The guiding principle to remember in regard to surviving in workplace environment is: ***The more I know about my workplace environment, the better I can prepare myself to deal with its demands.***

CHAPTER 10

Reinforcing Your Foundation

Over the years, I have had the occasion to check the references of innumerable candidates who my firm had recruited and placed in an assignment. It is common to encounter former bosses who had some performance-based issues with a candidate. However, when I drilled down to the heart of the issue, it usually became apparent the problems were related to the workplace environment rather than the candidate's character or capabilities. If placed in a Supportive Environment those same candidates would thrive and usually did. Likewise, I have had some miserable experiences with candidates who appeared to be superstars but when placed in non-supportive surroundings, they fell flat on their faces.

Situational Performance

How well you are able to perform depends greatly upon how supportive the environment is of a successful performance. This is known as *situational performance*. The quality of your performance is inextricably linked to the situation in which you find yourself. The truth is that *performance is always situational*. The concept of situational performance, however, should never be used as an excuse for poor performance. We mention it here simply to recognize that your environment has a strong impact on the quality and quantity of work you are able to produce.

Those individuals who appeared to be superstars in one environment but lost their luster in a different environment beg the issue of evaluating performance without considering the conditions of the environment. Let us go no further without defining an important term and explaining what we intend with its usage. ***Peak performance*** means doing your very best work in a Supportive Environment, where you have the backing of your manager, if not a whole team with common goals to assist you as needed. This is a measure of your true capacity to perform when unburdened with the added obstacles and distractions that are inherent to a non-supportive environment.

In a Supportive Environment, your manager and support team do their best to eliminate the obstacles for you, allowing you to fully accelerate your performance. If you do not have a strong support structure, you must eliminate each and every obstacle as it comes by yourself. This can be an overwhelmingly challenging burden and can place an extreme drain on time, energy, and motivation. It is easy to see how your performance could suffer.

Imagine, for example, the internationally acclaimed opera singer Sara Brightman. Place her in the Metropolitan Opera and she will send out crowd pleasing vocal vibrations to the far reaches of that magnificent hall. Put her in the 9th Ward of New Orleans without a speaker system, stage lights, and an orchestra as Hurricane Katrina rolled across the city and, obviously, she would struggle to perform at all. And, what would happen to her wonderful voice if she had to perform under such adverse conditions over and over again?

If the level of support your company provides is not adequate, it is still your responsibility to do your job to the best of your ability. However, you must realize and, to the degree possible, inform management that with more support you could be more productive. You certainly do not want to write a check your body cannot cash but there is almost always room for increased productivity given a stronger, more resourceful support structure. Keep in mind that unless you have a rock solid foundation that supports all the work for which you are responsible, and this usually only occurs in a Supportive Environment, then you will not be able to reach and sustain the same level of performance that you could if you worked in a Supportive Environment. As we mentioned previously, all performance is situational. All performance is dependent upon the conditions prevalent in your workplace.

A worker who is asked to do his job under adverse conditions in a non-supportive environment is placed in a similar situation. If he continues to strive to perform at the same level as he would in a Supportive Environment he will ultimately find that the burden of fighting the negative forces of the environment will have a deleterious effect on his overall ability to perform, and over time he will begin to erode his performance to the point he will eventually ask himself: *Why bother?*

I counsel an unusually large number of people who frustrate themselves, nearly to the point of insanity, by striving for sustained peak performance in non-supportive environments. While some particularly ambitious individuals may be able to elevate their performance in a non-supportive environment to near Supportive Environment levels, it is simply not possible to sustain such an effort in a non-supportive environment over an extended period of time even when supported by a strong foundation. Trying to achieve this impossible feat often results in burnout. In fact, I would go so far as to say, *always results in burnout!*

Therefore, it should come as no surprise that a Supportive Environment is not often found in companies that experience high rates of burn out and turnover. Unfortunately, the challenge of altering a well-entrenched culture in favor of a Supportive Environment may exceed the abilities of even the most well-intentioned executives at the helms of some of this country's large organizations.

Basis of Your Foundation

But let us keep the focus on you. The truth is you bring much more to the job than what can be documented on your resume. You bring the entire collective works of your time on earth. This includes the totality of your life experiences. It does not matter that you learned celestial navigation as a hobby and now use it as part of your day job. It does not matter if you learned to draw in the park on weekends, and now design web sites. What matters is that you have a large reservoir of skills and knowledge upon which to draw. Unless you are a hermit, you also have a network of contacts. You have problem solving abilities. No one gets to be your age without having encountered and solved thousands of problems. Every day you face something new and have learned how to adapt.

What you know, what you can do, who you know, your ability to solve problems, and how well you adapt to changing conditions, represent your *foundation* because these are the key elements that support your productivity. Specifically, your foundation includes:

- **Skills and Knowledge** – what you know and what you can do.
- **Network** – your relationships with other professionals and your access to resources.
- **Problem Solving Abilities** – your ability to analyze problems and implement effective solutions.
- **Adaptability** – your ability to adjust to new and changing situations.

Your foundation is a self-developed structure that helps support your ability to be productive. When you walk in the door on your first day of work, you bring your foundation with you. The more solid and expansive it is, the sooner you can be productive. The more weak and diminutive your foundation, the less able it is to support your productivity. It is the same with buildings. Notre Dame Cathedral in Paris has a

134

strong foundation which has allowed it to rise proudly above the Seine River since it was constructed in 1132. A circular bell tower on the western coast of Italy began slowly sinking even before construction finished in 1350 because its 17.4 metric ton frame rested on a weak foundation of sandy soil; thus, the nickname Leaning Tower of Pisa. In an effort to save this historic structure, the Italian government closed the structure in 1990. An engineering team devised a plan to excavate soil from under the high side of the tower and attach counterweights to help level out the tilt. Italian publication *La Nazione* reported in 2001, "Twelve years of interventions and 53 billion lire [approximately $25 million] have reduced the lean by 44 centimeters, bringing it again to that of 1838 and assuring the monument a calm life for another two or three centuries." Had the problems with the foundations of the Torre Pendente di Pisa, the bell tower's official name, gone unaddressed, the magnificent structure certainly would have suffered a less pleasing fate.

Massive skyscrapers which dot the horizon of New York City must be supported by foundations that extend to bedrock underlying Manhattan Island. The foundation of a modest-sized home may extend only four to five feet into the earth but that is sufficient for the amount of weight it must support. The stronger the foundation, the larger the structure you can safely build upon it and the longer that foundation will endure in the face of environmental forces which conspire to bring it down.

In terms of your foundation at work, think of it as the tools and resources you need to be productive. You need to know how to perform certain types of tasks. You need to know how to perform them safely and properly. You may need some supplies. If the supplies you need are not provided to you, then you need to know where you can go to procure them. You need to know how to analyze and solve problems or know who can help you develop workable solutions. We cannot emphasize enough that you need to know how to adapt to changing conditions in the workplace since all companies experience some ebb and flow of business activity.

All of these factors apply to any job you do, regardless of whether the environment is supportive or not. A Supportive Environment will simply enhance the effectiveness of your efforts while a non-supportive environment will challenge your fortitude.

The guiding principle to remember in regard to reinforcing your foundation is: ***The stronger my foundation, the more resourceful and productive I can be and the more able I am to perform in any environment.***

Skills and Knowledge: *Webster's New Universal Unabridged Dictionary* defines *skill* as "the ability, coming from one's knowledge, practice, aptitude, etc., to do something well" and *knowledge* as "acquaintance with facts, truths, or principles, as from study or investigation." Put simply, your skills are what you can do and your knowledge is what you know.

Your resume documents or implies that you have acquired certain skills during your working life. You are an accounting clerk in the oil and gas field and, therefore, able to code and process joint interest billings. You are a fireman able to recognize and prevent a BLEVE known in the industry as a *boiling liquid expanding vapor explosion*, the kind of violent explosion you see when a vessel such as a train tank car containing flammable liquid succumbs to the flames burning around it and self-destructs in a ball of flames. You can type 65 words per minute. You are able to drive a semi tractor-trailer rig cross-country over hazardous mountain roads and back it up to a loading dock in the Bronx. But how can someone verify that you really know how to do any of these things? It is relatively easy. Watch you do them!

Doing things well requires knowledge. You know what number to use to code a drill head. You know what protective gear is required to keep you safe when the air around you is burning. You know where the *J* is located on the QWERTY keyboard patented by Christopher Sholes in 1868. You know your phone number, your address, your age, and that rain is comprised of little droplets of water which have condensed from moisture in the clouds. There are literally thousands of useful and useless facts tucked away in your brain. Facts are easy to check. You either know the fact or you do not.

Where do you work? How long have you worked there? No explanation is required; a short answer will suffice.

But there is another component to knowledge. We will call it ***comprehension*** because it goes deeper than simply knowing facts. This kind of knowledge gets at the roots of understanding and there are no short answers. Comprehension is more abstract than simply knowing facts and, therefore, testing this type of knowledge usually calls for an explanation. How does electricity work? Why is the sky blue? Why is Geometry useful? While the explanations may be comprised of facts, you are not let off with a simple short answer.

Most people are not aware of the expansive quantity of skills and knowledge they possess for the simple reason that they do not use them or think about them very often. We will focus on skills, since doing things is at the root of your success at work. While knowledge and comprehension support your ability to perform; they alone are not the primary drivers of productivity.

An interesting exercise to help bring your skills to the forefront of your thought processes is to make a list of all the things you know how to do. Let us make this assignment more immediately useful. Make a list of all the things you know how to do that you could use at work. Before you hurry off to look at your resume, let us add one additional caveat. Make a list of all the things you know how to do that you could use at work but are not currently listed on your resume. *Why do that*, you ask? Because generating this list will force you to remember skills you have that might be useful if you dusted them off and tossed them in the tool kit you take to work each day. Once you have your list, review each item carefully to see if you currently have a need for that particular skill in your current job. You may be surprised.

Network: One of the responsibilities you have as an employee involves finding resources inside and outside of the organization that can help you perform your job. Depending upon the environment, your boss may be more or less attuned to assisting you in this endeavor. Either way, to be successful, you need to access certain resources to fortify your performance. This is where your network plays an important role. There is only so much you can accomplish by yourself. Your network of contacts represents relationships you have with other professionals who can help you gain access to resources which you might not be able to access on your own but need to do your job.

Have you ever noticed that in every office, every plant, every factory, and on every team, there is always someone who seems to be exempt from the daily turmoil, tirades, and taunts of a despotic boss? He seems to know everyone and run into friends and acquaintances wherever he goes. He could always find an extra computer when he needs one or a way to accomplish even the most impossible of tasks in an amazingly short amount of time. If you look closely, you will find that he is a master builder when it comes to building relationships. As such, he has created a network of friends and colleagues who are willing to help out when called upon to do so.

Before we delve further into the importance of relationships, let us clear up any confusion that might exist surrounding the distinction between building solid, stormproof relationships and schmoozing. No doubt about it, schmoozing is a good skill to master, but do not confuse relationship building with the short term self-promotional goals of schmoozing. Relationships built on schmoozing tend to be superficial, shallow, and short-lived. They fade quickly as the value of the alliance diminishes. Our experience suggests that relationships built on mutual respect and trust stand strong for years. The type of relationship that is strong enough to endure in a stormy workplace environment can be based on nothing less than mutual respect and trust.

I once had a co-worker who would voluntarily help me out on projects when he saw that I needed help. I very much appreciated the assistance. Unfortunately, he would follow his assistance with the sarcastic remark, "Wow, that was fun; you owe me big time." Needless to say, I was quite reticent to invite his assistance again. I do not know, and frankly I was unconcerned, whether he ever discovered that this approach did not generate many long term relationships.

Here is how it should work. The new teacher is back at work after being out sick for a week. You see him overwhelmed by a pile of tests that need to be graded. You approach him in the hallway between classes and introduce yourself then offer to score a few tests for him to help him catch up. It is a one-way transaction. You offer to help with no expectations of receiving anything but self-satisfaction in return. In doing so, you have made a new friend and created what could turn out to be an enjoyable long-term working relationship.

It is enough to treasure the relationship itself, rather than viewing the relationship as a means for producing goodwill and support. You can be certain that a solid relationship will produce plenty of goodwill and support but if you lust after the goodwill and support in an effort to enhance your own position, you may quickly find that the effort of maintaining the relationship will soon overshadow the perks. Abusing such relationships will also ultimately prove disastrous. Wisdom commonly passed down from veteran actors to newcomers in the entertainment industry suggests: *Don't step on people on the way up; you may need them on the way down.* We think this wisdom applies in a wider realm as well.

"Company parties, informal get-togethers, and business lunches mean interacting with people you rarely see or call. What's new with them? You can be certain that there are new career opportunities since the last time you spoke," suggests author and executive talent agent Debra Feldman in her article "It's Networking Season!" posted on careerJournal.com. "But don't make the mistake of disrupting the flow by aggressively selling yourself or monopolizing a group discussion."

People who are good at building relationships are relatively easy to spot. They are generous with their breaks, their lunch hours, and their leisure time. They gravitate toward up-beat, positive people like iron to a magnet. They avoid workplace cliques which tend to exclude people in favor of building relationships within as well as outside of their own department. They will also look to establish strong relationships outside the company with vendors, customers, and specialists. In general, they are genuinely interested in other people.

You may be familiar with the concept of a cross-functional team. Good relationship builders create a cross-functional network of contacts on which to draw for help with a tough assignment or people to whom they can go for advice. This is a good resource to have and an essential component of your foundation, particularly in a non-supportive environment where any kind of assistance may be in short supply. The person with a strong cross-functional network of contacts knows someone in accounting who can get the numbers that nobody else can get. She has a friend in shipping who can short-cut bureaucratic red tape to get a package delivered on short notice.

Positive comments sent by customers pleased with the treatment or service they receive as a result of the good working relationship they share with you may not go to you or your boss. Rather, they might go to the department head or higher. As your network of good relationships expands, it blocks more and more inclement weather offering you added protection regardless of which way the wind blows.

Problem Solving Abilities: Your ability to analyze problems and implement effective solutions is a key element of your foundation. You should constantly hone these skills to keep them sharp and ready for use at a moment's notice.

Interestingly enough, many people do not realize how adept they actually are at solving problems because they do it so frequently and without thinking about it that they do not realize they are, in fact, solving problems. Ask yourself: *Did I organize my closet recently? When my children get into a squabble, do I help mediate a workable solution to their problem? On weekends, do I tinker with that cantankerous engine on the lawnmower?* These activities require the use of problem solving skills.

The fact is that all problem solving skills developed or exercised outside of work hours are transferable to the workplace. The particulars of a given problem are much less important than knowing an effective process for analyzing the situation and arriving at a workable solution. An old Chinese proverb states: *Give a man a fish and you feed him for a day; teach a man to fish and you feed him for a lifetime.* As you might expect, we have a slightly different version: *Give a man a fish and you feed him for a day. Teach a man to solve problems and when he tires of eating fish, he can catch something else.*

Vision Works, a company that fosters innovative thinking, describes a ***problem*** as "the undesirable gap between the desired condition and the actual condition of something important." We use a similar definition to describe frustration which we discuss in more detail in the next chapter. They describe a ***solution*** as "taking corrective actions to close the problem gap by eliminating or mitigating the causes of the problem." Seems easy enough and it may very well be if you have an effective technique to identify and diminish the conditions that propagated the gap.

Additionally, Vision Works offers some useful thoughts in terms of causes. "For most problems, there are direct causes, which are near in time and distance to the problem effects they produce. These direct causes are more apparent and, therefore, easier to detect. There are also, however, additional higher level, or 'root' causes to a significant problem, and, therefore, much more difficult to detect."

A cautionary note is useful here. Do not confuse symptoms with causes. Suppose you have the common cold. As a result, your head may hurt, you might have a sore throat, and your nose may be dripping incessantly. While you may feel miserable, these are merely symptoms of the cold. Medication can reduce the negative impact of the symptoms without necessarily doing anything about the problem: you still have a cold. Likewise, you can mitigate the symptoms of a problem without actually ridding yourself of the problem. In some cases, this may represent the best approach to address the problem if the problem is too complex or pervasive to solve. Since there is currently no cure for the common cold, we can only hope to minimize the suffering we experience by addressing the symptoms till the cold runs its course.

If possible it is best to identify and attack the ***root cause*** of a problem as this is the primary reason the problem exists. If your yard is plagued by the Taraxacum Officinale (Family Asteraceae), a perennial weed commonly known as the Dandelion, simply plucking the flower and leaves is not enough. Only when the taproot is excised from the ground is the Dandelion truly eliminated. It is the same with problems in the workplace. Only when you eliminate the root cause will the problem finally go away.

To some degree, identifying the root cause of a problem is a matter of tracking backwards through cause-and-effect relationships based on facts uncovered during an investigation. For example, a car hits a light pole. The car hit the light pole because it skidded off the road which was wet. The road was wet because it was raining. If we stop here, we might conclude that the car hit the light pole because it was raining but would this be what really caused the wreck? Was it really the rain or were there other factors at work? This would depend on what other facts we could uncover.

Further investigation might lead us to the realization that the car was going too fast for the conditions because the driver was not paying attention to the speedometer. The driver was not paying attention to the speedometer because he was drunk.

While both the rain and the fact that the drunk driver are relevant factors, we can safely shift our attention to the drunk driver as the root cause of this wreck because the drunk driver was the reason that the vehicle was going too fast for the conditions. If it were not for the drunk driver, the fact that it had been raining would not, alone, have created this outcome. The rain was a contributing factor but the drunk driver was the root cause of this wreck. Knowing the root cause of this problem, you can now proceed to determine and implement an effective remedy to prevent its reoccurrence: *keep the drunk off the road!*

Most problem solving techniques utilize some combination of the following steps:

1. **Investigation** – because you need all the facts. You need to find out exactly what is happening. It would be useful to know whether something like this has ever happened before. You might also want to know what was supposed to happen if what did happen is not what was desired.

2. **Analysis** – because you need to understand the problem to the greatest extent possible. After gathering the facts, analyze them to determine what produced the gap between what was desired and what actually happened.

This can help you diagnosis the problem and perhaps determine a prognosis if one is not already apparent.

3. **Remedy** – because you want to solve the problem. At some point, you must shift from investigation and analysis to actually finding a solution. This is your best shot at what will resolve the problem. It should be based on your investigation and analysis of the facts and your experience as to what remedy has the best chance to cure the problem.

4. **Evaluation** – because your remedy may not solve the problem. It may have gotten you closer to the solution, maybe not. You must monitor implementation of your remedy and evaluate the results. If your course of action did not eliminate the problem, then you may want to reopen the investigation and revisit your analysis, so as to arrive at a more accurate prognosis.

If you noticed that these are the same steps that most people see their doctors take when they report to a clinic with an ailment, we commend you for your perceptive nature. Your doctor will meet with you and sometimes perform tests to investigate your condition. Next she will analyze the results of the test in an effort to identify your ailment. Then she will prescribe a remedy, if one exists. Finally, she will ask you to report back in a couple weeks to ensure that the remedy has worked as expected.

There are a number of effective problem-analysis or problem-solving techniques that are commonly employed in business situations. Some of them you may already know. Mind Tools Ltd. offers the following list of techniques on its web site:

*   **Brainstorming** – challenge a group to identify as many potential solutions as possible which are not critiqued until a suitable list has been generated.
*   **Critical Path Analysis** – calculate the minimum length of time in which the project can be completed by analyzing, sequencing, and prioritizing the required activities.

- **Decision Tree** – consider alternative decisions and evaluate the implications of making those decisions.
- **Pros and Cons Analysis** – evaluate ideas by categorizing relevant comments as plus, minus or interesting.
- **S.W.O.T. (Strengths, Weaknesses, Opportunities and Threats)** – identify the strengths and weaknesses of ideas and examine the associated opportunities and threats.

We encourage you to investigate other techniques available to you as well and choose the one that best suits the problem that confronts you and the conditions of your environment. Be aware that your boss and co-workers in a non-supportive environment may not share your enthusiasm for solving a particular problem. You should decide for yourself how severely the problem impacts your ability to be productive in your environment and act accordingly, often with discretion.

Adaptability: In the seminal work *On The Origin of Species by Natural Selection* of 1859, Charles Darwin states, "We have seen that man by selection can certainly produce great results, and can adapt organic beings to his own uses, through the accumulation of slight but useful variations, given to him by the hand of Nature." We suggest that in a process similar to the one described by Darwin that you, too, can evolve through a series of adaptations to be better suited to deal with the rigors of your current workplace environment.

Songster Elvis Presley promoted the idea that "Only the Strong Survive" in a hit by the same name penned by Kenneth Gamble, Leon Huff, and Jerry Butler. We think a more appropriate phrasing would be, "Only Those Who Adapt Survive." However, such a title might never have topped the charts with sales limited to a few enlightened members of the scientific community.

Fear of the unknown and fear of failure prevent many people from trying something new and ultimately will keep them from adapting to a new situation. Tom

Hopkins, author and sales trainer quoted on the web site ThinkExist.com, suggests, "Do what you fear most and you control fear." Whether learning new software or familiarizing yourself with new equipment, change is inevitable and adjusting to it is essential to your success in any job. "I am not judged by the number of times I fail," Hopkins explains, "but by the number of times I succeed; and the number of times I succeed is in direct proportion to the number of times I fail and keep trying."

Also quoted on ThinkExist.com, actress and television personality Oprah Winfrey advises, "Think like a queen. A queen is not afraid to fail. Failure is another steppingstone to greatness." We do caution that Supportive Environments are much more forgiving of failure than non-supportive environments but trying something new is not always followed by failure. The message suggested by Hopkins and Winfrey, and one with which we concur, is that letting fear dictate a course of inaction is an ineffective policy.

The external forces of globalization, an uncertain economy, and turbulence in the labor market certainly introduce unpredictable dynamics into your workplace. Compound that with the erratic nature of a non-supportive environment and you have uncertainty raised to the nth power. Remember the wisdom of Greek philosopher Heraclitus of Ephesus as quoted by Plato in *Cratylus*. "Everything flows, nothing stands still." You may have heard the more contemporary version: *The only constant is change.* How true. And so it is in the workplace. Your ability to adjust to new and changing situations can help your boat ride out storms that would certainly sink other vessels.

Regardless of market influences, technology is marching forward at breakneck speed. It has only been a little more than one hundred years since the Wright brothers flew their biplane over the sand dunes on the beach at Kitty Hawk, North Carolina, in 1903. Now commercial air travelers hurtle to their destinations at close to the speed of sound. The Electrical Numerical Integrator And Computer (ENIAC) built during the later years of World War II filled a thirty by fifty foot room and weighed 30 tons. Now the same computing power will fit on your wrist.

Pierre M. Coupet, founder and CEO of NetWEB Elite Solutions, Inc., on HR.com writes about how the personal computer, which arrived on the scene in 1974 and was widely distributed by IBM by 1981, reshaped the business world. "It took a number of years for most companies to catch on and realize that this was not simply a toy and that it would soon replace these huge mainframes and expensive workstations they were hooked into." These changes in technology are now history. The truth is all workplaces undergo constant change and your ability to adapt is essential to your ability to remain productive.

Some ability to adapt is founded in experience. You have learned what to do and equally important what not to do when the excrement hits the fan. Other ability to adapt is founded in an interest to learn new things, to make yourself usefully productive by applying all the skills and knowledge in your possession to the work at hand and by learning new skills and knowledge when required. One encounter with an obnoxious boss in an Antagonistic Environment may provide enough incentive for you to acquire the additional skills and knowledge necessary to keep your job.

You may want to learn not to fly off the handle when things do not go as expected. Step back, assess the situation and take productive action which may include doing nothing. There are innumerable situations in your workplace that require you to adapt. The sooner you accept this fact and develop an attitude that welcomes adaptation to change, if you have not already done so, the better off you will be.

Strength of Your Foundation Depends on You

How solid and expansive you build your foundation depends mostly on you. Its strength has everything to do with how much creativity and determination you can bring to the challenge of every new situation you encounter. How well your foundation serves you, depends on how strong you make it, how well you maintain it, and how deleterious the workplace environment is to it.

The Supportive Environment encourages you to build and maintain a strong foundation by providing you access to the components you need to do just that. This environment might be compared to the Metropolitan Opera. It supports best performances. When Ms. Brightman steps on stage, first of all there is a stage, the microphone is hot, the orchestra is ready, and all the seats are filled with an audience anxious to be pleased by what they are about to see and hear because someone went out and sold tickets. At the Met, the quality of the evening's entertainment depends solely on the entertainer's ability to perform.

The Benign Environment is ambivalent and somewhat indifferent. You can perform at your best if you are able but, first, you will need to find a stage and a microphone, then recruit an orchestra and figure out how to route power to the stage. You will have to print your own tickets and sell them yourself to fill the seats after you finish installing the lights.

The Contentious Environment is similar to the subway tunnel. Assuming you avoid getting mugged and do not accidentally step on the third rail, there is nothing that will lead to your demise but you will be trying to perform in an environment that prevents anyone from hearing you as one train after another rumbles through the station.

When contemplating the Antagonistic Environment, visualize the flooded 9th Ward of New Orleans during height of Katrina's fury. Here peak performance is nearly impossible to achieve due to the aggressive nature of the environment. As Friedrich Wilhelm Neitzche, a Prussian-born philologist and philosopher, is quoted as saying: "What does not destroy you, makes you strong." While experience is an excellent teacher, experiential learning is not without its risks.

A strong foundation should still be of interest to you even in a Supportive Environment. It all relates to the level of support your environment affords you. The more support your environment provides the less self-reliant you must be.

Regardless of the environment, it all boils down to the strength of your foundation. **The more solid and expansive your foundation, the less time and effort you will have to focus on shoring up your defenses and the more time and effort you**

have available to devote to your productivity. This is especially important in a non-supportive environment. The less stable your foundation, the less able you are to focus on your productivity and, therefore, the more the quality and quantity of your work may suffer.

CHAPTER 11

Strengthening Your Image

Many of us glance in the mirror to check how we look as we head out the door in the morning to greet the world. The mirror is a useful tool for us to use to verify that the preparations we have undertaken to make ourselves presentable have achieved the desired results. But the image we present to our friends, family, and co-workers is produced by more than how we look. Your image, as we speak of it here, is about everything that contributes to how you are perceived in the workplace.

Manage the Perception

The more you know about how you are perceived by your co-workers, the better prepared you are to make decisions and act in a manner that helps you shape a positive image. You can make a good image stronger. With will and determination, you can reshape a weak or tarnished image. And that is important because your professional image should present you in a positive light if you are to win the goodwill and support of your peers. If your image does not currently do that, you have work to do.

Being able to manage the perception that your co-workers have of you is extremely important, as your co-workers can be a very beneficial source of support. They can also be very critical if they do not like what they see. Their perception is comprised of a variety of elements which people commonly use to evaluate other people. These are all elements over which you have some level of control and, therefore, are able to improve. A positive image is a good thing to have and sustain in any environment but this is especially true in a non-supportive environment where it can serve to counter any erroneous charges leveled at you by your boss.

In my post-college travels around America, I once met a young man who hailed from the British Isles. He had moved to the United States in hopes of developing a musical career but did not seem to be making much progress. One evening we were chatting in his living room and I asked to use the bathroom. I must say that I was intrigued when I flipped on the light in the bathroom to find that the mirror above the sink had been taped over with newspapers. Upon returning to the living room, I inquired about the newspapers and he indicated that he had removed all the mirrors he could from the house and taped over those that were permanently mounted. When I asked, why, he explained that he believed he would not feel as bad if he did not know how bad he looked, particularly, in the morning. Whether you know how bad you look or not, those around you certainly know. If there is something wrong with your professional image it serves your best interests to know about it and correct it rather than ignore it.

Ways that you can positively influence your image and thereby influence how others perceive you in the workplace fall into the following categories:

- **Values, Ethics, and Integrity**
- **Attitude**
- **Productivity**
- **Communication**
- **Self-Management**

Pursuing a means to enhance your professional image can help you rule yourself out as part of the problem even if only to allay any element of self-doubt when confronted with a barrage of criticism from a hostile boss. It is natural for you to question whether you are at fault. A healthy sprinkling of introspection keeps you honest. Too much self-doubt places you in a weakened position. We certainly do not endorse the concept that says the employee is always right or the concept that says the employee is always at fault. We do, however, recognize that it takes two to tangle. It also takes two to Tango but, as statistics have unfortunately revealed, conflict is far more prevalent in the workplace than dancing.

The point here is that there may be some elements of your behavior which increase your vulnerability in non-supportive environments. Taking control over those areas of your professional life can produce results your co-workers can see, can help you reduce that vulnerability, and can help you to better establish yourself in a more defensible posture.

The guiding principle to remember in regard to strengthening your image is: *All of my decisions and activities should be consistent with what I would expect of my employees if I were a manager in a Supportive Environment.*

Values, Ethics, and Integrity: Since the implosion of Enron, concepts such as values, ethics, and integrity have flooded into the media spotlight. Values, ethics, and integrity come as a package deal. In order to keep from running afoul of corporate policy, the justice system, or your conscience, we recommend that you establish a solid understanding of how these concepts apply to the decisions and behaviors you bring to the workplace.

So that we are all clear on what these terms mean, we refer to the following definitions provided in *Webster's New Universal Unabridged Dictionary*:

- **Values** – the ideals, customs, institutions, etc. of a society toward which the people of the group have an affective regard.
- **Ethics** – a complex of moral precepts held or rules of conduct followed by an individual (ethical – being in accordance with the rules or standards for right conduct or practice, especially the standards of a profession.)

- **Integrity** – adherence to moral and ethical principles; soundness of moral character; honesty.

These definitions are a bit lofty, so let us bring them down to ground level and take a closer look at what these words mean in terms of your behavior at work. Values, ethics, and integrity are the starting point for self-management. More on the importance of self-management in a moment but for now, it is important to understand that your values, ethics, and integrity guide your behavior in all areas of life, not just in the workplace, and should be somewhat independent of any guidelines documented by the company or established by the corporate culture. The values, ethics, and integrity expected by the company should be viewed as a baseline that is common to all employees, not a lofty goal to which you should aspire. Your standards should be higher than those demanded of you by an employer.

Values, just as the word implies, are the things that are important to you. They are things that you value such as respect, truth, responsibility, and teamwork. If you think these are the kind of values you might find in a Supportive Environment, you would be right. This is the environment in which people work best, are the happiest, and are the most productive. However, you may hear these or similar values espoused in nearly all workplace environments. The sad reality is that in many companies, these values are given little more than lip service.

Ethics are the rules of conduct you employ to conform to your values. If you value respect, then you would want to respect yourself and others. If you value truth, then you would aspire to tell the truth even when it is inconvenient. If you value responsibility, then you would take responsibility for your actions even when you have made a mistake. If you value teamwork, then you would work in support of the team against all efforts to tear the team apart. Ethics are the fences that line the pathways of your behavior. They do not keep you from straying off the path but they do serve to let you know when you have strayed.

Integrity is a measure of how well your behavior aligns with your values. In other words, are you doing what you have told yourself and others that you would do? Integrity breathes life into your values and ethics. You can have values and you can have ethics but if you do not have integrity, your values and ethics do not much matter because they will be left gathering dust on the shelf. Your integrity is the vehicle that promotes your values and ethics. This is where the proverbial rubber meets the road. You can say that you value honesty and you can say that you behave honestly but it is your integrity that brings consistency between your values, your ethics, and your behavior. It is through your integrity that co-workers see you behave in an honest manner and, therefore, they are inspired to view you as an honest person. This alignment between values, ethics, and integrity is one of several qualities that helps portray you in a positive light.

Integrity is contagious. So is a lack of integrity. Just like the common cold virus, the lack of integrity has a nasty way of infecting those around you. It may happen slowly, at first. A senior procurement officer may take advantage of a pushy vendor, justifying the act with the idea that the vendor deserved it and besides, "I saved the company money." Who would argue with that? But it does not stop there. If the procurement officer gets away with cheating a bad vendor, next time, he may take advantage of a good and well-respected vendor when directed by his boss to cut expenses, making him appear to be the most budget-conscious procurement officer in the company. But his colleagues may know what he is doing. Even so, after he receives the Employee of the Month Award two times in a row, his peers cannot help but think that the boss condones this practice, so they begin following their co-worker's lead. Never mind that the company procurement policy demands fair and transparent negotiations with each and every vendor. In some companies, this disease has reached epidemic proportions. Not only are the customers fair game with manipulative sales schemes but bosses actually view stealing deals and poaching clients from fellow sales personnel as a good thing.

A sales representative for a service company headquartered in Kansas City confided in me several years ago that the sales personnel routinely padded customer invoices with additional charges and fees. The corporate bosses, she explained, thought that not every customer would complain. Those who did complain would be told that it was an accounting error and the charges would be promptly removed from the invoice or refunded if the invoice had already been paid. Those who did not complain, well, it was free and clear profit. Not really. In my opinion it was theft. No different then if the owners of the service company had hired cons to break into their customers' offices and steal cashboxes. It was clear that the owners of this company valued profits over honesty. I doubt they publicized that fact in their advertising as that would have highlighted their lack of integrity. It makes you wonder what other values they held that they would not want their customers to know.

"Pressure from management or the Board to meet unrealistic business objectives and deadlines is the leading factor most likely to cause unethical corporate behavior." This, according to an American Management Association survey performed in 2006. Speaking of Enron! When it collapsed, thousands of people lost their investments, employees lost retirement funds, and venders never got paid. All are very troubling stories. But in our opinion, the greatest tragedy and the one few people dare to mention is the large number of employees who must have known what was going on or at least sensed a problem and chose to do nothing about it.

The fact that Sheron Watson stood as the lone whistle blower is simply astounding. It is difficult for a rational person to believe that she was the only one in a multinational corporation who knew or suspected that something was amiss. There had to have been hundreds of people who were in a position to have known that the books were being cooked. Vice presidents, executive assistants, analysts, auditors, and sales and accounting personnel could have had some clue about what was happening. Was it the fact that they were making money and living the good life that bought their silence? Were they all afraid of losing their jobs? Why else would normally decent and morally conscious individuals decide to leave their integrity at home and turn a blind eye to the debacle unfolding in front of them? Those who quietly stand by and do nothing when they bear knowledge of illicit behavior own more than a few shares of culpability.

In the post-Enron era, virtually all companies have implemented some formal code of ethics. The Sarbanes-Oxley Act of 2002, commonly referred to as SOX, mandates certain conduct with regard to financial statements. And, MBA programs have added ethics classes to their curriculum. Beyond that, employees have an obligation to themselves and to their families to conduct themselves in an ethical manner regardless of what the company or the law requires.

The fact is that the person who does the right thing simply because it is the right thing spends a lot less time looking over her shoulder. In an Antagonistic Environment, that can make all the difference in the world. A boss who is out to get you has very little to get you with if you are not one to cut corners or shave the truth. It is more difficult to set someone up for public ridicule when that individual consistently chooses the high road.

If you are not a person of integrity, you might as well forget working in a Supportive Environment. First, it is unlikely that you could fake your way into that environment, and if by chance you did, it is highly unlikely that you would be welcome there for long.

Keep in mind that your values, your ethics, and your integrity are not those of the company and vice-a-versa. We do not recommend that you reject or ignore the values and ethics of the company unless they are patently unworthy of your respect. Set high standards, maintain your integrity, and you will easily exceed any expectations set by the company. Accept lower standards and you may find yourself to be part of the problem.

When you do not act in concert with your values and ethics, your integrity can be lost. Once it is lost, it is difficult, although not impossible, to regain. The reason many people hold politicians in such low esteem is that too many of them make promises during the campaign then conveniently forget their promises once they are in office. The fact that they always have a reason, or excuse which they seem to believe ameliorates their responsibility for this lack of integrity does not alter the perception this behavior creates in voters' minds.

Your co-workers' perception of you will be no better than that of a *forgetful* politician if what you do differs significantly from what you say you are going to do. Once people sense a loss of your integrity, their perception of you from that point forward is very difficult to change. A lack of integrity is viewed by most people as a negative quality regardless of any other characteristics you display even if the environment is tainted to such a degree that a lack of integrity is a part of the corporate culture. The American Management Association survey we cited earlier also revealed that "nearly a third of respondents (32%) said that their company's public statements sometimes conflicted with internal messages and realities." Should it be the case that the corporate culture where you work embraces dishonesty, irresponsibility, corruption, and other equally impoverished values, we recommend that you find your way out the door as quickly as possible. Your conscience will certainly let you know when that time arrives.

Not all unethical behavior merits a jail sentence. Some simply whittles away at your integrity. It may be as seemingly innocuous as not sharing credit with a co-worker who was instrumental in the success of your project. Even if no one else is aware of this oversight, your co-worker will know the truth of the situation and will certainly not be as willing to assist you in the future thus terminating your access to a valuable resource. Others may know the truth as well. The image your co-workers have of you may suffer and if you have a functioning conscience your image of yourself will likewise be diminished.

Obviously, not all of your choices are going to be black and white. There are a lot of gray areas when it comes to ethical issues. Even so, it is crucial that you recognize when your actions meet the letter of the law but skirt the intent for this is the entrance to the danger zone. Set high ethical standards and when circumstances arise where your actions and the decisions that prompted those actions are called to appear under the intense light of public scrutiny, you will be able walk away with your head held high.

Attitude: Your attitude helps your co-workers predict how you will respond to a given situation. It is a major part of what guides them in deciding whether they like you, and whether you are an enjoyable person with whom to work or to be around. A positive attitude may entice them to share useful opportunities with you while a negative attitude may convince them to withhold an opportunity.

Webster's New Universal Unabridged Dictionary defines **attitude** as the "manner, disposition, feeling, position, etc., with regard to a person or thing." We view it as the part of your personality you share with others every time you encounter them.

It is often said that hiring decisions are based 50 percent on experience and 50 percent on attitude. These numbers may skew more heavily toward attitude if the common advice from recruiters is true: *Hire for attitude, train for skills.* The bottom line is that a positive attitude is an important quality for you to exhibit during the interview process as well as throughout your tenure in whatever job you are hired to perform.

The kitchen in your house has a light switch on the wall. Flip it up and the light comes on. Flip it down and the light goes off. You control access to the switch. You decide when to turn it on so you can see where you are going and move around without bumping into the counter, stove or refrigerator.

Now suppose the light switch, instead of being conveniently located on the wall in the kitchen, is mounted on a post by the street where anyone passing by can switch it on or off at will. Imagine the difficulty of preparing the evening meal or the danger of slicing a roast when you could suddenly be plunged into darkness at the whim of someone else. Obviously, no one would tolerate this situation, so why would you allow other people to control your attitude in this manner? Someone flips your *attitude switch* up, and you have a happy day. They flip in down, and suddenly you are pissed off at everyone around you. Unfortunately, that is exactly how many people in the workplace and elsewhere behave.

How much control do you exert over your attitude? Do you let your co-workers flip your *attitude switch* on and off at will or do you keep that switch well out of their reach?

"One of the hardest things for us to learn in our relationships – both work and personal – is that we can operate independently of other people's bad moods, but we have to work at it. Unless you mentally immunize yourself, you can be infected by other people's crankiness," advises Leslie Charles, speaker and author of *Why Is Everyone So Cranky?*

Presenting a positive attitude to those around you even in the face of adversity, especially in the face of adversity helps your co-workers shape a positive perception of you. It works much like a mirror, show a good attitude to others and they will reflect a good attitude back to you. That is the theory anyway. Be advised, it may not always work but it is always worth the effort. What is the alternative? Present a negative attitude? You probably know co-workers who do that consistently. They cannot be bothered to help anyone regardless of the situation without a tirade of complaints. They fly into a rage with the least provocation. Their "hot buttons" are out for everyone to see. Push one and the results are predictable. What is your perception of them?

"So many people struggle with negative attitudes and self-defeating behaviors because they fail to realize that what you think about comes about," explains Mark Victor Hansen, public speaker and author of *The One Minute Millionaire: The Enlightened Way to Wealth.* "If you don't discipline yourself to be positive by tuning into positive messages and hanging out with positive people, then the world tends to suck the life-force out of you." A chronic negative attitude puts you on the fast lane to disaster.

First, few things will give a boss in an Antagonistic Environment a better excuse to unburden himself of your services than a negative attitude. It is a position you cannot defend. What are you going to say? "Yes, I have a bad attitude but it is your fault!"

Second, a negative attitude is damaging to your self-esteem. Sometimes in a non-supportive environment, all you have to bolster your self-confidence and ability to motivate yourself day after day is a positive attitude. Let your attitude slip and you are more susceptible to a boss who may characterize you as incompetent and unworthy of the position you hold.

Third, your positive attitude helps buoy the attitudes co-workers who may be subjected to the same environmental influences as you but be less capable of sustaining a sense of self-confidence and inner peace. A positive attitude might help improve everyone's situation while a negative attitude almost certainly will make it worse.

It is not always easy to maintain a positive attitude which is why so many people opt out. **Frustration** is the culprit. It can have a debilitating influence on your attitude. If you are frustrated with your job, your relationships or any element of your life the resulting frustration can surface as a negative attitude. The good news is you are not alone. *The Gallup Management Journal's* semi-annual "Employee Engagement Index" reveals the results of surveys performed between October 2000 and April 2004. The most recent survey indicates that 60 percent of actively disengaged workers "often feel frustrated." This represents a significant portion of the workforce that experiences frequent frustration at work.

But if you are not one of the top quartile of employees who enjoys the benefit of working in a Supportive Environment, you may be challenged to flip your *attitude switch* to positive day after day. Being able to control frustration allows you to take a major step forward in making it easier to leave your *attitude switch* in the positive position.

Frustration can be caused by a disconnection between your current state of affairs and where you would like to be with regard to your job, relationships or life. Let us focus on your job. If you believe you are overworked, underpaid, and unappreciated, you may convince yourself that you have sufficient grounds for feeling frustrated. Frustration often results from a disparity in how you would like to be treated and the reality of your current situation.

Chronic frustration can breed undue **stress** which can easily taint your attitude. But not all stress is negative. The butterfly that does not have to struggle to free himself from the cocoon begins life with an underdeveloped set of wings and is domed to an early demise. Just as with the butterfly, a certain amount of stress is essential to our mental and physical health and wellbeing. But at the same time, excessive stress can also be debilitating. Therefore, it is useful to be able to identify the symptoms of stress and know ways to reduce the negative impacts stress may have.

Dale Collie, a professional speaker and former US Army Ranger, identifies the following symptoms of stress:

- Anxiety
- Indecisiveness
- Irritability
- Complaining
- Forgetfulness
- Loss of self-confidence
- Argumentativeness
- Insomnia
- Rapid emotional shifts
- Physical exhaustion

"Symptoms such as these," comments Collie, "cost companies billions of dollars each year in health care costs, absenteeism, accidents, quality control, personnel turnover, and various interpersonal relationship problems." In extreme cases, stress can have deadly results. Your ability to manage stress is essential, especially if you work in a non-supportive environment.

Try putting the issue related to your stress in perspective with these questions: *Is it a matter of life or death? Will the outcome impact my career? Is it the most important issue I will consider this week?* You get the idea. Many people stress themselves over rather insignificant issues. Once an issue is resolved, whether by you or your boss, do not linger over it. If you were at fault, apologize, forgive yourself, and move on. If your boss was to blame, forgive him, and move on.

This advice is particularly true if you are moving on to a new job. Latent anger with your previous boss can easily show up during an interview prompting a hiring manager to doubt the wisdom of bringing you on board regardless of your skills set. Remember, attitude accounts for at least fifty percent of a hiring decision.

If you feel the need to complain or let off some steam that inevitably builds up in a non-supportive environment, do not do it at work around your boss or your co-workers. You will regret it. Do not generate steam at work and blow it off at home. That is not fair to your family. Hit the stair climber. Hit a volleyball. Take a soothing bath or meditate to calm the raging inner beast. Let the steam blow down in a safe manner where no one gets burned. When these techniques are not enough, sometimes you simply need to remove yourself from the environment. Take a vacation to recharge. You might extend your respite by staggering your vacation with the time your boss plans to take off should your boss be your primary source of workplace stress.

"Stress management techniques begin with becoming aware of your stressors, recognizing what you can change, and learning to moderate your emotional and physical reactions to your stressors," advises the *Helpguide*, an online source for non-commercial information on mental health and lifelong wellness. "Stress management comes down to finding ways to change your thinking and manage your expectations."

Check the reality of your ***expectations***. If you expect your boss to give you a raise and the reality is that she will never give you a raise no matter what, then you leave yourself vulnerable to frustration. Why would you expect supportive behavior from a boss in a non-supportive environment? As the popular television psychologist Doctor Phil would say, "Get real!" Once you recognize that your boss will never give you a raise and adjust your expectations to reflect that reality, you have started to alleviate one source of your frustration.

Reigning in expectations, however, does not resolve other sources of frustration. For instance, it does not address the fact that you want a raise but find yourself in an environment where that is not going to happen. It simply removes from contention the idea that this boss will grant you one which should make it clear that you have a decision to make.

The remedy for frustration is often a ***decision*** that drives a course of action which can potentially extricate you from an undesirable situation. A good friend called me one day during a break in a real estate class he was taking to prepare for reinstatement of his license. He said a young woman in the class had just stood up from her laptop computer and said, "There, I did it!"

"What?" my friend asked.

"I resigned," the woman said displaying a huge grin.

"You did?"

"Yeah. I just emailed my resignation."

"You resigned by email?"

"Sure! Why not?"

"What'd your manager say?"

"Nothing. I am the manager. I had six people working for me."

"And you didn't give any notice."

"Why should I? Do you think the company cares about me? Radio Shack just laid off two hundred people by email. If they can do it, so can I," she said with the look of elation that only comes from making a decision which demonstrates a sense of having regained control over her future.

A brief note to CEOs: you cannot treat employees like excess inventory and expect them to have any sense of loyalty or respect for you or the company. OK, we are wrong! You can do this but be advised that the young lady who resigned by email with no advance warning has provided you a glimpse of the future you are creating if you demonstrate, by example, no sense of loyalty to *your most valuable assets!*

Before you rush to your computer and start typing an email resignation, we feel obligated to remind you that every action has consequences. If you are not currently in a position to resign, step away from the keyboard. This simply means that, at this time, resigning is not the right decision to address your frustration. It does not mean that you do not have other options.

Making a decision that properly addresses your situation is the key. Using the problem solving techniques discussed earlier can help you identify and make a good decision. Once you make that decision, you will find that your frustration begins to dissipate. Regardless of the eventual consequences, simply the act of deciding on a course of action places control of your future in your hands and alleviates the frustration regardless of how prudent the decision turns out to be. Wallowing in indecision allows frustration to fester like an infected sore.

But some people have difficulty making decisions especially when surrounded by uncertainty. Jonah Lehrer, author of *How We Decide*, writes in *The Boston Globe* in 2008, "The best decisions occur when people take the time to study their decision-making process, and not just the decision itself." Lehrer suggests it is not just a matter of considering all the choices and cites work by Dutch psychologist Ap Dijksterhuis who advises people to analyze their options then pause, and give their unconscious mind, or intuition, time to consider the problem. The resulting decision often turns out to be the best option.

Not everyone, however, has time for a long deliberative process. Lehrer considers the situation faced by Capt. Chesley B. "Sully" Sullenberger III, pilot of U.S. Airways flight 1549, who decided the Hudson River was his best choice for an emergency landing after striking a large flock of geese moments after takeoff. Training teaches pilots "how to draw upon an optimal blend of reason and emotion. They learn how to ignore their fear when fear isn't useful and how to make quick, complicated decisions in the most fraught situations." In other words, they practice *deliberate calm*, a phrase pilots use to describe how they control their emotions to make complex decisions in harrowing situations with little time and incomplete data. Many of the decisions you make in the workplace are not weighted with such grave consequences as the one made by pilot Sullenberger when he set his plane down on the Hudson River but you will certainly benefit by introducing an increased level of *deliberate calm* to your decision-making process.

While the decision alone can often reduce or eliminate your frustration, at least temporarily, you would be wise to formulate a decision that prompts an action which has a positive outcome for you. For instance, you might decide to strengthen your foundation by registering for night classes to pursue a degree or specialized certificate which could make you more marketable. With a certificate or degree in hand, the idea of removing yourself from the source of irritation is much more viable.

You should be aware that risk is a partner of any decision you make or any plan you pursue. Any plan certainly involves some combination of time, money, and resources. As many people often discover, money is scarce in a volatile economy. Domestic issues sometimes cut into the amount of time you have available to pursue your plan. Anything that delays reaching our goal can breed additional frustration. If you do not pace your expectations and realize that you will encounter delays and setbacks along the way then you place undue stress upon yourself to achieve the desired results.

The truth is you have total control over your attitude, once you reign in your expectations and exert control over frustration by making a decision to remove yourself from an undesirable situation or improve your ability to deal with it. This has nothing to do with who your boss is or how he behaves. It is all about you taking charge of your attitude by reigning in your expectations, keeping a lid on frustration, and venting stress in a healthy, safe manner.

Productivity: Research on productivity compiled by the Impact Achievement Group, a training and performance management company, has led Senior Managing Partner Rick Tate and colleague Julie White to state that "employee morale and happiness are not the critical path to productivity—but productivity and employee achievement are the critical path to high morale and a happy work environment." This reasoning contradicts the long-held believe that employee recognition programs and pizza luncheons improve morale and leads to improved productivity. Rather, Tate and White indicate that management "can only create working conditions that provide opportunities for people to seek these things [which motivate them] for themselves." In other words, you determine for yourself the level of productivity that makes you happy. The company can only create the conditions that help you achieve and sustain that level but you have to provide the motivation.

You may recall a quotation attributed to Russian novelist Vladimir Voinovich, "They pretend to pay us, and we pretend to work!" While denoting the persistent, yet satirical nature of the Russian people in the face of overbearing hardship, this self-destructive bargain is profoundly damaging to the workers.

All of us know someone who is always in motion but rarely gets anything done. They keep themselves busy by involving themselves in activities that rarely produce results and they drag down the performance of those around them. Combine them with those who are rarely in motion and you have the low performers.

Janet H. Cho of the Newhouse News Service reports on the results of a survey of 16,237 workers performed by Leadership IQ based in Washington, DC. The survey identified the following qualities of low performers:

- Negative attitude
- Stirs up trouble
- Blames others
- Lacks initiative
- Incompetence

How you perform in the workplace is a reflection of who you are as a person and, regardless of the environment in which you find yourself, it is in your best interest to demonstrate the strength of your character by meeting the demands of your workplace environment for as long as you decide to work there.

The Leadership IQ survey also identified characteristics of high performers.

- Creative
- Highly engaged
- Reliable
- Goes above and beyond
- Productive

It should come as no surprise that high performers are productive. It is inherent in the term *high performers*. But how do you go from being a low performer to a high performer? The director of Space Shuttle Flight Design and Dynamics used to tell me: *If you can't measure it, you can't fix it*. Ignore the implication that something is broken and focus on the desire to improve performance in terms of increased productivity.

The Australian Government defines ***productivity*** as "a measure of the rate at which outputs of goods and services are produced per unit of input." This measure is accepted worldwide. "Productivity is calculated as the ratio of the quantity of outputs produced to some measure of quantity of inputs used." Productivity can also be expressed as a percentage rate by dividing the number of widgets produced by the number of *wobits* it took to produce them.

For instance, if you can produce 5 widgets for every 10 *wobits* you put into the process, divide 5 by 10. You have demonstrated a productivity rate of 50 percent. The inputs, what we are calling *wobits*, do not necessarily need to be objects. They can be hours worked to create the 5 widgets. Maybe you worked 80 hours to produce those 5 widgets. In this case, your productivity rate would be 6.25 percent. If you are able to decrease the number of hours required to produce the 5 widgets then your rate will increase. If for some reason it takes you longer to produce those 5 widgets, your productivity rate will decrease.

It is not assumed that 100 percent is a perfect productivity rate. The productivity rate is only useful as a comparison. If your productivity rate was 6.25 percent last month and increased to 6.32 percent this month, you have shown an improvement. Your value to the company has increased. Depending upon the type of work you do, even a small increase in your productivity rate can mean a big increase in production quantity. If you continue to increase your value to the company, this is evidence that you can use to your benefit during a performance review to lobby for a promotion or a raise.

Suppose you are an instructional designer for web-based content, you might measure productivity in terms of the number of hours it takes to produce one page of training material. I used this measure of productivity in one of my jobs. My manager did not require that I do it; in fact, she did not even know that I was measuring my productivity. I did it as an exercise to see if was improving either as a result of modifications to the process I designed or my increased familiarity with the subject matter.

According to the Australian Government, "evidence of productivity growth usually means that better ways have been found to create more output from given inputs." The Australian Productivity Commission indicates that there are essentially two ways to promote growth in output. You can bring additional inputs into production or you can increase productivity.

Suppose you are a technical writer. You are paid by the number of pages of written work you produce. Currently, you spend 6 hours per day writing and turn out 10 pages of completed work per day. Your daily productivity rate is 167%. One way to increase that rate is to bring additional inputs into production. Your inputs are the number of hours you spend writing. If you spent 8 hours per day instead of 6, you might be able to turn out 12 pages of work. This would increase your daily production rate to 200%.

Working faster or more efficiently, are other ways to increase your productivity. Suppose as a technical writer, you currently use an old IBM Selectric typewriter. If you upgraded to a computer with a contemporary word processing program and spell checker capability, you might be able to turn out 12 pages in 4 hours. This would give you a daily productivity rate of 300%.

Some companies set productivity targets that employees are expected to meet. Many grocery stores measure how many items a checkout clerk scans per minute. Secretaries are assessed on how many words per minute they can type. Auto retailers have sales quotas. Manufacturers have production quotas. Your job may have standards for measuring productivity. The key is the ratio of outputs to inputs. Do some research and find out what the measurement is for your job.

To be effective, productivity targets must be realistic. They are meaningless unless founded upon industry baselines or past performance. There must be a valid reason to believe that the targets are achievable.

STRENGTHENING YOUR IMAGE

For example, Hicham el Guerrouj, according to the International Association of Athletics Federation, runs a mile in 3 minutes and 43.13 seconds. That is his productivity rate. Suppose your boss set your target for the mile at 3 minutes and 25 seconds. Is it credible to believe that you could achieve that rate, since el Guerrouj set the current world's record for the mile on July 7, 1999, in Rome, and no one has yet beat it?

A friend of mine ran the mile in an average time of 12 minutes and 18 seconds at the Little Rock Marathon. Would it be reasonable for her to shave 5 minutes off her time given her past performance? Your performance target must be reasonable given your past performance, your access to necessary resources, and freedom from restrictions or obstacles. Suppose that my friend had to run the marathon barefoot. That would certainly impact her time. In fact, she may not even be able to finish the race if she had to compete without the proper footwear.

There are a variety of factors that can impact your productivity in the workplace, some over which you have no control. Suppose the person providing your inputs resigns and her replacement does not have the slightest idea what he is doing. Certainly, your productivity rate drops for reasons that are outside your sphere of influence. A misdirected boss can negatively impact your productivity as he has a great deal of control over your access to resources. He can limit the inputs at your disposal. He can create obstacles or introduce disruptions. He can set impossible productivity targets to ensure that you always fall short.

Some companies may use a backdoor approach through unpaid overtime to increasing productivity by coercing you to contribute more of your hours to the company cause. This may not be bad on an occasional basis but when done on a regular basis, it is simply an unethical effort to obtain more work for less money without renegotiating your compensation. Candy companies discovered a long time ago that they could increase profits without raising prices by reducing the amount of candy while leaving the size of the box unaltered. Company executives calculated correctly that customers would either not notice the reduction in candy or would not complain about it. Unpaid overtime,

168

couched as extra effort for the team, accomplishes the same result. Less candy for you, more profit for the company.

How your boss behaves or the punitive nature of your workplace environment you endure provides you no justification for being a low performer. You must still find your own source of motivation to drive your performance. The bargain you are obligated to respect as long as your stay in your position, even if your employer falls short, is: *A fair day's work for a fair day's pay.* Even so, there is only so much work that you can accomplish in the standard 8-hour workday. Trying to push past that limit for an extended period of time will quickly lead to burnout.

You will recall that we previously defined ***peak performance*** as doing your very best work in a Supportive Environment, where you have the backing of your manager, if not a whole team with common goals to assist you as needed. To reach peak performance, you must be unburdened by the obstacles and distractions that are inherent to a non-supportive environment. By definition, peak performance is only possible in a Supportive Environment. That does not give you *just cause* to slack off in a non-supportive environment.

It means that you need to perform at your best, given the prevailing workplace environment while diverting a certain amount of your attention and effort from production to self-protection. Do you drive slower on roads soaked with rain or covered with ice? We hope so. Does it take you longer to reach your destination? Of course! Safely navigating the obstacles present in a non-supportive workplace environment requires a similar reduction in productivity.

Some environments are so hazardous that the Occupational Safety and Health Administration (OSHA) mandates employees receive training and don personal protective equipment (PPE) before performing any work in those environments. The costs of this training and equipment are expensed as part of the overhead required to safely and properly perform the work.

While your company is not required by OSHA to tell you that you must have proper training and a well-stocked workplace survival kit before entering a non-supportive workplace, you would do well to ensure your own preparedness. For this reason your best in a non-supportive environment will not measure up to your best in a Supportive Environment. The losers here are the customers you serve and the shareholders as any loss in productivity equates to a decline in shareholder value.

Given all the challenges of non-supportive environments, you still have ways to improve your productivity. In a client case study reported by Productivity Inc., Mike Shanahan, president of Cadco Ltd., explains that increasing productivity is "all about finding the simplest way to accomplish a task or an operation." It does not matter if you are the CEO or a line employee; you can increase your productivity by looking for ways to streamline your work. Obviously, if the company has written procedures that you are expected to follow that may not be an area where you can implement changes. But nearly every job has some tasks that can be performed at your discretion. You can enhance your productivity by finding the simplest way to perform these tasks. "All it takes is a commitment and a willingness," says Shanahan, "to look at things a little differently."

Think of yourself as a crime investigator. Someone is stealing your productivity and you must find the culprit. Interview witnesses if you are able. Ask yourself lots of questions until you find something that does not make sense. Use the problem solving techniques we discussed earlier to home in on the problem and see if another way of performing that task is more efficient.

We would offer a cautionary note here. In a non-supportive environment, your realm of control may be limited. You may want to exercise prudent judgment before interviewing others or changing process that may impact your co-workers until you are certain those changes promote efficiency and that you have the authority to implement them. Use your own discretion to determine the risk of such actions. To the degree that you are able to streamline your processes, you gain an increase in productivity which allows you more latitude in diverting attention and effort toward protection and defense.

It may be hard to believe but there is a problem with being overly productive in a non-supportive environment. The bottom line here is to maintain your high level of productivity but don't advertise it. If your star shines too brightly in comparison to your co-workers, you may end up with a lion's share of the work being dumped on your desk. Why? The reason is simple. You get the work done while those around you are blissfully inefficient. Keep it up and you may draw the ire of slackers who fear an increase in their workload as you continue to show what performance levels are possible.

Another danger is that your boss may argue that since you are performing so well that certainly he cannot be the problem. There is both benefit and danger in that expression of skewed logic. The benefit is that your boss has stated that your performance is not a problem. He will either have to document deterioration of your performance or risk contradicting himself, if he tries to make your performance an issue at some point in the future. The danger is that when you need help you may be in the untenable position of being the only one crying wolf over a problem that is conveniently not visible to anyone else.

In any case, remaining quietly productive might be your best course of action in non-supportive environments. First, you continue to offer value to the company. Second, your voice carries more weight if you are a high performer. Any drop in productivity plays into the hands of an unscrupulous boss. Plus, it places in doubt the credibility of your voice in questioning workplace processes or behaviors. Who listens to the runner who finishes last when he denounces the condition of the track?

Communication: An unhindered exchange of communications is critical to the success of any organization. Marshall Goldsmith, global business consultant and author, puts it this way in his article "Failure to Communicate" in *Talent Management Magazine*, "The quality of information flow within an organization often is a good indicator of the quality of the organization, period." Unfortunately, effective communications surfaces as a consistent problem for a large number of companies as it is for a number of individuals. Carter McNamara, a principal with Authenticity Consulting. Communications, adds that "too often, management learns [of] the need for communication by having to respond to the lack of it." Jeff Harlig, founder of Words@Work, caps this thought. "After all, when information isn't flowing down and out, it often isn't flowing up, either."

Just because management does not insure lines of clear and honest communication, this does not mean that you must queue up with that protocol. It is your responsibility to manage all of your communications which take place in a workplace environment regardless of the turbulence swirling around you. This includes formal as well as informal exchanges. It does not matter whether you are the sender or recipient. If the information is important enough to share, it serves you well to ensure the process is effective. This is particularly important in non-supportive environments where what you communicate or do not communicate can have extremely negative consequences.

A key component of how you are perceived in the workplace relates to how well you communicate with others as well as how you receive and process information provided to you. This includes both verbal and non-verbal forms of communicating throughout the various levels of your organization. Effective communication with superiors as well as subordinates is essential to your success in all areas you pursue. Exhibition of poor communication skills makes you part of the problem experienced by so many companies while the display of effective communications positions you as part of the solution.

Effective communication is a two-way process whereby one individual sends a message to another individual and the receiving individual indicates that the message was properly received. This is how facsimile machines *talk* with each other. The conversation between two facsimile machines goes something like this:

FAX 1: *Hey FAX 2! I have some important information for you.*
FAX 2: *OK, FAX 1. I'm ready to receive it.*
FAX 1: *Here it is.*
FAX 2: *Got it. Is this what you sent?*
FAX 1: *Yes, that's right.*
FAX 2: *Good! Thank you FAX 1!*
FAX 1: *You're welcome FAX 2! Good-bye!*

Of course, facsimile machines do not speak English. Rather, they use an audible code to communicate with each other over telephone lines but this exchange represents the content of their conversation.

Notice that FAX 1 does not send the information until FAX 2 indicates a readiness to receive it. Even after FAX 2 receives the information, FAX 1 does not terminate the session until FAX 2 verifies that the information was accurately received.

Imagine if the exchange were not so interactive and went something like this:

FAX 1: Hey FAX 2, here's some information. Hope you got it. Good-bye!

FAX 2: Wait, I'm not ready. What did you send me?

FAX 1: [Silence]

FAX 2: FAX 1, are you there? Can you send that again?

FAX 1: [Silence]

FAX 2: Oh well! I guess it wasn't that important. I'm out of here!

Effective communication is more than tossing information out a figurative window during a drive-by and hoping that it lands in the right hands. But this is how many people communicate with each other. They have in mind what they want to say; the fact the intended recipient is not ready to receive the information or does not understand it rarely enters into the picture. This is one-way communication and there is no guarantee that the message actually arrived at its intended destination.

Conveying your message to the desired recipient is much more effective when the following components of communication are properly observed:

1. **Formulate your message in terms best suited for the recipient**
2. **Select the most appropriate and reliable delivery method**
3. **Ensure the recipient is ready to receive your message**
4. **Deliver your message**
5. **Verify it was accurately received**

These may seem like rather simple steps to take to ensure the effectiveness of your communications with others, and they are simple. But far too many people slip into the realm of miscommunication by skipping one or more of these steps.

An extremely important point that Jeff Harlig, who we quoted earlier, makes is that "good communications requires us to think very deliberately and very consciously about something we can easily accomplish with almost no attention whatsoever: speaking." In other words, do not neglect the wisdom of this age old advice: *Do not open your mouth without first engaging your brain.*

The simple steps listed above provide you the means to ensure that your message is clear, accurate, and completes the journey from your brain to the intended recipient. However, these steps also require that you put some thought into the process of communicating as well as the effort it takes to construct your message. The importance of your message should guide you as to how much time and effort you devote to the entire endeavor. Speaking from experience, I would suggest that *quality of your communication increases with the rigor of your editing process.* This applies whether you are writing a book or asking for a raise.

1. Formulate your message in terms best suited for the intended recipient. When constructing your message, keep the focus on the intent of your communication. Ask yourself: *What do I want this exchange of information to achieve? Am I simply informing the recipient with an FYI message or am I trying to sell the recipient on an idea? Do I want the recipient to take action based on the information I am conveying? What do I need to communicate to achieve the desired outcome?* If your purpose is to inform, you may want to present your news upfront. If your intent is to inspire the recipient to take action, then it may be more prudent to build your case, first, and close the message with your request.

There is an abundance of material available on the topic of *business communications* to guide you in how best to present the different types of messages you may want to send in a business environment. Entire courses of study are presented on how to tune your message to the recipient's perspective. We recommend a little research in this area to augment any weaknesses you may have. Additional consideration should be given to vocabulary and grammar. Numerous sources are available to help you enhance your skills in these areas as well.

In an effort to avoid being misunderstood when communicating, it is useful to consider what differentiates you from your intended recipient. Language can be an obvious barrier but it is also useful to consider gender, race, culture, education level, and socioeconomic class to name a few. All the things that make us unique individuals also make us different and can come into play when attempting to communicate with each other. It is probably not reasonable to assume that anyone truly takes all of these factors into consideration when sending an interoffice memo. The point is that when the differences are known, we should be sensitive to them. Otherwise, we risk being misunderstood.

Other questions you would be well advised to ask yourself include: *Is this an appropriate communication for a business environment? What are the chances that it will be misunderstood? How could this information be misused? Do I really want to share this information?* If you are the least bit unsure about your message, then it is best to delay opening your mouth, dropping off your note, attaching the stamp and dropping your letter off in the box or clicking the Send button. Nothing can compensate for the damage you may do to your reputation, career or relationships if you abdicate the use of your brain in formulating the content of your communication.

2. Select the most appropriate and reliable delivery method. Basically, you have two modes of delivery: oral and non-oral. Each method offers some benefits as well as drawbacks. Though either means can be perfectly effective in carrying your message to the intended recipient, there are important differences. Some methods of delivery are more personal than others. For example, a formal letter sent to a friend might be considered rude as would an informal note slipped to someone you hardly know.

Oral communications, which involve spoken words, are of an immediate nature in terms of delivering your message and carry the possibility of receiving an immediate response from the recipient. This includes face-to-face exchanges, videoconferences, and telephone calls. If your issue requires a detailed explanation or an immediate response, then a face-to-face meeting may be the best approach unless the other face is located halfway across the country or is otherwise not easily accessible. Depending on the relationship you have with the recipient, a videoconference may provide an alternate solution or a simple phone call may suffice. Each option that moves further from a face-to-face exchange adds distance between you and the recipient and, therefore, increases the possibility for miscommunication.

Any oral exchange invites the opportunity for the recipient of your message to ask questions. If you are not prepared with answers, unskilled at thinking on your feet or not adept at deferring your response to a later date, you may want to consider a non-oral method of delivery. This is especially true in a non-supportive environment.

Non-oral communications including texting, emails, letters, and notes are predominantly comprised of written messages which often offer your recipient more time to digest the contents of your message before responding. Voice mail, while oral in nature, offers the same distance between you and the recipient as other forms of non-oral communication.

Keep in mind that well-written messages require as much skill if not more than artfully articulated verbal messages. By their very nature, however, they often offer you the luxury of checking and double checking what you have written to ensure that it actually matches what you really intended to convey to the other party. Unless your message is typed, penmanship counts. We all know the challenge of reading written instructions from a doctor.

3. Ensure the recipient is ready to receive your message. This step applies more to verbal communications. It is common to start job interviews and business meetings involving parties who have not previously worked together with idle chit-chat. This serves two purposes. First, it lets each party learn something about their counterpart; and, second, it helps make sure that the communication processes are in full gear before the parties start exchanging important information. Less skilled speakers will attempt to grab the ear of their audience with *look, well, hey, uh* or some other *throw-away* word intended only to attract your attention before they deliver the information they really want you to know. A better approach is to command the attention of the person to whom you are speaking by the power of your presence and the importance of your message.

4. Deliver your message then verify it was accurately received. This step completes what scientists call a *feedback loop* which provides you some assurance that your message arrived at the desired destination. The recipient of your message will provide an acknowledgement, send a response or perform some action that lets you know your message was received. But such feedback may not be forthcoming unless you request it.

In a written communication, you may want to add the lines: *Let me know as soon as you receive this. What are your thoughts on this subject? If you have any questions, contact me as soon as possible.* The importance of your message should dictate the importance of confirming that your message was received. Many email systems can generate a confirmation email which informs you that the recipient opened your message. Many delivery services also provide confirmation of delivery. In some cases, it might be appropriate to follow up your written communication with a phone call to ensure your message was received and to inquire if there are any questions.

In a verbal exchange, you could simply ask: *What do you think about this issue? Do you have any questions?* Confusion in responding to these requests could indicate confusion in regard to the reception of your message. Be aware, however, that some people will look you in the eye and pleasantly acknowledge receipt of your message while not having the foggiest idea of what you just told them. They may think they are being polite. Some do not wish to reveal that they do not understand while others may not have the slightest interest in your message. It certainly depends on the situation, the individuals involved, and the nature or complexity of the message you wish to deliver. Use your judgment to determine if following up with a more specific question is appropriate. Pressing the issue or asking the recipient to restate your message is often effective at determining if the message was received but can also be viewed as offensive.

Regardless of any request you make of the recipient, the responsibility for confirming the delivery of your message lies with you, the sender. How could it be any other way? Would you insert in a written communication the request: *Let me know if you do not receive this letter.* Of course not! How could the recipient read your message until it actually arrives?

Unfortunately, far too many people omit this essential component of effective communication. Consider the implications of not confirming that your message was received. Any thought that the recipient will act upon a message she does not receive is an unreasonable expectation.

Having discussed the process for sending messages and the importance of confirming their receipt, we have yet to mention the advisability of communicating certain information in the workplace. You should communicate fairly openly with your manager in a Supportive Environment as your manager serves to assist you in solving problems and overcoming obstacles. However, we would caution you to be careful about providing too much information to a boss in a non-supportive environment.

Remember, you have total control over most information until you share it with your boss, a co-worker, a vendor, friends or others. Once you release it to the universe, it is out of your control regardless of the promises of confidentiality that the recipient may offer. Your confidant may talk in his sleep and his jealous spouse, who never liked you, may dish your information to your boss's spouse at the company party. Believe us, it happens. This does not mean that you should withhold vital information from your boss or others in the workplace. You cannot and should not withhold information that is relevant to the proper execution of your work-related responsibilities. It simply means that you should use discretion in deciding what information to share as well as where and when to share it.

All work-related information that you disseminate in the workplace should represent a truthful, accurate portrayal of your activities and decisions. While even negative information directly related to your area of responsibility should not be withheld, it can be provided in a context that factually conveys the circumstances associated with what happened. Do not exacerbate the situation through distortion or omission. Not providing essential information would be a dereliction of your duties and we do not recommend that course of action even when the information reflects negatively upon you. If you were responsible for what happened, in the long run, it is best to take responsibility and face the consequences even if it means you may be fired. To do anything else would erode your integrity.

However, you often have control over when, where, and how you release such information and we do recommend leveraging that control to the fullest extent possible, especially in a non-supportive environment. This means managing the release of the information in the same manner as a public relations expert would strive to enhance the impact of good news and minimize the damage of bad news.

When the news is negative, what you communicate should represent only the facts and not be skewed by suppositions, guesses or rumors. It is far better to say, *I do not know*, than to be wrong and have to try to explain why you misspoke.

Remember, you are not responsible for explaining everything that happens in your workplace. Others are responsible for the results of their actions and decisions. While you may need to reveal those actions, you do not need to offer an explanation for them. You may politely direct such inquiries to the individual who holds responsibility for that particular piece of the puzzle should you know who that might be. Sometimes that individual may be a co-worker or your boss. If you do not know, say so. Do not speculate or guess especially in a non-supportive environment.

I know of one boss who would storm down the aisle, plant her feet in front of some subordinates, and toss out a rhetorical question about a work-related issue. One unfortunate soul always spoke up. Rarely did he have direct knowledge of the situation but rather made an honest effort to share with her what he know about it. She would light into this guy with the full frontal force of an exploding Howitzer shell then stomp off in disgust leaving the bewildered *team member* wondering what hit him. What the poor soul never seemed to realize was that he did not need to answer every question posed by the boss. Neither do you. It is important to know when to speak up and equally important to know when keep quiet. You are not a radio disc jockey who is obligated to fill the void. If pressed for a response and you do not have accurate, verifiable information, you can always say, *I don't know.* If pressed further, you can add: *I'm certain you would not want me to provide erroneous information. I'll have to get back to you.* Then keep your mouth shut.

In some situations, it is better not to accept delivery of the question in the first place. This is especially true if you are neither in a position to know nor in a position to find out. If this is the case, you may want to respond with: *I'm not the right person to answer that question.* But be ready for the inevitable follow-up question: *Then who is the right person?* If it is not your responsibility to know who the right person is then offering that information keeps you linked to the problem. Suppose the person you "finger" denies that he is the culprit. It is often better to leave investigative responsibilities in the hands of your boss. A simple sideways shake of your head may help you disengage from this exchange more effectively than responding verbally with: *I do not know?* Your boss can always follow that response with: *Why don't you know?* And so on. Be aware that not falling for this trap may prompt your boss to escalate the conflict which if not managed effectively can easily lead to some undesirable results. Rest assured that we will revisit this subject, later in this chapter, with ways for you to keep the lid on conflict you are certain to encounter in non-supportive environments.

How helpful you should be by way of volunteering information to a superior depends entirely on the level of risk present in the environment. As you know, everything, including the sharing of information, is more risky in a non-supportive environment. We will cover this area in more detail when we discuss how to manage responsibility.

But now, who among us has not sent an email in haste then wished to have it recalled? While some email systems have the capability to recall an email, usually the recall must be executed before the recipient opens your message. Suppose you exchange emails with a friend or co-worker and the content gets a little out of control. Now you want to eliminate any record of this exchange. Is it possible to completely remove an email from the system? Do not make the mistake of thinking that deleting an email from your inbox completely purges it from the system. The same is true of any computer file once it finds a home on your computer's hard drive or on a network fileserver.

Consider the case of Lt. Col. Oliver Laurence North. Better known as Ollie North, he is now infamous for his role in the Reagan Administration's clandestine sale of arms to Iran in an illegal scheme to aid the Contras in Nicaragua. Military support for the Contras had been specifically forbidden by Congress with the Boland Amendment. North "got into some trouble with the U.S. Congress when erased computer files were recovered as computer evidence," reports Armor Forensics, an electronic data recovery company, on its web site. Many people think that once a file or email message has been deleted that is it is gone forever. Not so. Once prosecutors gained possession of North's computer, they found a wealth of incriminating information. North is reported to have commented quizzically that he thought he had deleted those files.

What North learned too late was that hitting the Delete key on the computer does not necessarily mean that the data cannot be retrieved by a computer forensics specialist. Armor Forensics reveals that "as much as 50 percent of the computer hard drive may contain such data types in the form of email fragments, word processing fragments, directory tree snapshots and potentially almost anything that has occurred in past work sessions on the subject computer."

A Guide to Understanding Data Remanence in Automated Information Systems, issued by the National Computer Security Center, suggests that to ensure complete destruction data on electronic storage media that the media should be destroyed through "smelting, disintegration, pulverization, or incineration." Doubtful you are going to do that to your company computer without some serious repercussions.

Our best advice is simply not to keep or share personal information at work that would embarrass you if it became public. We would also advise that you not engage in illegal activities on the company's computer system. Once you send an email or save information as a document file, it is too late. If you have personally sensitive or embarrassing information at work, remove it from the premises as soon as possible. Keep in mind that simply tossing something in the waste basket is a gamble. Your trash may pass through several hands before being incinerated.

Useful to remember, too, is that most large companies have retention policies that guide you in regard to how long certain work-related information must be retained whether for legal or business reasons. You should adhere to those policies when discarding company information.

When it comes to personal information, what you share is entirely at your discretion. Know, however, that once you release details of your personal life to the universe via email, Facebook, MySpace, LinkedIn or any of the common social media sites, that information is entirely out of your control and you could be sharing with a larger audience than you intend.

Remember the emails FEMA Director Michael D. Brown sent from his wireless BlackBerry as Hurricane Katrina hit New Orleans? In these communications with his associates, he commented, "I just feel like I'm getting the s—t beat out of me, but hey, we're working our butts off down here..." In another email he wrote, "Can I quit now? Can I go home?" While Brown did not try to conceal these communications, they were obviously not intended for public consumption. Now, however, they are public record thanks to CBS News which obtained copies and posted them on its web site. CBS News may not have interest in your emails but the lesson should be clear.

Executive coach and organizational consultant Joan Lloyd advises avoiding the following types of communications in the workplace:

- Criticizing one peer to another peer
- Talking about one employee's performance to another employee
- Socializing with one employee but not others
- Discussing family matters
- Expressing dissatisfaction about your employer
- Going over your boss's head to complain to his or her boss
- Revealing departmental problems to people outside the department

Some of these communication *faux pas* apply more to someone in a management position but all are good for anyone to consider in terms of what information they communicate in the workplace.

It needs to be said and here is as good a place as any. Avoid all vulgarities, questionable jokes or sexually-oriented information in your communications. This type of content is not appropriate for workplace communications and many companies have policies that prohibit this type of information. You would be well-advised to augment any such company policies with your own rules as to how you manage personal and professional communications in the workplace because what you chose to communicate, when you chose to communicate, where you chose to communicate, and to whom you chose to communicate can make a difference. The good news is that the choice of what, when, where, and to whom is often entirely yours.

Self-Management: In considering the idea of self-management, let us define what it means to be an effective manager as opposed to a boss. A ***manager*** acts in a professional manner to provide guidance, access to resources, and support for subordinates in overcoming obstacles to productivity. Regardless of the outcome of the work performed by subordinates, a manager remains at least partially responsible for the results. If we alter this statement slightly, we have a good definition of what it means to be self-managed. A ***self-managed individual*** acts in a professional manner to provide guidance, access to resources, and support for his activities in overcoming obstacles to his productivity. As a self-managed individual you do the same things that a manager in a Supportive Environment would do only you do them for yourself.

What does this mean for you? It means that it matters less whether your boss is an effective manager and matters more whether you are self-managed. If you are self-managed and your boss fails to serve as an effective manager, it means that you have the skills and motivation to step in and fill the void. You perform the work; you manage your performance. When you need additional resources, you locate them. When you need assistance overcoming obstacles, you identify a solution or find someone to help you.

And, you evaluate everything that you do in terms of how you as the *acting manager* would assess your performance. Does this require extra effort? We think of it as the required overhead that comes with the job. It is simply part of being a professional and taking enough pride in what you do.

Assuming a leadership role as your own manager has benefits. As a result of learning to effectively manage your activities, you become a much more self-reliant individual and increase your value as an employee as well as your sense of self-worth. You learn flexibility and adaptability that allow you to deal with changing and possibly adverse circumstances. You learn to address challenges that may seem beyond your capabilities or out of your control by determining a strategy to overcome them. In addition, you continue to be productive. This gives you less time to complain. To whom would you complain? Your manager? That's you! Are you going to pull yourself aside and moan about the lack of resources or are you going to go find what you need to do the job. The plain fact is that each of us is far more capable than we imagine ourselves to be. We encourage you to tap into that capability.

While there are benefits to being self-managed, there are also challenges. One of these challenges lies in the area of managing conflict. As a self-managed individual, you are responsible for dealing with any adverse interpersonal relations you encounter in the workplace. In a non-supportive environment, many of these conflicts may result from encounters with your boss.

First, let us note that not all conflict is bad. Public speaker and author Les Brown writes in an article entitled "Resolving Conflict" circulated by the DailyInBox.com, "Don't be afraid of conflict. Too many of us become agitated when we encounter conflict or disagreement out of concern and fear. It's odd when you think about it, because conflict is a part of nature, a part of life." It is also a part of all workplace environments regardless of how supportive they may be. "Unless you are a hermit," Brown continues, "odds are that conflict is inescapable. And so, you need to approach conflict calmly, as an expected part of dealing with others. Consider conflict a way of learning to see things more clearly." The challenge is to manage it effectively and not let it escalate out of control.

While we discussed communications earlier in terms of formulating content, selecting a delivery method, and ensuring the recipient is ready, and verifying that your message was received, we revisit the topic here since your ability to manage conflict is heavily influenced by your ability to self-manage how you communicate with people in stressful situations. This has more to do with your ability to control your emotions than it does with the style or substance of your message.

Katherine Crowley and Kathi Elser, authors of *Working with You Is Killing Me*, write, "We teach our clients that the key to dealing effectively with difficult people and situations at work is to manage our internal response first. By internal response we mean the automatic reaction that someone else's behavior triggers inside of you." Such self-control is termed by the mental health community as *emotional intelligence*.

Controlling your anger and rationally moving toward a well-conceived response maintains your roll as the professional in the interaction where a hasty reaction does not. Let us make an important distinction between the words *reaction* and *response*. *Webster's New Universal Unabridged Dictionary* defines **reaction** as "an action in a reverse direction or manner" and **response** as "an answer or reply, as in words or some action." While the distinction may be slight, it is an important distinction none-the-less.

Reaction occurs in direct relationship to what someone else did. Someone presses one of your "hot buttons." You react. Your reaction is hasty and unreasoned. *You insult me; I'm going to insult you. You hit me; I'm going to hit you.* It is done without thinking and demonstrates a loss of self-control. Most often how you react is not in your best interest.

A response is different. Think in terms of how someone who maintains self-control would respond when confronted with an adverse situation. *You insult me; I walk away allowing those present to share my loss of respect for you. You hit me; I defend myself then call 911 and have you arrested.* The response depends on the situation and demonstrates your efforts to generate an outcome that is in your best interest.

"Communication is a funny thing," says Robert Bacal, a conflict management consultant with Bacal & Associates. "It is something we do without thinking or reflecting about what we are doing." This is certainly one of the reasons why conflict management skills are essential in the contemporary workplace. Imagine the soldier sent out toward enemy lines with a red flag instead of the commonly accepted white flag to negotiate terms of a cease fire. Such confusion could produce catastrophically fatal results for the messenger if not the two armies posed to annihilate each other.

"Most of us don't consciously manage conflict situations," Bacal continues. "It's normal to get caught up emotionally, and just jump in without thinking. The core of conflict management involves slowing down, and using your head to think through what you should do, rather than reacting in a knee-jerk fashion." In other words, respond instead of react.

In any interaction with another person, what you do or say can increase, avoid, diffuse, or reduce the level of conflict. You can manage conflict by choosing which of the following ways of responding makes the most sense:

- **Confront** – increase conflict by disagreeing
- **Ignore** – diffuse conflict by ignoring the comment
- **Postpone** – diffuse conflict by postponing your response
- **Divert** – diffuse conflict by diverting attention to another topic
- **Acknowledge** – diffuse conflict by acknowledging the comment
- **Agree** – reduce conflict by agreeing

For purposes of illustration, let us envision a conversation between a co-worker named Sally and you in the lunchroom at work. Sally sees a woman in a colorful dress, comments that it is the most beautiful dress she has ever seen, and asks you what you think about it. You have six possible ways to respond. You can confront her, ignore her comment, postpone your response, divert attention from the dress to something else, acknowledge the comment without giving your opinion or agree with her.

If you ***confront*** her with a statement that disagrees with her position, then you may encourage her to defend her position more strongly. Such a response might be something like: *I wouldn't be caught dead in a dress like that. I hope she can get her money back?*

If you ***ignore*** her question by acting as though you did not hear her, you force her to repeat her position or move on to another subject of conversation. If she returns to the question about the dress, you have the same six options as before.

If you ***postpone*** your response by taking a sip of your juice or another bite of food, you delay having to agree or disagree. Once you swallow, you might say something non-committal like: *I'm not sure whether I like it or not.* Sally has nothing with which to disagree since you have postponed your assessment of the dress.

If you ***divert*** attention away from her question by stating something not related to the dress, then she is forced to move on to the new topic with you or repeat her question to elicit a comment from you. In this case, your response might be: *Oh, look at the time! I've got to get back. Are you going to see Brian this evening?* You have guided the conversation in a totally different direction without providing a response to her question about the dress. You can also divert attention from your assessment of the dress without straying from the topic by diverting to a detail of the dress with a comment like this: *Look at all the flowers in that pattern.* Sally must either revisit her question or move on with you to the flowers. You leave her nothing with which to disagree since you have only offered an acknowledgement of the flowers not stated an opinion of them.

If you acknowledge the comment, you let her know you hear what she said and stop with that without providing your own opinion.

If you ***agree*** with her, then you can minimize the potential for conflict with a response like this: *Oh Sally, you're right! I just love that dress.*

To respond to you, Sally has the same six choices and so it goes back and forth. How you respond to each other's comments and questions determines the level of conflict present in your exchange.

This is an effective tool to use at work. When your boss or a co-worker confronts you in an antagonistic manner, you can choose, depending on the situation, how to respond. Continued confrontation can quickly increase conflict. Ignoring, postponing, diverting, and acknowledging tend to avoid or diffuse conflict. Agreeing obviously minimizes conflict.

If your desire is to minimize conflict, then avoid confrontational responses. We do not mean to suggest that you agree simply to lessen conflict. You have the option to withhold a contradictory point of view until conditions are more favorable for the delivery of that information.

It is useful, especially in a non-supportive environment, to have a professional response ready for those times when your boss throws something really unexpected at you. You may find that the following comment serves that purpose: *Excuse me. I'm not sure I understand what you are saying.* This forces your boss to repeat or defend his statement while providing you time to formulate a response that best serves your interests.

In terms of any confrontation with your boss, the more you align yourself with facts and the less you align with rumors, suppositions or opinions, the better off you will be. Your boss will be hard pressed to argue with facts. He may realize the difficulty of sustaining such a position with his superiors and relent. This avoids a battle of personal opinions, in which case your boss will almost always prevail simply because he out ranks you and his opinion carries more weight in the organization.

Being self-managed means you are in charge of your own morale, motivation, collaboration, goal setting, productivity, and quality assurance. You crack the whip when a deadline approaches. You reward yourself for excellence and a job well done. You encourage yourself to get back up when your best, most well-intentioned efforts fail.

Obviously, it is easier to be self-managed in a Supportive Environment. It may also be expected. The truth, however, is that is it more essential to be self-managed in a non-supportive environment. And, of course, there are limitations that you should observe. We will go into more detail on that when we discuss the assumption of responsibility in the next chapter.

Professional Image

Maintaining a professional image in the workplace is really a matter of pursuing opportunities for personal growth and taking charge of the following key elements of how people assess your professional image:

- **Values, Ethics, and Integrity**
- **Attitude**
- **Productivity**
- **Communication**
- **Self-Management**

Any deviation from managing these key elements of your professional image provides a boss in a non-supportive environment with ammunition to use against you. Just because your boss or any of your co-workers choose not to behave in a professional manner, this should not be seen as justification for you not to maintain a professional demeanor in all of your work-related activities.

Do not take your boss's bad behaviors personally. He would most likely direct his abuse at anyone in your position. Do not let his failings be your downfall. Maintain a positive self-image and pride in your work in spite of what your boss does or what may be going on around you. *Consider the source* is a useful mantra to repeat silently to help put his comments in perspective.

You can probably imagine how you might be perceived if you fail to take charge of your affairs. What is your perception of someone who lacks ethics, integrity, and values? Do you enjoy working with people who have a bad attitude and are not productive? Do you respect people who cannot control how they communicate in the workplace? Would you hire someone who always waits to be told what to do? Of course not!

The bottom line is that you must take the high road and be professional at all times, regardless of how your boss or other employees behave. **If you take charge of your affairs, your co-workers, at least those whose respect is worth having, will perceive you as a capable professional.**

CHAPTER 12

Assuming Responsibility with Less Risk

Assumption of responsibility is a double-edged sword that can give you greater power to slice through the bureaucracy and accelerate your career or it can just as easily be used by an unscrupulous boss to cut you off at the knees. If you assume responsibility for clearing a backlog of orders and you successfully complete the assignment then you are the hero, right? If you assume responsibility for delivering a report to upper management on time and the report is late, are you in trouble? Maybe. It all depends on the environment. If you assume responsibility and do not deliver the goods, you may be history or you may be right in sync with the culture of the organization. Regardless of the outcome, assuming responsibility means assuming risk and you need to be cautious, especially in a non-supportive environment.

Risk Accompanies Responsibility

In the workplace, accomplishment and failure play at opposite ends of the bell curve. A few good employees are known for their accomplishments while a few bad apples are known for their failures. The careers of the good employees make steady forward progress while the bad apples are working themselves out of a job. Meanwhile, most employees ring in and ring out the work day from the center of the bell with no notable accomplishments and no notable failures. They hover in that *safe zone* near the middle by not assuming too much responsibility and, therefore, not taking on too much risk. That is how most employees think it works. Remember the bargain: *a fair day's work for a fair day's pay?* You put in more than a *fair day's work* and you should be suitably rewarded for it. A Supportive Environment typically works that way. In a non-supportive environment, whose career makes steady forward progress can depend on the agenda pursued by your boss.

Just as the laws of physics dictate that *for every action there is an equal and opposite reaction*, the forces governing the workplace suggest that *for every work assignment, your boss expects a particular result.* We cannot state more emphatically that your acceptance of any work assignment comes with a responsibility for generating the result your boss wants. This is the case, whether that result is logical, is in the best interest of the company or is even possible. Your responsibility for producing that result may not be clearly stated but it is certainly implied and you would be well advised to determine what your boss wants and the full extent of your responsibility before tackling the assignment.

When you assume responsibility in the workplace, you are actually promising to produce some result. It might be recalling a date and time when your boss asks you for it tomorrow, next month or who knows when. It might involve filling an order for a persnickety client. You could be asked to organize the file room. That one leaves plenty of room for interpretation. Would you think to ask what organize means to your boss? If you pursue the activity without a clear understanding of the outcome your boss desires, how will you know which path leads to success? You are flying blind if you launch into an assignment without having a clear picture of what your boss expects the outcome of your efforts to be.

You should also be certain that you are capable of generating the expected outcome. How closely you come to achieving the desired results will be used to determine whether your efforts in completing the assignment were successful. It is like not asking your boss before you flip a coin whether she wants heads or tails. Imagine flipping a silver dollar and after the coin comes in for a heads-up landing you ask your boss, *do you want heads or tails?* By then it is too late to change the outcome. If she selects tails, *you failed!*

Webster's New Universal Unabridged Dictionary defines **risk** as "exposure to the chance of injury or loss." Except in environments where actual physical danger is an inherent component of the job, "injury or loss" applies to the consequences of failure to accomplish the desired results your boss desires. Such consequences in a non-supportive environment can be harsh. Therein resides the risk.

In every workplace, there is an invisible line that marks the acceptable ***threshold of risk***. Below that line, the risk of failure is low enough to be tolerable. The further above that line you tread, the more you risk failure. The more the risk, the more caution is warranted before blindly accepting an assignment. You have to know where this line resides in your workplace environment. We mention this point because most people are not even aware there is such a line. They are simply not accustomed to evaluating risk as a normal course of their work.

Your challenge is to assess quickly and accurately whether a given assignment surpasses your threshold of risk. Whatever method of assessment you employ to make this determination, it should be readily available and relatively foolproof. The following two questions serve this purpose and should pop into your consciousness whenever your boss presents you with an assignment:

1. ***What happens if I fail?***
2. ***What are my chances of failing?***

First, ask yourself: *What happens if I fail?* If there are no consequences for failing, there is no need to consider the chances of failing. Unfortunately, there are almost always consequences for failing and they often correlate with the environment. The less supportive the environment, the more harsh the consequences may be.

In a Supportive Environment, your manager may not like the fact that you failed but she may understand that certain circumstances were out of your control and act accordingly. Do not expect any such consideration in a non-supportive environment. If you work in a Benign Environment the consequences of failure depend almost entirely on whether your boss or anyone in a position of power notices that you have failed. In a Contentious Environment, your boss may be privately pleased at your failure while lighting into you for your incompetence. In an Antagonistic Environment, a substantial failure could very well spell the end of your tenure in that organization.

Let us back up a moment to clarify an important point. Do not confuse failing to complete the assignment with failing to achieve the results your boss wants. These are two different factors. Failing to complete the assignment may be precisely what your boss in a Contentious or Antagonistic Environment wants you to do but do you think she would ever tell you that? Not on your life. She will make the assignment as ambiguous and vague as possible if you let her.

Regardless of what logic dictates, your boss may very well have her own agenda. Therefore, something that you view as mundane or quite insignificant may be perceived by her as an end-of-the-dinosaurs-and-life-as-we-know-it event. The problem is, you are thinking logically in terms of what is in the best interest of the organization. You are following the guidance that management recited at the last employee meeting. You are not thinking like your boss, in a Contentious Environment, who needs you to mess up every once in a while or your boss, in an Antagonistic Environment, who wants to get rid of you. If you try to point out that it really is not a major issue, you will quickly be informed by the boss that she, and not you, is privy to the big picture and, therefore, she, and not you, is in the best position to interpret the ramifications of what you did. Even the most trivial of things can be blown totally out of proportion by a boss who feels she must make an example out of you to demonstrate the error of your ways to the rest of her staff. Bosses who thrive on turmoil are always on the prowl for ways to keep the pot boiling and you in the middle of it.

Other bosses, and even some managers in a Supportive Environment, are poor communicators. With no mal intent, they simply lack the skill to clearly express their expectations.

This is why you must clarify, before assuming responsibility for an assignment, precisely what your boss or manager wants the outcome to be. You want her name right next to yours on the *contract* or more realistically the email that spells out what she wants you to achieve. Your first level of protection against failure is to ensure that she concurs with the targeted objectives of your activity and, therefore, your success in achieving those objectives will not be turned into a failure. If necessary, you must coerce her into becoming a partner in your success by documenting the details of her request. Consider this as an essential part of your job in any environment and an especially important key to your survival in a non-supportive environment.

Just because you have your boss's name on an email that defines what outcome she wants you to generate does not mean that you are failsafe. Therefore, you must also ask yourself: *What are my chances of failing?*

Your chances of failing to achieve the desired results depend upon the strength of your foundation and the circumstances prevalent in the environment in which you work. A Supportive Environment works in your favor. The less supportive the environment, the harder the environment works to thwart your best efforts. Your foundation which encompasses your skills and knowledge, your network, your problem solving abilities, and your adaptability must be strong enough to carry you through to success regardless of the forces that a non-supportive environment musters to make you fail.

Assessing Risk

It is useful to categorize your risk of failing to achieve the results your boss desires in the following manner:

- **Low risk** – the assignment falls below your threshold of risk and you can easily guarantee a successful outcome. Low risk assignments often involve simple and relatively common tasks where the expected outcome is clear and consistent with past experiences.
- **Moderate risk** – the assignment rises above your threshold of risk and you cannot guarantee a successful outcome because the assignment involves challenging tasks and questions of access to necessary resources. Even though failure may seem unlikely there are still enough unknowns that it is not out of the question.
- **High risk** – the assignment rises above your threshold of risk and you cannot guarantee a successful outcome because the assignment includes tasks that may exceed your experience level and present significant limitations on your access to necessary resources. Your ability to generate the desired outcome is extremely uncertain.

You simply cannot accurately assess your ability to generate a successful outcome unless you know what outcome you are supposed to generate. The less you know about the outcome and your access to the necessary resources, the more risk you assume if you accept the assignment.

An assignment which you might otherwise assess as low risk slips out of the low risk category when important questions about the desired outcome and your access to the necessary resources are left unanswered. The more unknowns there are, the higher your risk of failure. The more information you have about the assignment, the better able you are to assess your risk of failure.

Risk management experts often utilize a *bowtie chart*, named for its shape, which is comprised of three elements: an undesirable event (center of the bowtie), barriers to that event happening (left side), and measures to mitigate the severity of the event if is should happen (right side). The left side of the bowtie chart is formed by a triangle pointing to the right. The right side of the chart is a triangle pointing the left. Where the points of the two triangles meet a statement inside a circle documents the undesirable event. In your case, the undesirable event is your failure to successfully achieve the results your boss wants for a particular assignment. With each new assignment, you will need to reassess the risk of failure.

On the left side of the bowtie chart is your first barrier against failure, your depth of skill and knowledge applicable to the assignment. Maybe you have been trained to perform this kind of assignment or you have previous experience which should prevent you from failing. Should the challenges of the assignment breach that barrier, you have your ability to adapt to different situations and solve problems. If that barrier is also not sufficient to prevent failure, then finally, you have a network of contacts that may be able to guide you toward success. All the various elements of your foundation serve as barriers on the bowtie chart to prevent the undesirable event, failure, from occurring.

On the right side of your bowtie chart are the measures you have in place to mitigate the consequences you may face should the undesirable event actually occur. Your primary measure for mitigating the consequences of failure relates to the question, how much responsibility did you assume? Did you deflect some of the responsibility back to your boss because too many questions were left unanswered or she limited your access to necessary resources? Did you get her to acknowledge this fact in an email that she knows you have on file? If so, then she may be inclined to temper the intensity of her dissatisfaction with your failure since she knows she shares in that failure. We will go into more on documentation in the next chapter. Your second measure of mitigation is the strength of your image. How well are you respected by your co-workers and others in the organization? How easily can your boss attack your failure without generating too much of a reaction from the rest of the troops?

Your Response to Risk

Risk management experts may take weeks or months to study a situation before issuing a report on the perceived level of risk and how to address it. You don't have that much time. You must be able to quickly and easily assess the risk of accepting a work assignment. This means while you are still standing in front of your boss if the request is delivered in person.

Your assessment of risk should result in an immediate response, either *OK* or *wait a minute*. Never say, *OK*, if you are uncertain as to the level of risk you will assume by accepting the assignment. It is better to say: *I may not be the right person for this assignment. Let me think about what all would be involved and get back to you with some questions before I commit to this assignment.* You must be able to determine when it is in your best interest to accept responsibility for a particular outcome, and when and how to tactfully decline the assignment or deflect the responsibility back to the boss. When you are unable to ensure that you can complete the assignment successfully, you should not accept full responsibility. Sometimes you are given no choice by your boss. In which case, you must clarify that others, including your boss, share responsible for achieving the outcome your boss desires.

If you work in a non-supportive environment, we advise that you accept responsibility for outcomes that are high risk only after you have received explicit written approval or authorization from your boss. This could be an email that your boss sends to you asking you to perform a given assignment. Before accepting the assignment, assess the risk and respond to your boss with any questions you have. Should you receive the assignment verbally, in person or by phone, ask any questions you think of at the time then document what you have been asked to do in an email to your boss with the request that she correct anything you may have misunderstood and add any additional information she may have that will help you complete the assignment. This is a good approach to take whether the request comes directly from your boss or arrives via a third party. If a co-worker informs you that the boss has asked you to do such and such, the risk of miscommunication escalates and it becomes even more essential to confirm the assignment, the desired outcome, and your limits of responsibility in writing. The email should go to the boss with a CC to the party who conveyed the request. Yes, this requires extra effort but so does donning a flack jacket before flying over enemy territory. The less supportive the environment, the more steps you may need to take to protect yourself.

Please be advised that there is no *statute of limitations* for problems at work. Something you did last quarter could suddenly resurface as a problem today, especially in a non-supportive environment. Your boss assigns you to train a co-worker to set up new accounts and the co-worker ends up wiping out several active customer accounts on his first solo effort. The boss verbally throttles the co-worker but while she is normally quick to jump on everything you do wrong, for some reason, this time she does not mention your involvement. *Whew! I skated free on that one*, you think. Not so fast. Your boss might have simply let the situation ride until she thinks she has enough ammunition to knock you down a peg or two.

Some readers may remember *Candid Camera* hosted by Allen Funt until he retired after a stroke in 1993. The show, which first came to television in 1948, featured a hidden camera to catch-on-tape people reacting to unusual, although staged situations when they believe no one was watching. The unsuspecting characters were then held up to public ridicule on national television. Funt's frequent warning for the viewing public was: *When you least expect it!*

But maybe you should expect it. According to a promotional email distributed by Undercover Corporate Solutions, a management consulting firm modeled after the popular TV Show *Undercover Boss*, "increasing numbers of employers are using Undercover Business Consultants to monitor employees and get valuable information, not otherwise attainable."

Even if your boss never saw *Undercover Boss* and does not have an actual video tape record of your actions, she may decide *when you least expect it* to throw the proverbial book at you for something that happened weeks or months ago. Be ready. It may serve your interests to preempt her efforts by confessing and facing the music on your terms rather than hers.

Even when all suitable precautions have been taken, delivering the right results to an unreceptive audience can still be risky. An extreme case of this occurred to a former client of mine who was at the time a senior marketing manager with a large corporation. She presented well-documented data from focus groups that clearly contradicted the corporate expectation. The company had invested a lot time and money, and the executives had invested a great deal of ego into a new product. The focus groups were virtually 100 percent negative in their response to the new item. One might think that someone at an executive level would look at that and say, *kill this turkey and, by the way, thank you Ms. Marketing Manager for saving us from a really bad idea.* But it did not play out that way. Instead, my client's report was buried never to see the light of day and she was not given any more assignments. Each day she reported to her office but was provided nothing to do. When her annual review rolled around, her boss recommended her dismissal, since in the last six months she had contributed nothing to the organization.

Risk in Lots of Other Places

Our entire discussion on accepting or reflecting responsibility has centered on work assignments but it has just as much application to the receipt and transfer of information. Any time your manager shares business-related information with you it carries an implied obligation of responsibility. That responsibility might encompass remembering the information on behalf of your manager, keeping the information confidential, or acting upon the information in some manner. As such, all the same considerations that applied to the success and failure of work assignments applies to the management of that information. The distinction is that the information may be passed to you in a rather inconsequential manner and potentially inconvenient form. Additionally, the instructions for what you are supposed to do with it might be quite obscure. All the same considerations come into play relative to the receipt or transfer of physical items such as packages, tools, equipment, etc. Responsibility will pass to your hands upon acceptance of these items unless you purposefully deflect it.

You should also be aware that you hold full responsibility for any activities you undertake on your own. If you see something that needs to be done and you do it without your boss's authorization, you hold full responsibility for the outcome. When consulted in regard to employees taking initiative, a high-level director in the space shuttle program used to say, *ask forgiveness, not permission!* Consider the implications of that in an Antagonistic Environment. Before pursing any program of unilateral action that skirts the scope of your general activities, you should be reasonably certain that the outcome you may generate holds little or no potential for being viewed as controversial as you may be at risk whether you fail or succeed. If anyone in authority takes exception to the outcome of your efforts, you will certainly stand alone in defending your decision to act alone.

Note that both the success and failure of your actions are tools a misguided boss can and very well may use against you to cause, as the Webster definition of risk states, "injury or loss." Failure to produce the desired results can be the reason you do not get the office with a window, it can justify why you do not receive a promotion, or it can be the rationale for why you are laid off or terminated. Certainly, failure in the workplace can have dire consequences. But success may be no better because some bosses view it in the same vein as failure. This is why we recommend that you memorize our modified version of the Miranda mantra recited by police officers upon the arrest of a suspected criminal. We believe it will serve you well on good days as well as when things go terribly awry. *Anything I say or do may be used against me by my boss in a non-supportive workplace environment.* This simple statement summarizes why it is essential to your professional wellbeing for you to fully evaluate the risk of failure before assuming responsibility for an assignment.

Responsibility and Risk in Your Environment

Since the risk of failure tends to increase as support decreases, the guiding principle to remember in regard to assuming responsibility with less risk is: ***The more supportive the environment, the more responsibility I can safely assume; the less supportive the environment, the less responsibility I should assume.***

We advise utilizing the following guidelines for accepting responsibility:

- **Antagonistic Environment** – accept responsibility with extreme caution for all risky assignments and if possible obtain explicit instructions, preferably in writing, from your boss stating the desired outcome and the limitations of your authority.
- **Contentious Environment** – accept responsibility with caution for all risky activities and if possible obtain explicit instructions, preferably in writing, from your boss stating the desired outcome and the limitations of your authority.
- **Benign Environment** – involve your boss before pursuing activities with uncertain outcomes.
- **Supportive Environment** – accept full responsibility for your decisions and actions but ask for clarification or guidance when in doubt and request help as needed.

Antagonistic Environment: Accepting responsibility in an Antagonistic Environment is somewhat like shooting at a moving target. At the very least, it can be difficult. Therefore, you must always consider the risks associated with acting upon any request your boss makes. You must quickly evaluate whether the request is an honest assignment of work that you should expect as part of your job or whether it could possibly be something designed to set you up for failure or position you for blame should something go wrong.

Once again Enron serves as a fertile field for examples. Numerous ex-Enron employees have horror stories centering on tasks assigned to them that smelled to high heaven from an ethical standpoint. You do not seriously think that Enron CFO Andrew Fastow personally made every bookkeeping entry in the General Ledger himself, do you? In most cases, questions from employees disturbed by the "smell" were deflected with a perfunctory assurance that everything was in order. Did anyone not think to say: *Great, then you won't mind putting that in writing for me, will you Mr. Fastow?* Are you thinking that posing this question to your boss might place you in a somewhat awkward position? Sure it does but hopefully we have made you aware of the fact that if asking your boss for written clarification or authorization produces undue anxiety, then you are already in an awkward position and probably have got much bigger issues about which to worry. Even if your boss's request seems straightforward and honest, it is simply a good habit to request your assignment instructions in writing unless the request is as innocuous as bringing your boss a ream of paper for her printer.

In an Antagonistic Environment, clarity is your friend. Exactly what outcome or result you are taking responsibility for should be crystal clear to you, your boss, and all parties involved. This often includes writing a statement detailing the desired result. For instance, the boss may sit down with you and begin a conversation by saying, *I have been watching you closely and I am very impressed with your progress. I think you are ready for a major assignment.* If you are in an Antagonistic Environment, this conversation alone should be reason enough to raise a cautionary flag as it has the form and feel of a set-up. Your boss goes on to say that she has some concerns for the sales numbers. Interpret this to mean that someone higher up has aimed a blowtorch at her backside. She explains: *I want you to design and execute a plan to increase sales and get the numbers up.* This, of course, is music to your ears. It is exactly what you wanted: a chance to make a real difference. This could be your ticket to the top. You jump at the chance. Then, a few months down the road, you realize that your carefully thought out plans are headed down the commode. No one but you is taking your project seriously because no one in management announced publicly that you were anointed as the savior of the sales numbers.

You also observe, with growing panic, that anything you propose, which has a price tag attached, is doomed to failure because you have absolutely no budget authority. Finally, at the end of several weeks of hard work, you discover with a sense of pride that you were able to inch the sales numbers up a bit. In spite of the opposition, the lack of support, and no budget, you made a measurable difference in the sales numbers. Once more, you are summoned to your boss's office. You assume you are there to accept a spot bonus or at least an "at-a-boy." Instead, the boss dresses you down for making *absolutely no difference at all in the sales numbers.* You protest that the numbers are up but she quickly shoots that idea down. *You call that up? I've seen a bigger blip in those numbers from someone flushing the toilet,* she screams. *Get out of here. I don't know why I thought you could do anything worthwhile.* Reeling from the shock, you stagger out of your boss's office knowing that it will be a cold day in Hell before anything close to good happens to your career as long as you work for her.

It should be clear to you that accepting a challenging assignment without clearly documented instructions, expectations, and authority in an Antagonistic Environment can be tantamount to career suicide. Even if the boss thinks you might be able to do a good job, if you are not in sync with her, the results may not satisfy her expectations.

Suppose you are just trying to be helpful. Bring a problem to your boss and the likely response will be: *Thanks! I am glad you brought that to my attention. Would you mind taking care of it?* With no direction, guidance or common expectations, you are stepping out on that limb alone if you say, *OK.*

Can this happen in other non-supportive environments? Yes. Can happen in a Supportive Environment? No. Even if you fail miserably, she will deal with you directly and fairly and counsel you as to where you fell short. When you fail, she fails, too. Even if her superiors are unhappy with the results, your manager will try to deflect some of the heat. Whereas, in non-supportive environments, the boss will hang you out to dry on a whim.

Additionally, you should consider the possibility that your boss will abuse the results you generate. Could she *forget* what she asked you to do? Would she lie about what she asked you to do in order to make her look good or you look bad? If you have that email with her name right next to yours, then chances are she will think twice about it. Could or would she _____? You fill in the blank. Figure out what she could possibly do to abuse the results that she has asked you generate. Then put a plan in place to involve her sufficiently in what you are doing so that she cannot use those results against you without implicating herself in the process.

The more antagonistic the environment, the more likely your boss is to delegate responsibility freely without delegating a corresponding level of authority. This is a potentially dangerous situation for you and a no-lose situation for your boss. If you succeed against all her efforts to sabotage your work, then she is a genius for selecting you for this assignment. If you fail, you are an idiot.

Contentious Environment: Accepting responsibility in a Contentious Environment is not as risky as accepting responsibility in an Antagonistic Environment but the danger of failure is still a significant and relevant factor because the environment itself does not provide a solid support structure that encourages success. If you have not developed a functional foundation, then you are less able to produce the desired results when doing so requires resources that may be beyond your immediate reach.

The consequences of failure may not be as severe in an Contentious Environment as they are in an Antagonistic Environment. Even so, the risk of failure remains just as high and continued failure will only serve to perpetuate the abusive relationship between you and your boss that defines this environment. It can also quickly lead to burnout. To avoid positioning yourself for failure, we recommend employing the same techniques for evaluating the risk of assuming responsibility that are essential to your survival in an Antagonistic Environment.

Strive for extreme clarity in any communications with your boss. Additionally, you should consider and thwart any ways your boss could misuse the results of your work. This should apply both to successes and failures.

While the boss is not out to fire you, she may strive to keep you in failure mode as a misguided effort to preserve the illusion of her superiority. This is why accepting responsibility without clearly defining the desired result, without proper access to resources, and without the necessary support is not a wise move in a Contentious Environment.

Benign Environment: A Benign Environment offers an intriguing challenge with regard to the acceptance of responsibility due to the fact that your boss is effectively disengaged. Chances are you do not receive assignments. You may not receive instructions of any kind from your boss. Often you are left to your own devices unless something bad happens. But when something bad does happen, who do you think is going to be held responsible? Your boss who was not aware of what you were doing? Or you? Of course, you are the responsible party. You decided what needed to be done and did it without authorization. You are completely responsible.

Reflect for a moment on our discussion about taking unilateral action in a non-supportive environment. Most of what you do in a Benign Environment will be self-inspired and unmonitored. We recommended that before moving forward with any unilateral action, you should be reasonably certain that the outcomes you plan to generate hold little or no potential for being viewed as controversial as you will certainly stand alone in defending them. The same holds true for any actions that rank above your acceptable threshold of risk.

Your best defense is to keep your boss well informed of your work, especially for activities that might be considered controversial or ones that may hold significant potential for failure. In this manner, you receive implied authority from your boss to proceed. If your boss is non-responsive, an email that details your intended actions in a given situation followed by the phrase: *Please let me know if you have any questions or if you would like me to pursue a different course of action.* This gives you tacit approval to move forward as planned. The fact that your boss does not respond implies her concurrence with your intended course of action. Her only way out is to claim that she did not receive your email. Many email systems now provide you the means to request a confirmation when the recipient opens your communications. This may be enough to show that she was in the loop should problems arise.

Supportive Environment: In a Supportive Environment, you can safely accept more responsibility because you can tolerate a higher level of risk than you can in a non-supportive environment. By definition a Supportive Environment provides you greater and easier access to the resources and support you need to successfully complete your work assignments. In word and deed, your manager is part of your support structure.

Communications with your manager are also more honest and straightforward than in a non-supportive environment thus contributing to a clearer understanding of what the desired outcome of an assignment should be.

While failure should never be considered an acceptable option, if the desired outcome of an assignment was pursued with honest zeal, failure may be better understood in a Supportive Environment if as a result of failing you learned something from the experience that makes you a more valuable asset to the organization. Known as *experiential learning*, this method of self-education is often costly but has proven to be very effective. Hit your thumb with a hammer a couple times and you quickly learn to keep your thumb out of the hammer's path. No book, no video, or no classroom instructor can teach that lesson more effectively than the hammer itself.

Risks Don't Announce Themselves

The risks associated with an assignment may not always be obvious at the time you accept the assignment. However, as you continue to perform in your position, you will gain an increased awareness of what can and often does go wrong, whether by design or default.

When you are uncertain in regard to any assignment, it is always to your benefit to request additional guidance. In a Supportive Environment the guidance should be readily forthcoming. In a non-supportive environment, it may be harder to obtain. In such cases, always put your marching orders in writing if your boss does not do it already. If the assignment comes with an unacceptable level of risk, do not proceed without shoring up your defenses.

If you do not have the means to ensure that you can perform the assignment successfully, you might politely suggest to your boss that *someone with more experience may be better suited to tackle the assignment.* If that does not work, tactfully deflect responsibility for the outcome back to your boss.

There is risk in everything you do in a non-supportive environment. Does this mean that you reject all assignments in a non-supportive environment outright? That would win you a quick trip to the door. Your challenge is to determine at what point low risk passes into the unacceptable range. If you cannot shed yourself of a high risk assignment and are given no other choice by your boss then you have to move forward with the assignment but you must do so cautiously and complete it as best you can. To the degree possible, attach conditions that clarify that your control over the outcome is limited and that you cannot be held completely responsible for what happens.

Would a power company manager assign an untrained lineman to fix a short on a pole out behind your house? Certainly not a manager with the best interests of the company in mind or one that had any concern for the safety and wellbeing of the lineman would not make such an assignment. Fortunately, not all work assignments are accompanied with life and death issues for you, but many can quickly kill a career. The good news is, the more high risk assignments you complete without problem, the more experience you gain and the higher your tolerance for risk will become. Some people welcome risk. Regardless of your affinity for risk or lack of it, the point is to be aware of the risk of failure associated with each assignment and make every effort possible to maximize your chances for success.

Whenever you do have to proceed with a risky assignment, it is wise to implement a plan to save all communications between you and your boss or other significant parties regarding the assignment, associated expectations, and any other relevant factors. **Documentation may be the only defense you have if things go terribly wrong or as we have shown, even if everything goes terribly right.**

CHAPTER 13

Using Documentation to Your Advantage

Companies use documentation to their advantage. You need to use it to your advantage, too, especially in a non-supportive environment. At times it may seem like a time-consuming bother and totally useless unless, of course, something catastrophic happens and your boss is looking for heads to roll. Then, you will be ever so glad to have kept that email.

Benefits of Documentation

The intent of documentation is to provide an accurate record of what actually happened. It is useful to have in a Supportive Environment and genuinely essential in light of accusations, innuendos, and rumors that frequently occur in a non-supportive environment. Things will certainly go awry in any workplace but since non-supportive environments seem more prone to the propagation of problems, an accurate record of your actions is a vital tool you can wield to defend yourself and one that could very well prove essential to your survival.

Documentation can be as simple as saving an email from your boss or writing a note to yourself about when you handed a project file off to a co-worker. Or it can be as complex as a complete record of every action of everyone involved in completing a year-long project. Documentation is simply a record of who did what, when, and why.

Ever had your spouse ask you to recall how the two of you spent New Years Eve of 2004? *I don't remember, Sweetheart*, may generate a disappointed frown but you probably will not be asked to move out. Now imagine your boss foaming at the mouth to know where you put the requisition he gave you two weeks ago. *What requisition*, you ask feverishly pawing through your desk trying to figure out where it might be or whether you even have it. What if he demands to know why you put blue dresses on the mannequins in the display window instead of red as you were initially instructed? Or any number of things. Will you be able to recall every detail that he may demand to know during a meltdown? If you have accurate documentation of your work-related actions, you will be able to locate the important details in a calm professional manner. Simply pull out the file you created on display window issues and show your boss a copy of the email he sent you instructing you to put blue dresses on the mannequins. End of story. How might the story end if you did not have that email?

The pet refrain of an office manager from my distant past was *do you know where _____ is?* No doubt you can fill in the blank with an experience of your own. One day it would be a list of names and phone numbers. The next day it would be a client file, CD or invoice. After a while I realized that what was lost did not really matter. On any given day, something was lost. The fact that this item would not logically be part of your normal workflow was of no consequence. If she had misplaced it and you were within her sight, she viewed you as a suspect.

The fact was that the environment she had been instrumental in creating ensured that things would get lost. One day she ordered her assistant to pull half the files beginning with *Association of* and re-file them under the association name because there were too many files in the *A* drawer. Not all the association files, mind you, only half of them! This guaranteed confusion. It quickly became clear that only those individuals who documented what they did with anything that passed through their hands were provided some immunity from her condescending stare and huff of exasperation which invariably followed when someone could not answer the where-is question quickly enough.

While the benefits of maintaining adequate documentation may be obvious, it is still useful to review some of the more important ones here:

- Having the facts readily available when you are being interrogated by an angry or frustrated boss.
- Being able to convey the facts and dispel unfounded speculation which can easily lead to confusion, flashpoints or confrontation rather than bringing resolution to a problematic situation.
- Position yourself in a positive, professional light by knowing with reasonable precision exactly what you did, when you did it, and why.
- Having a comprehensive record of what you accomplished during the year always ready for a performance review.

Details that a misguided boss might fabricate or misconstrue can often be deterred or countered by facts if you have them readily at hand. Additionally, information in the form of printed or written documents weigh heavily in your favor if a higher power is required to mediate a dispute between you and your boss, especially if your boss has no such documentation to support his case. Your boss may actually be inclined to moderate or forego an attack on you if he knows that you maintain accurate records of your work activities.

How Much Is Enough?

The process of deciding how much information to preserve touches on the subject of risk assessment which we discussed in the previous chapter. The underlying concept of risk assessment hinges on the idea that anything which obstructs your view of what an assignment entails elevates your risk of failure. Those obstructions could be self-imposed, not by design but rather as a result of your level of inexperience. The more experience you have, the more familiar you are with all the necessary requirements of an assignment. Other obstructions involve unknowns that could occur in any workplace environment such as how easy will it be to work with a new group of people or to locate necessary resources not available through the traditional supply chain. Unfortunately, some obstructions could be purposefully perpetrated by your boss who withholds important information relative to the assignment or surreptitiously blocks your access to resources. Again your experience comes into play. The more experience you have, the more able you are to spot critical gaps in the information provided by your boss or clear alternative paths to the resources you need.

Let us just say that once you gain some experience at determining risk in terms of each assignment, we are certain you will not find the process all that onerous. In fact, we believe that you will become so comfortable with the process of risk assessment that you do it as a normal course of your work activities, much like looking both ways before crossing the street.

For those readers who feel challenged by the risk assessment process, consider all assignments in a non-supportive environment as falling in the danger zone of significant risk. Once you become more comfortable with assessing the risk of accepting an assignment, you can easily slack off on documentation of low risk assignments and shift your attention toward ones with a higher risk of failure.

It is difficult to say exactly how much documentation is enough and how much is too much but it is safe to say that your documentation process should start with the first mention of a new assignment. And if you are uncertain, more is usually better than not enough. You do not want to learn the hard way that you have not maintained enough documentation to cover your *Activities and Serious Situations*. Astute readers will be able to decipher the relevant acronym. They will also learn what they need to know so as not to get caught running naked through the office.

Here are some of the things that you should consider documenting when the associated activities exceed your tolerable threshold of risk:

- **Assignments** – Write a clear description of the assignment. This can be as short as one sentence or quite length depending on the size and complexity of the assignment. Consider including the following information: *Who gave me this assignment? When will it start and when should it be completed? Why is it important? What did I actually commit to do?*

- **Contacts** – document contacts whether in person, by phone, or via email where there is a transfer of information, tools, equipment, or work products. Consider including: *Who did I contact or who contacted me? When? Why? Was something transferred? If so, what? What was said? Did I commit to do something? If so, what?* You are responsible for any information or material as long as it is in your possession. You may also be responsible for where it goes when it leaves your hands. If you do not know or cannot remember then you place yourself at risk if something goes missing or the wrong parties obtain access to sensitive information.

- **Redirection** – Write a clear description of the desired redirection. Consider including: *Who asked for it? Why was it wanted? What did I do as a result?* Before accepting redirection, consider how it will impact your ability to complete the assignment. This is particularly important as redirection can easily change the scope of an assignment and your level of responsibility. As any project manager knows, redirection can impact manpower, resources, budget, delivery date, and even whether the project is still possible to complete. A seemingly small change could end up having a significant impact on your career if you approve the change without following accepted protocol, without proper authorization or if you fail to complete the assignment successfully.

- **Completions** – Write a clear description of what was completed and when it was completed. Consider including: *Who did I notify? When?* This is extremely important since it usually marks the termination of your responsibility for that activity and can be just as important as the point at which you initially assumed responsibility. Other than for tasks that are of a maintenance or perpetual nature, most activities have a precise point at which they begin and a precise endpoint. Between these two points, you are the responsible party.

In addition, retain most if not all communications especially if they are in the least bit controversial. The issues that they address may not have been resolved by your exchange of communications and if you believe they have, your communications may help document what resolution was agreed upon by other interested parties.

Easy Retrieval Is the Key

The key to an effective documentation regimen is to create a mechanism whereby the information that you need to conserve is collected as a matter of routine. This may mean creating a checklist for your more common processes that provides an easy means of recording key elements of your process. It may mean keeping a journal where you log relevant activities. It may mean setting up an electronic directory or physical file structure where you name and save emails in an orderly fashion for easy retrieval. If you receive verbal instructions from your boss, you can document them in an email which you send to him to confirm that you properly understood his instructions then save to your email archive. Whatever mechanism you decide to employ, it should not significantly interrupt or overburden your normal work processes.

Keep in mind that the ease of retrieving the information you need is an essential component of whatever system you establish. A process that requires you to spend time searching through a box full of papers to find out why you thought you had the authority to change the assignment requirements may not be your best approach. You need an organized process for collecting and maintaining relevant information so that it is readily available when you need it.

A word of warning is appropriate here. You should be aware that all such information that you collect and maintain as part of your job is, in a legal sense, owned by the company. Therefore, limit your notes and comments to a factual nature. Remember, anything that you preserve in written form may be accessed by an authorized company representative at any time and could become public knowledge against your most strenuous protests.

Since the risk of failure tends to increase as support decreases, the guiding principle to remember in regard to using documentation to your advantage is: ***The less supportive the environment, the more I need to document; the more supportive the environment, the less I need to document.***

You will notice that this runs opposite to the assumption of responsibility. The less supportive the environment, the less responsibility you can safely assume and the more you need to document. The more supportive the environment, the more responsibility you can safely assume and the less you need to document. As you decrease responsibility, you should increase documentation and vice-a-versa.

Documentation in Your Environment

The need to document your assignments and activities differs with the type of environment in which you work. We advise utilizing the following guidelines for documentation:

- **Antagonistic Environment** – document all activities including decisions, actions, and interactions associated with all assignments.

- **Contentious Environment** – document all significant decisions and activities associated with all but the most routine or non-controversial assignments.

- **Benign Environment** – document all significant decisions and activities associated with all but the most routine or non-controversial assignments.

- **Supportive Environment** – document key milestones and accomplishments associated with significant assignments so as to have a readily available record of progress for your manager.

Antagonistic Environment: Protecting yourself with accurate and easily accessible documentation is part of your job. If you work in a non-supportive environment, you are a soldier on a mission of productivity in hostile terrain. You cannot accomplish your mission if you do not protect yourself.

Remember, you are in defensive mode. Your boss in an Antagonistic Environment would like nothing better than to find that you have screwed up so he can fire you. In a Contentious Environment, your boss simply wants you to screw up. Bosses in a Benign Environment are missing in action leaving you to defend yourself. You need to exercise caution in regard to how much responsibility you assume and protect yourself in non-supportive environments by documenting what you did and why.

You must be able to respond to the accusatory question: *Why did you do that?* Not having a ready answer or making something up on the spot that turns out to be wrong leaves you vulnerable. This includes collecting information related to nearly all of your work assignments and should be considered as normal overhead for operating in such a compassion-challenged environment. Of course, this means that you will not be as productive as you would in a Supportive Environment but the plain fact is that you have to document all your significant activities, interactions, and milestones precisely because you are not in a Supportive Environment.

Suppose, for instance, that your boss calls you into his office and gives you unclear and contradictory instructions for your next assignment. You know that he has a reputation for coming down hard on any employee who fails to divine his true intent. This is a common mechanism used by bosses in non-supportive environments to set you up for failure. Our recommended response to this boss's ambiguous instructions would be to return to your office and shoot him an email stating your understanding of his instructions in as clear and concise language as you can produce, then in the same email request that he either confirm or clarify your take on it. You can be certain that none of these emails ever gets deleted from my hard drive. Rather, I save them in a specially labeled folder for quick and easy reference when needed.

Recently a client contacted me and painted a very dire picture of her situation with respect to her boss. It was obvious that he was out to get her. She is a manager at a health care organization and reports to a director. To put things in perspective, she has an MBA and numerous industry certifications. The director has an associate degree and no certifications. What he does have, however, is a strong political base and a reputation for browbeating anyone who crosses him. I strongly advised her to copy him on all her email communications and to document everything.

Not long after our meeting, what I had feared happened. The director dismissed my client with the observation that she simply did not fit the culture of the organization. Lucky for her, she had saved all her email communications with him, including those in which she reported the steps she was taking to eliminate long standing practices that were in clear violation of state law and could have resulted in a loss of license for the institution. As of this moment, her situation is a bit uncertain, but clearly if she decides to contest the dismissal, she has a record that her boss knew and concurred with her actions.

When it comes to documentation, the bottom line is accurate documentation may not save you but, at least it gives you a fighting chance.

Contentious Environment: A Contentious Environment has its own challenges. Your boss is not your friend, your colleague, or your supporter no matter what he tells you or how chummy he occasionally acts. He will do whatever he needs to do to ensure that he has the control that he wants to have over you.

Regardless of how submissive you pretend to be, he may not be satisfied unless he can find fault with your work. The distinction is that deep down and it may be so deep that it is beyond his consciousness he knows that he needs you to do the work and he needs you to justify his position as the supreme problem solver. Therefore, he is on the hunt for problems and if they do not manifest naturally, he is more than willing to create them for you.

Documentation of your assignment-related activities, interactions, and milestones is essential to help you navigate your way around any trouble that you may encounter. Notice the implication that you are already in trouble. That is how your boss views you. You are the problem. He knows it and simply does not have the goods to prove it. Yet! You must always be ready to disprove each and every accusation. Documentation is your weapon of choice.

Benign Environment: In a Benign Environment, your boss is disconnected from what you do. For better or worse, you are on your own. You hold full responsibility for nearly everything you do. Therefore, it is of paramount importance that you document what you did and why you did it.

Your actions must hold up under the light of scrutiny because if anything goes wrong it will be you facing the hard questions at the inquisition. Accurate documentation will help refresh your memory regarding decisions you may have made months ago.

Supportive Environment: While the need for documentation as a defensive measure is not an issue in a Supportive Environment, it can still serve a useful purpose as a quick and easy tool when questions arise as they invariably do in any workplace environment. Additionally, an effective documentation archival process melds well with ongoing efforts to keep your manager apprised of your activities and accomplishments. Such is the mark of a self-managed professional and demonstrates a sense of pride in the work you do.

Managers in a Supportive Environment like to see employees exhibit a sense of pride and ownership in their work and look for opportunities to reward significant accomplishments. Your documentation can facilitate this process. Having an easily accessible record of your activities also serves a useful purpose when it comes time for a performance review. With the information you need to document your work activities and accomplishments close at hand, you can easily save yourself the time and frustration it would otherwise take to gather or reconstruct that information weeks or months after the fact.

Documentation Is Your Insurance Policy

We cannot be overzealous in our insistence that documentation serves both to your benefit and in your defense. Like an insurance policy, it is there if you need it. If you do not need defending, it is useful to facilitate your reporting of activities and accomplishments during a performance review. However, when adverse situations arise, as they invariably do in non-supportive environments, a strong defense is essential. **Accurate documentation of what you did, when you did it, and why bolsters your ability to deflect unjustified accusations.**

CHAPTER 14

Recognizing Traps and Manipulation

The ancient lore of an Indonesian tribe reveals that when the great tree of life shakes it is the time for them to retreat to the hills for a tsunami is on its way. They recognize that the sea and the land will then battle for control of the shoreline. When the battle is done and the forces of nature once again agree on a new boundary between the water and the land, life can continue as before.

During the devastating tsunami of December 26, 2004, nearly 700,000 people in a host of different nations were killed while no members of this Indonesian tribe died. Without an advanced-technology tsunami warning system and speed of light communications, members of this tribe recognized the signs that a tsunami was on its way. They removed themselves from its path and they lived while many of those who did not recognize the signs perished.

Techniques Used in Your Environment

Your survival in the workplace may very well hinge upon your ability to recognize the signs that danger is at hand. Bosses in Antagonistic and Contentious Environments often employ techniques to trip up the unwary employee. Techniques? Let us call them what they are, *traps*. Your boss may use traps with the intention of ensnaring you in an embarrassing situation. You are vulnerable to such tactics if you are unable to recognize the telltale signs of the traps a cunning boss may unleash on you.

Antagonistic Environment: In such a hostile environment as this, your boss seeks nothing less than your removal. Getting caught in one of her traps may prove to be immediately fatal to your career.

Contentious Environment: Here your boss seeks to maintain control over you and your co-workers by any means possible. Capturing you in one of her traps lessens your perceived status and degrades your reputation in the organization. It makes you susceptible to the whims of your boss whose merciful nature, she would like you to think, allows you to keep your job as long as you do her bidding without question.

Benign Environment: Bosses missing-in-action tend not to use traps or other techniques to control employees. They do not need to use them, since they are generally uninvolved and uninterested in their employees' activities. They need you there to do the work but that is the extent of it. If something goes wrong, they are not responsible. They were not aware of your activities. They can easily point the finger at you.

Supportive Environment: Managers do not need traps and would not use them anyway. Traps are a tool for bosses who lack the ability to motivate and inspire employees usually as a result of some deficit in their personality or professional skill set. Managers in a Supportive Environment help their employees overcome obstacles and back them up in challenging times. Traps and manipulation techniques are antithetical to the process of inspiring and motivating workers. Managers in Supportive Environments know this and, therefore, avoid them altogether.

Control Is the Goal

Unfortunately, an amazingly large number of companies encourage or, at least, tolerate Antagonistic and Contentious Environments. Why else would so many studies reveal such a high percentage of unengaged workers? If you work in one of these trap-rich environments, your ability to avoid traps set by unscrupulous bosses may determine whether you are able to keep your sanity as well as your job. Your tenure may very well depend upon your ability to distinguish between valid directions from your boss and a trap intended to set you up for failure.

Many traps have a recognizable sequence intended to ensnare you much like the sweet fragrance of sap lures insects to their death in the clutches of the carnivorous Dionaea Muscipula, commonly known as the Venus Flytrap.

Under one entrapment scenario, you may think that your boss has finally recognized your talents and abilities and is tapping you for that big, important assignment that will finally put your name on the leader board of rising stars. Fat chance! Unless you are in a Supportive Environment, you are being lured into a trap.

Remember the old story about a scorpion and a frog relayed again a few years ago in the movie *The Crying Game?*

A scorpion and a frog encounter each other on the bank of a river. The scorpion asks the frog if he would be so kind as to carry him across the water on his back.

The frog, wary of the scorpion, inquires, "How do I know that you won't sting me?"

"Because if I do, I will also die," the scorpion replies.

Satisfied with the scorpion's answer, the frog invites him to climb upon his back and off they set across the river. In midstream, the frog feels a sharp pain in his side.

"Why did you sting me?" the frog cries. "Now, we're both going to die."

"It's my nature," replies the scorpion as he and the frog sink beneath the water.

In Antagonistic and Contentious Environments, it is your boss's nature to set traps and to employ manipulation techniques regardless of the fact that this inhibits the productivity of the organization that she manages. What is at issue is her ability to maintain control through whatever means necessary. Therefore, unless you learn to recognize how these traps work and avoid falling prey to them, your career will hang by a thin thread that your boss can snip whenever she likes.

Most misguided bosses will use one or more of these techniques from time-to-time. Usually, bosses fall back on these techniques because they have reached their level of incompetence by potentially devious means and know no other way to retain their positions. They simply cannot excel in an honest, open competition where a genuine ability to lead always wins.

You should also be aware that some bosses will use these techniques for no other reason than to *play* with people. They believe that the *game* is there for the sake of the *game*. In the 1970s, *winning by intimidation* became a favored management technique. Even though intimidation is, as are the other traps and manipulation techniques we reveal here, so clearly counter to a productive workforce and attainment of organizational goals, we are sad to report that things have not changed much in this regard since the seventies.

Intimidation is a common technique employed by a boss. In fact, when we first used the word *boss*, you will recall that we highlighted corrupt politicians Boss Tweed and Boss Tom as examples.

Webster's New Universal Unabridged Dictionary indicates that **intimidate** means "to make timid; fill with fear." In other words, it implies a threat of some kind. While Boss Tweed and Boss Tom did not earn their reputations by making idle threats, laws have changed and prosecutors are much more inclined to enforce the law than when corruption saturated the political culture. While some bosses certainly do back up intimidation by breaking bones and bodies, the practice is no longer as widely accepted in the workplace as it might have been a hundred years ago. Even so, it still exists.

Bosses will only use intimidation if they think it will work. Whether it does work depends to a great degree upon you and how you respond to it.

Blackmail with its threat of public embarrassment through the release of incriminating information is a specialized form of intimidation. In the case of blackmail, the best remedy is to avoid placing yourself in the position of being blackmailed. A rational assessment of whether the boss can actually carry out the threat that underlies her effort to intimidate you may lead to the conclusion that the threat is little more than bluster and you can let it roll off your back like rain off a duck's feathers. Even if the boss could carry out the threat, would she? Remember MAD, commonly known as mutually assured destruction? It works both ways and your boss knows it.

You will find this discussion of intimidation along with other traps and manipulation techniques in Appendix C. You may notice upon completion of your review of the traps and manipulation techniques that many of them require some element of confusion or distraction. Confusion keeps you from thinking straight. Distraction pulls your attention away from where it should be focused. In either case, your full capacity for straight thinking is not focused on what is actually happening behind the smoke screen or off in the wings. Confusion and distraction are used, in business as in warfare, because they work by creating opportunities to steal, misappropriate resources, or prevail over forces might otherwise present significant resistance.

Other authors writing on this subject characterize a misguided boss with what they may see as the boss's signature trap. For instance, one boss may favor *delivering a gift before dropping the bomb*. Labeling this boss the "Gift Giver" ignores the fact that she will pull out any number of other tricks at a moment's notice if she believe they will achieve the desired results.

The more in control of your work-related affairs, the less susceptible you are to falling for one of these traps. In addition, a little analysis or evaluation of the situation goes a long ways. Are you someone who enters national marketing sweepstakes without reading the fine print to determine your actual chances of winning? Are you often tempted by an email from a stranger offering you a large cut of a fortune if you will only help him transfer the money to a bank near you by providing your social security number? If so, then you are particularly susceptible to manipulation by a misguided boss and must be extra vigilant in a non-supportive work environment.

Recognize the Signs

The key to not falling victim to a trap or manipulation is recognizing the signs. Here are some clues to help you avoid running into trouble. Answer *yes* to any of the following questions and your caution flag should be flapping vigorously at the top of the mast:

- Does it seem too good to be true?
- Will it delay what really needs to happen?
- Is it in the best interests of the organization?
- Does it require you to take the first step?
- Does it unrealistically redirect blame?
- Does it promote confusion or distort the facts?

Your best defense is to learn to recognize the traps and how they can be used to set you up for failure, so when you encounter any of them in the workplace you will be less apt to become a victim. Be aware that new techniques are being developed every day while old ones are often dusted off and revised. Sadly pessimistic? Yes. Realistic? Absolutely!

The guiding principle to remember in regard to traps and manipulation techniques is: ***The less supportive the environment, the more cautious and prepared I need to be to deal with a full range of traps and manipulation techniques.***

Once you become familiar with how these devices are generally used to snare you, you will, in all likelihood, learn to smell the trap a mile away.

CHAPTER 15

Establishing Your Workplace Survival Plan

We have presented you with ways to characterize the threat level present in your environment by identifying your workplace as an Antagonistic, Contentious, Benign, or Supportive Environment. We have shown you how to defend yourself and leverage increased influence over your environment by reinforcing your foundation, strengthening your image, assuming responsibility with less risk, and using documentation to your advantage. We have even discussed the importance of recognizing traps and manipulation techniques that unscrupulous bosses will use to inhibit your success. It is time now to bring it all together into a comprehensive plan that you can formulate and implement yourself. This will be your **Workplace Survival Plan** and it will serve to address your specific situation.

Be advised that your Workplace Survival Plan will only be as strong and enduring as your weakest element. If you build your Workplace Survival Plan enduringly strong and fortify it with an unyielding resolve, it should offer you good shelter and defense from the turmoil and confusion that abounds in even the most hostile environments. In fact, if used effectively your Workplace Survival Plan can help you create a supportive enclave where you can work productively while being relatively free from the destructive distractions that surround you. You may also notice that the results of your efforts will begin to change you, not your boss or the environment. As you take charge of your professional life, you will become more confident and capable. You will also begin to align yourself with other professionals.

But, first, you need to develop your Workplace Survival Plan. To help focus your efforts, we have organized the necessary preparatory activities into the following sequence of six logical steps:

1. **Identify Your Workplace Environment**
2. **Manage Your Acceptance of Responsibility**
3. **Implement Your Documentation Process**
4. **Strengthen Your Image**
5. **Establish Your Foundation**
6. **Update Your Workplace Survival Plan**

How quickly and aggressively you develop and implement your Workplace Survival Plan depends on you. The urgency of the development process should be driven by how supportive your workplace environment is and the level of risk you face on a daily basis. Some people believe in making changes slowly and thoughtfully. Other people jump into a new skin and, from day one, begin doing what it takes to own that skin. If you work in an Antagonistic Environment, then you have no time to waste in developing your plan and putting it to use.

You may have noticed that the sequence of these steps differs from the order of how these topics were presented earlier. That is because it is useful to understand all the elements that contribute to your foundation and image before discussing acceptance of responsibility and documentation. However, when implementing your Workplace Survival Plan, especially if you work in a non-supportive environment, there is a valid sense of urgency in managing your acceptance of responsibility and implementing your documentation process as soon as possible.

1. Identify Your Workplace Environment

First and foremost, you must identify the type of environment in which you work. An Antagonistic Environment requires a different approach to survival than a Benign Environment or a Contentious Environment.

You should recall from our previous discussion the following characteristics that define the four workplace environments:

- In an Antagonistic Environment, your boss sees you as the enemy and provides strong negative attention.
- In a Contentious Environment, your boss views you as the problem and provides non-supportive attention.
- In a Benign Environment, your boss ignores you unless confronted with a serious issue and provides little or no direction.
- In a Supportive Environment, your manager treats you with respect and values your contribution.

Do not confuse the fact that similar behaviors may be exhibited in each of the four environments. Sometimes a boss in an Antagonistic Environment will act like your best friend and confidant. Do not let that sway your assessment. It is the frequency and egregious nature of the behaviors that color the environment.

Think in terms of trends. Workplace environments are defined by an overall trend of behaviors that are exhibited, particularly by authority figures such as your boss. You cannot accurately identify the environment by seeing only a snapshot; you have to watch the movie which may take days if not weeks.

Enter the following information on my Workplace Survival Plan.

- *My name*
- *My job title*
- *Type of industry in which I work*
- *Job title of my manager.*

Write a brief background statement on my situation at work.

Check the environment which best matches my workplace.

List up to four key issues I encounter in the workplace.

Can I map each action in my Workplace Survival Plan to one of these issues?

Yes – Map all of the actions you add to your Workplace Survival Plan to one of the issues listed above.

No – Seek the council and guidance of a career coach to help you develop solutions to those problems that you are unable to map to actions in your Workplace Survival Plan.

For example, if you frequently get into *arguments with your boss*, map this problem to the *Communication* area of *4. Enhance Your Image*. The actions you develop under this area as part of your Workplace Survival Plan will help you formulate a solution to this problem. You should be able to map most of the problems you list to one or more of the topic areas presented in the Workplace Survival Plan Checklist.

Being able to identify your environment and knowing something about it is essential to your survival in the workplace because the environment sets the tone for how you should behave. The less supportive the environment; the more risk you face. The more risk you face; the more your behavior must shift toward surviving. Of course, this means you are less productive in a non-supportive environment than you would be in a Supportive Environment but that is simply the way it is.

The following list provides a quick and easy way of connecting the appropriate behavior that you should employ with the environment:

- In an Antagonistic Environment, be **extra cautious**.
- In a Contentious Environment, be **cautious**.
- In a Benign Environment, be **reserved**.
- In a Supportive Environment, be **proactive**.

The remaining steps in developing and implementing your Workplace Survival Plan will help you bring out the details associated with each of these behavior modes. Even so, this list will serve you well as a quick reference for when you encounter a new or unusual situation but do not have time to plan out what course of action would represent your best interests.

Remember, everything you do, all decisions and actions, from this point forward must take into consideration the potential hazards or lack of hazards of the workplace environment that surrounds you.

2. Manage Your Acceptance of Responsibility

Managing acceptance of responsibility requires that you have a constant awareness of when you are being placed in the position to accept or reject responsibility. With responsibility comes risk and with risk comes danger, especially in a non-supportive environment. Your acceptance of responsibility makes you responsible for accomplishing a particular result. Your level of risk depends on your ability to achieve that result regardless of access to resources or anything else you may need to complete the job. Not achieving the desired result is problematic in any workplace environment but even more so in a non-supportive environment.

Responsibility can come knocking at any time and be dressed in a variety of disguises. Underneath any of its masks lies a request for you to do something, take care of something, check into something, monitor something, or work with somebody, and on and on. In another form, it can be couched as a request to make sure something does not happen. *We need to keep this quiet; don't let finance know what's going on. Don't let your co-worker mess up. Don't let the customer see that report.* If you accede to any of these requests you have assumed responsibility for preventing a particular event. Problems occur when you have no reasonable way to guarantee that that event will not happen.

We suggest the following thought process to guide your acceptance of responsibility for the outcome of an assignment.

Are all assignments and the expected outcomes clearly defined?

Yes – Continue to the next question.

No – Ask for clarification of the assignment and the expected outcome:

- If clarification is provided, continue to the next question.
- If clarification is not forthcoming, reject the assignment or reflect responsibility for the desired outcome back to your boss.

Am I able to differentiate between the task and the expected outcome?

Yes – Continue to the next question.

No – Practice analyzing tasks in terms of possible outcomes that could be generated and potential problematic issues.

Am I able to differentiate between the task and the expected outcome?

      Yes –   Continue to the next question.

      No –   Practice asking for more explanation with a supportive colleague or a family member.

Do I have adequate skills and knowledge to complete all assignments successfully?

      Yes –   Continue to the next question.

      No –   Ask for or find the necessary training or mentoring to provide you those skills.

- If training is provided, continue to the next question.
- If training is not forthcoming, reject the assignment or reflect responsibility for the desired outcome back to your boss.

Do I have access to adequate resources and assistance to complete all assignments successfully?

      Yes –   Continue to the next question.

      No –   Ask for or find adequate resources and assistance to complete the assignments and achieve the expected outcome:

- If adequate resources and assistance are provided, continue to the next question.
- If access to adequate resources and assistance are not forthcoming, reject the assignment or reflect responsibility for the desired outcome back to your boss.

If you answered any of these three questions in the negative and a follow-up with your boss does not resolve these concerns, then a cautionary light should immediately start flashing in the corner of your eye. That light is your warning sign that if you accept the assignment, you are placing yourself in a vulnerable position and face a reasonable possibility of failing to complete your assignment.

Failure has different implications in different environments. This is why the first step in development of your Workplace Survival Plan is to identify your workplace environment.

In a Supportive Environment, your manager inherently shares the risk of failure on any assignments you are given and should be willing to provide within reason whatever you need to be successful. Proceeding under these conditions may present a tolerable risk knowing that your manager has provided you all the information that is currently available and more details will be forthcoming. In a non-supportive environment, proceeding without having all the facts clearly delineated can range from risky to suicidal. If you fail to achieve the desired results, you can find yourself standing alone with your boss pointing an accusatory finger in your face while peppering you with intimidating questions. Better that you ask him, up front, the questions necessary to clarify what you are being asked to do.

Never accept full responsibility for the outcome of an assignment or, for that matter, any action you pursue in a non-supportive environment if the assignment and outcome are not clearly defined, or if you do not have adequate skills, knowledge, resources, and assistance to complete the assignment successfully unless your boss adequately addresses each of the previous concerns to your satisfaction. Then and only then, proceed but do so with caution. Your success is always contingent upon knowing what you have been asked to do and having the skills, knowledge, resources, and assistance necessary to do it. Without these things, you are obligated to reject the assignment or reflect responsibility for the outcome back to your boss.

Here is another important question to ask yourself:

Are any assignments controversial?

      Yes – Ask for clarification regarding the consequences of success and the consequences of failure to achieve the desired results.

   No – Continue to the next question.

If the assignment contains an element of controversy, then there are forces somewhere in the organization that will not be happy if you succeed and others that will not be happy if you fail. This creates a problem. In such a case, you need to have a clear idea of which perspective is held by whom and the implications of your bringing a frown to their face. If your success means alienating a powerful executive than do you really want full responsibility for that? Your boss, in a non-supportive environment, might be inclined to deflect any blame that comes his way to you. Once again, you are standing out there on your own.

The purpose of your Workplace Survival Plan and, in particular, the questions we suggest you ask yourself before assuming responsibility for an assignment are intended to minimize the chances that the hot spotlight of scrutiny falls on you.

Am I in a Supportive Environment?

   Yes – Assume responsibility for pursing best approaches, request assistance when needed, and look for opportunities to contribute to achievement of organizational goals.

   No – Continue to the next question.

Am I in a Benign Environment?

   Yes – Evaluate assignments, clarify and document questionable requests, and negotiate possible alternative approaches when a successful outcome is uncertain.

   No – Continue to the next question.

Take note that in a Benign Environment, you may not be given actual assignments by your boss, since your boss is missing in action. Your approach under such conditions should be to turn all of your actions that might be in the least bit questionable into assignments. You can do this by keeping your boss apprised, in advance, of your activities with the caveat that you should be notified by a particular date or time if there is any disagreement with any of your proposed actions. You can also do this in person and follow up with an email to document the communication. No notification or questions from your boss and you have implied approval to proceed as planned.

Am I in a Contentious Environment?

Yes – Shift responsibility back to management by clarifying and documenting questionable assignments, following instructions, and not suggesting questionable alternative approaches.

No – Continue to the next question.

Am I in an Antagonistic Environment?

Yes – Shift responsibility back to management by clarifying and documenting assignments, following instructions with strict precision, and not suggesting alternative approaches.

No – Continue to the next question.

Are you thinking: *How do I shift responsibility back to management? My boss is in control. He can tell me to do anything he wants.* True but you certainly do not have to do everything you are told, do you? What if your boss says: *Go get $1000 from petty cash, don't sign for it, and don't let anyone know.* Are you going to do it? What if he says: *Go fire the lady in 1535.* Are you going to do that? Does he have the authority to delegate this task to you? Maybe. Maybe not! You may go tell her that the boss wants to see her; however, that should probably be the extent of your involvement.

The point is there are a lot of things your boss might tell you to do that might be illegal, do not make sense, you do not have authority to do, you do not know how to do, or you do not have the resources to accomplish. And this is assuming that your boss has clearly explained to you what he wants you to do. You can reject responsibility by declining to accept the assignment. If that does not work or you decide that as a reasonable part of your job you must at least attempt the assignment, then you can still reflect responsibility for the outcome back to the boss.

To reflect reasonability back to the boss, you must make yourself very clear. *If I accept this assignment, I cannot accept responsibility for achieving the results you desire since x, y, and z are out of my control.* If this exchange occurs verbally then quickly follow up with an email to document your conditions for acceptance of the assignment.

Unconditional acceptance of an assignment leaves you completely vulnerable to blame should your best efforts to generate the desired results fall short. Additionally, if you are unclear on what the desired results should be, it is tantamount to shooting an arrow before the boss tells you the target. Shoot, ready, aim! How much sense does that make? If you trust your boss, this might be an alright approach. In a non-supportive environment, however, you certainly cannot trust your boss. Therefore, letting your boss define the desired results after the fact offers you no chance of altering your aim and sets you up for failure. Success at this point would depend entirely on the boss's prevailing mood.

The guiding principle to remember in regard to assuming responsibility with less risk is: ***The more supportive the environment, the more responsibility I can safely assume; the less supportive the environment, the less responsibility I should assume.***

Use this guiding principle as a general rule of thumb for acceptance of responsibility in the workplace. When employed in conjunction with the questions we have suggested that you ask yourself when facing a work assignment or a request that involves the assumption of responsibility for a particular outcome, this approach will help you to minimize your risk of failure.

3. Implement Your Documentation Process

Any business process that is extremely important or ones that hold a high potential for confusion or conflict often have policies, procedures, and an audit trail to ensure proper handling of information and assets. Every deposit, withdrawal or other transaction involving your bank account is recorded by the host institution with you receiving a receipt for your records. Why is this important? Can you remember exactly how many checks you wrote from your checking account last year on what dates, to whom, and for how much? If a discrepancy occurs, an accurate audit trail of the transactions allows both you and bank personnel to retrace the history of transactions to see what happened. This is the logic behind implementing a documentation process as part of your Workplace Survival Plan.

In the workplace, you face an unending array of transactions with your boss and others. These transactions can include a wide range of activities and transfer of information and assets. Lacking an efficient and effective means to document these transactions, it is nearly impossible to recall with any level of certainty precisely what you did or did not do. The problem resides in the fact that you never know which transactional detail will be important tomorrow or next week. Two months from now will your boss want to know why you sent that confidential report to a client or when you sent it? Do you have an email record that indicates your boss directed you to purge critical information from the database or did you take it upon yourself to do so? Did you really think it was part of your job to approve purchase of new equipment?

If you have a steel-trap mind with perfect recall, you do not need to document anything; you remember it all. For the rest of us, a documentation process is an essential component of an effective Workplace Survival Plan. Until you need it, it is simply overhead. No one likes sending in monthly payments to the insurance company. But once you are lying in a hospital bed staring up at astronomical medical costs or standing in front of the home that a tornado inconveniently moved down the block then you are glad you had the forethought to buy insurance.

Your documentation process serves a similar purpose. In all likelihood, no one will ask you about most of your workplace activities. It is the one time that someone in a position of authority has a question that makes some little tidbit of information so extremely important. Imagine the benefits of having the facts when you are being interrogated by an angry or frustrated boss. Unruffled, you check your notes to report that your boss authorized you by email on such and such a date to purge all records for client Jones.

In Antagonistic and Contentions Environments, which are rife with conflict, having the facts readily available is essential to your survival. Life is not perfect. Even in Supportive Environments, there will be disagreements or speculation. Imagine being able to convey the facts and dispel unfounded speculation which could easily lead to confusion, flashpoints or confrontation. Having access to the facts, allows you to position yourself in a positive, professional light by knowing with reasonable precision exactly what you did, why you did it, and when.

What information you decide to retain as part of your documentation process is dependent upon your unique situation and your level of risk. We recommend that you consider keeping records on any or all of the following:

- Assignments
- Contacts
- Redirection
- Completions

From our previous discussions, you know that you are at more risk in a non-supportive environment. Therefore, it would make sense that your documentation process be more rigorous in a non-supportive environment. This does not mean that we advocate not having a documentation process if you are in a Supportive Environment. A good documentation process is simply one quality of being a professional.

The following questions are intended to guide your development of a documentation process that will help you survive a probing inquiry of your work-related activities.

Is my job comprised of project-related activities?

Yes – Establish a mechanism to document the project description, scope, key personnel, schedule with key milestones; to track progress; and to retain all significant project-related communications.

No – Continue to the next question.

Project-related activities have a specific start time and completion time. They usually have interceding milestones that address the key step-by-step activities that are required to complete the overall project. An effective method for retaining project-related information includes use of a projects archive on your computer with a unique folder for each individual project. This gives you a place to store all electronic information, including emails from your boss or the client, associated with the project. An accordion folder for each project provides an organized means to retain key hardcopy materials.

Is my job comprised of cyclical activities?

Yes – Establish a mechanism to retain all relevant communications to document policies and procedures, any deviations from standard practices, and irregular routing of information or materials.

No – Continue to the next question.

Cyclical activities are ongoing; there is no start time or completion time. For example, accounting processes like processing accounts payable vouchers. It is an unending process of review, approval, and entry of the voucher into an accounting system but not necessarily in that order. You could document each voucher that you process but that might be a bit overbearing and unnecessary since the accounting system records that you entered a record and when. Additionally, most accounting processes have well established procedures. Retain a copy of the established procedures and any directives that document deviations from standard practices, particularly those commanded by management as well as irregular routing of vouchers if that is even possible. Note that manufacturing or maintenance processes tend to be cyclical activities.

If you have easy access to a computer, you can retain policies, procedures, and communications directing any deviation from standard practices on your computer. Factory or field workers without easy access to a computer may need to keep a pen and notepad handy to jot down relevant information.

Am I in a Supportive Environment?

Yes – Document significant activities and milestones associated with significant assignments so as to have a readily available record of progress for your manager.

No – Continue to the next question.

Am I in a Benign Environment?

Yes – Document your actions, interactions, and milestones associated with all but the most routine activities for any assignments that might be perceived as controversial.

No – Continue to the next question.

Am I in a Contentious Environment?

Yes – Document your actions, interactions, and milestones associated with all but the most routine activities for any assignments that might be perceived as controversial.

No – Continue to the next question.

Am I in an Antagonistic Environment?

Yes – Document your actions, interactions, and milestones associated with all but the most routine activities.

No – Continue to the next question.

Your documentation process for capturing relevant information associated with your work activities should be easy and routine. By determining what information you need to retain and establishing specific locations for retaining this information, you avoid the hassle of deciding what to keep and remembering where you put it in each individual instance. A significant characteristic of your documentation process should be that the information you collect makes sense and is easy to retrieve when you need it. Cryptic notes may be confusing when it comes time to decipher them.

The information you gather serves additional purposes as some of it will document your contribution to the organization. It will prove very useful in preparing for your performance review or in updating your resume should you receive an unsolicited offer or decide to seek employment elsewhere. You never know when opportunity will knock on your door. Your resume should be a living document that you update as you continue to notch your belt with additional skills and accomplishments.

Some of the information you should consider retaining includes:

- **A list of projects that were completed successfully.** This means on-time, on-schedule, and to the satisfaction of the customer.
- **Any positive comments you received from customers or colleagues** regarding their satisfaction with your work or their pleasure in working with you.
- **Any awards, certificates or positive recognition you received in regard to your work** including employee of the month, highest sales volume, fewest errors, etc. Even if the company does not track rates relative to your performance, there is no reason for you not to track your rate if that places you in a favorable light or provides you useful feedback to help you improve your productivity.
- **Any special achievements, actions, ideas or contributions that made the company, your organization or your group look good.**

In many ways, a performance appraisal is similar to a job interview. In the case of the performance appraisal, it is consideration for a possible promotion or bonus. In the case of a job interview, you are placing yourself in consideration for a new job. Many of the same criteria apply to both situations. It is always to your benefit to be prepared with the right information.

No one needs to know the specifics of your documentation process or the details of what information you document. Those around you, including your boss, will simply know that you are able to retrieve the information you need, when you need it.

The guiding principle to remember in regard to using documentation to your advantage is: ***The less supportive the environment, the more I need to document; the more supportive the environment, the less I need to document.***

Use this principle for deciding when and what to document in the workplace. When employed in conjunction with the questions we have suggested that you ask yourself, it will help you to minimize your risk of being improperly blamed by documenting why you made a particular decision or took a particular action.

4. Strengthen Your Image

Your image in the workplace is the collective reflection of how your peers see you. Are you competent, energetic, self-motivated, a joy to be around or not? A positive image can go a long way toward helping you build or strengthen your network of support, something that can serve you well particularly in a non-supportive environment. Some of the best ways that you can positively influence how others perceive you in the workplace fall into the following categories:

- Values, Ethics, and Integrity
- Attitude
- Productivity

- Communication
- Self-Management

Let us examine each of these areas in terms of how they contribute to your Workplace Survival Plan. Your answers to the questions in each of the following sections will help you identify where you may need to focus additional effort in fortifying your image.

The guiding principle to remember in regard to strengthening your image is: *All of my decisions and activities should be consistent with what I would expect of my employees if I were a manager in a Supportive Environment.*

Values, Ethics, and Integrity

Am I familiar with the letter and intent of each of the policies and procedures, including a Code of Conduct, that apply to my area of work?

    Yes – Continue to the next question.

    No – Obtain copies and familiarize yourself with the letter and intent of all the policies and procedures that apply to your area of work as well as the corporate Code of Conduct to avoid potential conflicts through any of your work-related activities.

This means that you must know the written and unwritten policies and procedures that govern your workplace environment. Any dispute with management will ultimately prompt someone to inquire whether you followed the rules. While it is not advisable to quote the rules to your boss, *if* you do not know the rules you leave yourself vulnerable.

Do I value mutual respect, truth, responsibility, and teamwork?

    Yes – Continue to the next question.

No –   Determine why you do not value these qualities in yourself
and your co-workers. It is likely that you are facilitating or
enabling a non-supportive workplace environment and should
seek the counsel and guidance of a career coach to help you
work through these issues.

Would I be willing to explain the reasons for my work-related decisions, actions or lack of actions in a public forum?

Yes –   Continue to the next question.

No –   Evaluate the basis for your decisions, actions or lack or actions
in favor of a more publicly defensible posture. If necessary,
seek the counsel and guidance of a career coach to help you
determine why you would not be able to defend your work-
related activities in public.

Am I aware of blatantly unethically or illegal activities in my workplace?

Yes –   Quickly distance yourself from any unethical activities and
illegal activities. You might also want to contact an attorney,
report these activities to the proper authorities, and give
serious consideration to removing yourself from this
environment.

No –   Continue to the next question.

Your values, ethics, and integrity should stand above and be independent of any guidance provided by your manager or the company. It should be a matter of self-respect that guides you to do what is right in all situations, not company policy or the threat of punitive consequences.

Attitude

Am I often angry, disgruntled, accusatory or upset at work or do I frequently exhibit any other key indicators of excessive stress?

        Yes – Implement a strategy to reduce stress and work to differentiate your mood from the negative influences of those around you or seek professional help to deal with your specific situation.

        No – Continue to the next question.

Do I have trouble motivating myself at work?

        Yes – Find a reason, not related to management or the company, that inspires you to do a good job or seek the counsel or guidance of a career coach to help you deal with your specific situation.

        No – Continue to the next question.

A good attitude is a fundamental characteristic of a content and productive worker. Do not let the fact that you may happen to work in a non-supportive environment damage your attitude to the degree that a misguided boss could use it as a reason for downgrading your performance assessment or terminating your employment.

Productivity

Am I always busy but seem to get little actual work done?

        Yes – Find effective ways to evaluate and prioritize your various work-related activities, limit distractions, and focus on the completion of important, high priority work.

        No – Continue to the next question.

Do I have a means to measure my level of productivity?

> Yes –   Continue to the next question.
>
> No –   Find a way to measure your level of productivity in terms of money, resources or time, then assess it periodically with the goal of maintaining or improving it. Seek ways to streamline any parts of the process over which you have control.

It is to your benefit to remain as productive as possible regardless of the turbulent nature of the environment. Of course, a non-supportive workplace environment will diminish your ability to perform compared to what you could accomplish in a Supportive Environment. Nonetheless, it is essential that you not use this as an excuse not to do your job to the best of your ability.

Communication

Does the content of each of my communications convey a clear, concise, and truthful message that is appropriate for the workplace and how well I know the recipient?

> Yes –   Continue to the next question.
>
> No –   Determine when and why your communications lack clarity, conciseness, and honesty or are inappropriate for how well you know the recipient, then strive to remedy the situation. Seek opportunities to learn from experienced co-workers, take a class on business communications or seek counsel and guidance from a career coach.

Do I consider whether each communication will enflame conflict or diminish it?

> Yes –   Continue to the next question.

No – Evaluate your written, verbal, and non-verbal communications in terms of whether your response will enflame or diminish conflict and the ways you have of managing conflict to serve your best interests.

Do I follow up on my communications?

Yes – Continue to the next question.

No – In person or on the phone, ask if the other person understands what you are saying or ask if there are any questions. Embed within written messages a request for a response, even if only to acknowledge the receipt of important communications.

In the workplace, information can work in your favor or against you depending upon how you use it. What you choose to communicate, when you choose to communicate, where you choose to communicate, and to whom you choose to communicate are all important considerations.

Self-management

Am I willing to take full responsibility for my actions at work?

Yes – Continue to the next question.

No – Determine why you are unable to take full responsibility for your actions at work. If necessary, seek the counsel and guidance of a career coach to help you work through this issue.

Accepting full responsibility for all actions you take at work may at first glance seem to run contrary to our cautionary note on accepting responsibility. Not so. Being self-managed does not require you to place a target on your back in a non-supportive environment. Being self-managed means that when you do accept full responsibility for a result or outcome that you stand behind your actions whether you succeed or fail. In the situations where you deflect responsibility back to your boss, you still take full responsibility for faithfully executing the directives of your boss. Responsibility for the implications of those results and outcomes remains with your boss.

For example, your boss directs you to produce a report with incomplete data. You take responsibility for producing the report based on the data available. You may even want to note on the report that the data is incomplete. Responsibility for the fact that the report is not based on a complete set of data and all the implications of the decision to produce such a report remain with your boss.

As a self-managed employee, your goal is to take charge of all areas of your professional life. Ask yourself: *What would a manager in a Supportive Environment have me do?* Then evaluate all of your activities in terms of that guidance. Deviate from this approach only when specifically directed by your boss. But do it only on a case-by-case basis. Your ability to manage your decisions and actions effectively is one key to your success in any workplace environment.

5. Strengthen Your Foundation

Your foundation underlies your ability to be productive and supports your ability to make certain that good decisions drive all of your work-related activities. A good way to evaluate the strength of your foundation is to evaluate yourself. *Am I the best person for the job I currently hold? If I were the manager and had to hire someone to do my job, would I hire me? If not, why not?* No need for a lack of confidence or an over inflated ego here. Be honest with yourself. *Do I have the necessary skills and knowledge or the necessary network of contacts to do my job? Do I have the ingenuity and ability to analyze and solve the problems that I might encounter? Am I able to adapt to new and changing situations?* Can you provide concrete examples?

Let us revisit these questions and others in a more organized fashion to help you evaluate the strength of your foundation as part of developing your Workplace Survival Plan.

Am I competent to perform all of my work-related duties?

Yes – Continue to the next question.

No – Seek opportunities to learn from experienced co-workers or enroll in classes that can provide you the skills and knowledge you lack.

Am I familiar with most significant issues or problems associated with my work-related duties and do I know how to resolve them?

Yes – Continue to the next question.

No – Seek opportunities to learn from experienced co-workers or enroll in classes that can assist you in identifying and resolving work-related issues and problems.

Do I have reliable contacts with co-workers who can provide assistance in each of my areas of responsibility?

Yes – Continue to the next question.

No – Identify a co-worker who would be willing to provide assistance in each of your areas of responsibility.

Do I have reliable external contacts as part of my network who can provide valuable assistance when I need it?

Yes – Continue to the next question.

No – Identify people in each external organization with which you work and elsewhere who hve proven to be reliable.

Am I familiar with most of the new technologies and processes associated with my line of work?

Yes –   Continue to the next question.

No –   Read industry publications, seek opportunities to learn from experienced co-workers or enroll in classes that can assist you in familiarizing yourself with new technologies and processes associated with your line of work.

You should work and act as if you are the best person for your job. If you are being honest yourself and you would not hire yourself for your job, then you have some work to do in establishing a much stronger foundation than the one that currently supports you. Do not forget, a strong foundation underlies the overall effectiveness of your Workplace Survival Plan.

The guiding principle to remember in regard to reinforcing your foundation is: ***The stronger my foundation, the more resourceful and productive I can be and the more able I am to survive in any environment.*** Being resourceful and productive is definitely in your best interest.

6. Recognize Traps and Manipulation Techniques

The more in control of your work-related affairs, the less susceptible you are to falling for a trap or manipulation technique that a boss in a non-supportive environment may employ to trip you up. If it seems too good to be true then it probably is. If the bargain requires you to complete your end first then what leads you to believe the boss will complete his end once he has what he wants from you? Surviving in a non-supportive environment means that you must develop a healthy level of awareness.

Are you familiar with most of the common traps and manipulation techniques used by bosses in non-supportive environments?

Yes –   Continue to the next question.

No – Study the techniques and manipulation techniques documented in this text. If necessary, seek the counsel and guidance of a career coach to help you learn how to avoid falling victim to them.

Your best defense against traps and manipulation techniques is to learn to recognize them and how they can be used to set you up for failure.

7. Update Your Workplace Survival Plan

The preceding steps are the starting point to establishing an effective Workplace Survival Plan that addresses your specific situation. They are not the end. You may find that your preliminary efforts do not work as well as you would like. This is not an exact science and your workplace is an ever changing environment with new duties, new challenges, new policies and procedures, new technologies, and new personnel. Unfortunately, you cannot tune into the Weather Channel to check on current conditions in your workplace to see if anything has changed since yesterday. It is your responsibility to monitor the environment and to review, periodically, each element of your Workplace Survival Plan to see if it needs to be updated, tweaked or refined to address some change that has occurred in the workplace or to improve its overall effectiveness.

The guiding principle to remember in regard to *Your* Workplace Survival Plan is: ***The more current my Workplace Survival Plan; the more prepared I am to adapt to the changing demands of my workplace environment.*** The fact is that your Workplace Survival Plan will only be as effective as you make it.

Has it been more than 6 months since I reviewed and updated my Workplace Survival Plan?

Yes – Review all elements of your plan and update as necessary. Use the Workplace Survival Plan Checklist as a guide.

No – Continue to monitor the environment for changes that will necessitate a modification to your plan.

All of the questions we have presented in this chapter to help guide in the development of your Workplace Survival Plan can be found on the Workplace Survival Plan Checklist located in Appendix B. Use this checklist to develop your Workplace Survival Plan.

Benefits of Your Workplace Survival Plan

While others run around the office "naked," your Workplace Survival Plan will help you to defend yourself against unwarranted attacks and accusations, to improve your ability to identify and overcome obstacles, and to increase your overall worth as an employee. It will serve you best if it is current and comprehensive. While an effective Workplace Survival Plan is essential in a non-supportive environment, it can also benefit you in a Supportive Environment.

In a Supportive Environment, your Workplace Survival Plan helps you model professional, supportive behavior regardless of the environment. It positions you as part of the solution, not part of the problem. It helps you ensure that you are prepared to deal with any situation that arises.

Think of your Workplace Survival Plan as your guide for continuous professional development. You did not think that you could find a job then glide gently into retirement, did you? The workplace is constantly changing and you must change with it, irrespective of whether the individual to whom you report acts like a boss or a manager. In a sense, your goal is to make your boss or your manager redundant or, at least, to reduce your dependence upon him. Your goal is to remain productive while out maneuvering the misguided machinations of your boss in a non-supportive environment or more fully complement the backing you receive from your manager in a Supportive Environment. In effect, your Workplace Survival Plan guides you in constructing your own Supportive Environment to the degree possible regardless of what occurs around you.

You will be better able to recognize good management behavior, even in an otherwise non-supportive environment, and support that behavior without leaving yourself vulnerable. No doubt, you've heard it said that criminals target weak individuals who are ill-prepared to defend themselves. We surmise that this logic is transferable from the street to the workplace. If you act like a victim, you are many times more likely to be victimized.

With an effective Workplace Survival Plan, you will be better prepared to protect yourself. You will be able to disable your "hot buttons" and disengage more quickly from conflict. The fact that the boss sees you not respond when he tries to find and press your "hot buttons" will weigh in your favor. So will the fact that you will always have a valid explanation for what you did and why you did it. He will have little reason to complain, knowing that you received and documented his authorization before you proceeded with any potentially controversial project. No matter how poorly he performs, he will see you behave like a professional who is prepared for anything and this may prompt him to reconsider the advisability of trying to pull something over on you.

Bosses in a non-supportive environment are more likely to target employees who do not act professionally and who do not know how to defend themselves. These employees are more easily set up for failure by an unscrupulous boss. If you thwart your boss's every effort to find a weakness, he may eventually leave you alone and move on to torment an easier target. This does not mean you can let your guard down, nor should you. It simply means that you have implemented your Workplace Survival Plan and it is working.

As a former educator, I know that positive reinforcement of good behavior tends to propagate good behavior. Your Workplace Survival Plan will help you model professional, supportive behavior. It is certainly up to each and every individual to decide how to behave in the workplace. However, **as a result of having developed your Workplace Survival Plan and using it to guide your actions, you may be able to inspire an increase in professional, supportive behavior amongst your co-workers and maybe even your boss.**

Workplace Survival Plan and Checklist

Use the Workplace Survival Plan Checklist to help you develop your Workplace Survival Plan. The answers to the questions on the checklist should spur sufficient thought to guide identification of specific actions you can take to strengthen your position in your workplace environment.

Workplace Survival Plan Checklist

1. Identify Your Workplace Environment

Guiding principle: ***The more I know about my workplace environment, the better I can prepare myself to deal with its demands.***

Enter the following information on my Workplace Survival Plan.
- *My name*
- *My job title*
- *Type of industry in which I work*
- *Job title of my manager.*

Write a brief background statement on my situation at work.

Select the environment which best matches my workplace.

List up to four key issues I encounter in the workplace.

Can I map each action in my Workplace Survival Plan to one of these issues?

Yes – Map all of the actions you add to your Workplace Survival Plan to one of the issues listed above..

No – Seek the council and guidance of a career coach to help you develop solutions to those issues that you are unable to map from at least one action in your Workplace Survival Plan.

2. Strengthen Your Foundation

Guiding principle: ***The stronger my foundation, the more resourceful and productive I can be and the more able I am to survive in any environment.***

Am I competent to perform all of my work-related duties?

      Yes –   Continue to the next question.

      No –   Seek opportunities to learn from experienced co-workers or enroll in classes that can provide you the skills and knowledge you lack.

Am I familiar with most significant issues or problems associated with my work-related duties and do I know how to resolve them?

      Yes –   Continue to the next question.

      No –   Seek opportunities to learn from experienced co-workers or enroll in classes that can assist you in identifying and resolving work-related issues and problems.

Do I have reliable contacts with co-workers who can provide assistance in each of my areas of responsibility?

      Yes –   Continue to the next question.

      No –   Identify a co-worker who would be willing to provide assistance in each of your areas of responsibility.

Do I have reliable contacts in each of the external organizations with which I work on a regular basis?

      Yes –   Continue to the next question.

      No –   Identify someone in each external organization with which you work who has proven to be reliable.

Am I familiar with most of the new technologies and processes associated with my line of work?

        Yes –   Continue to the next question.

        No –   Read industry publications, seek opportunities to learn from experienced co-workers or enroll in classes that can assist you in familiarizing yourself with new technologies and processes associated with your line of work.

3. Enhance Your Image

Guiding principle: ***All of my decisions and activities should be consistent with what I would expect of my employees if I were a manager in a Supportive Environment.***

Values, Ethics, and Integrity

Am I familiar with the letter and intent of each of the policies and procedures, including a Code of Conduct, that apply to my area of work?

        Yes –   Continue to the next question.

        No –   Obtain copies and familiarize yourself with the letter and intent of all the policies and procedures that apply to your area of work as well as the corporate Code of Conduct to avoid potential conflicts through any of your work-related activities.

Do I value mutual respect, truth, responsibility, and teamwork?

        Yes –   Continue to the next question.

        No –   Determine why you do not value these qualities in yourself and your co-workers. It is likely that you are facilitating or enabling a non-supportive workplace environment and should seek the counsel and guidance of a career coach to help you work through these issues.

Would I be willing to explain the reasons for my work-related decisions, actions or lack of actions in a public forum?

Yes – Continue to the next question.

No – Evaluate the basis for your decisions, actions or lack or actions in favor of a more publicly defensible posture. If necessary, seek the counsel and guidance of a career coach to help you determine why you would not be able to defend your work-related activities in public.

Am I aware of blatantly unethically or illegal activities in my workplace?

Yes – Quickly distance yourself from any unethical activities and illegal activities. You might also want to contact an attorney, report these activities to the proper authorities, and give serious consideration to removing yourself from this environment.

No – Continue to the next question.

Attitude

Am I often angry, disgruntled, accusatory or upset at work or do I frequently exhibit any other key indicators of excessive stress?

Yes – Implement a strategy to reduce stress or seek professional help to deal with your specific situation.

No – Continue to the next question.

Do you let other people control your mood as though it were a light switch that can be turned on or off?

Yes – Work to differentiate your mood from the negative influences of those around you or seek professional help to deal with your specific situation.

No – Continue to the next question.

Do I have trouble motivating myself at work?

Yes – Find a reason, not related to management or the company, that inspires you to do a good job or seek the counsel or guidance of a career coach to help you deal with your specific situation.

No – Continue to the next question.

Productivity

Am I always busy but seem to get little actual work done?

Yes – Find effective ways to evaluate and prioritize your various work-related activities, limit distractions, and focus on the completion of important, high priority work.

No – Continue to the next question.

Do I have a means to measure my level of productivity?

Yes – Continue to the next question.

No – Find a way to measure your level of productivity in terms of money, resources or time then assess it, periodically, with the goal of maintaining or improving it. Seek ways to streamline any parts of the process over which you have control.

Communication

Does the content of each of my communications convey a clear, concise, and truthful message that is appropriate for the workplace and how well I know the recipient?

    Yes –   Continue to the next question.

    No –   Determine when and why your communications lack clarity, conciseness, and honesty or are inappropriate for how well you know the recipient, then strive to remedy the situation. Seek opportunities to learn from experienced co-workers, take a class on business communications or seek counsel and guidance from a career coach.

Do I consider whether each communication will enflame conflict or diminish it?

    Yes –   Continue to the next question.

    No –   Evaluate your written, verbal, and non-verbal communications in terms of whether your response will enflame or diminish conflict and the ways you have of managing conflict to serve your best interests.

Do I follow up on my communications?

    Yes –   Continue to the next question.

    No –   In person or on the phone, ask if the other person understands what you are saying or ask if there are any questions. Embed within written messages a request for a response, even if only to acknowledge the receipt of important communications.

Self-management

Am I willing to take full responsibility for my conduct at work?

Yes – Continue to the next question.

No – Determine why you are unable to take full responsibility for your conduct at work. If necessary, seek the counsel and guidance of a career coach to help you work through this issue.

4. Manage Your Acceptance of Responsibility

Guiding principle: ***The more supportive the environment, the more responsibility I can safely assume; the less supportive the environment, the less responsibility I should assume.***

Are all assignments and the expected outcomes clearly defined?

Yes – Continue to the next question.

No – Ask for clarification of the assignment and the expected outcome:

  - If clarification is provided, continue to the next question.
  - If clarification is not forthcoming, reject the assignment or reflect responsibility for the desired outcome back to your boss.

Am I able to differentiate between the task and the expected outcome?

Yes – Continue to the next question.

No – Practice analyzing tasks in terms of all the possible outcomes that could be generated and potential problematic issues.

Are you comfortable asking your boss for more explanation for an assignment?

    Yes –   Continue to the next question.

    No –   Practice asking for more explanation with a supportive colleague or family member

Do I have adequate skills and knowledge to complete all assignments successfully?

    Yes –   Continue to the next question.

    No –   Ask for or find the necessary training or mentoring to provide you those skills.

        •   If training is provided, continue to the next question.

        •   If training is not forthcoming, reject the assignment or reflect responsibility for the desired outcome back to your boss.

Do I have access to adequate resources and assistance to complete all assignments successfully?

    Yes –   Continue to the next question.

    No –   Ask for or find adequate resources and assistance to complete the assignments and achieve the expected outcome:

        •   If adequate resources and assistance are provided, continue to the next question.

        •   If access to adequate resources and assistance are not forthcoming, reject the assignment or reflect responsibility for the desired outcome back to your boss.

Are any assignments controversial?

    Yes –   Ask for clarification regarding the consequences of success and the consequences of failure to achieve the desired results.

No –   Continue to the next question.

Am I in a Supportive Environment?

Yes –   Assume responsibility for pursing best approaches, request assistance when needed, and look for opportunities to contribute to achievement of organizational goals.

No –   Continue to the next question.

Am I in a Benign Environment?

Yes –   Evaluate assignments, clarify and document questionable requests, and negotiate possible alternative approaches when a successful outcome is uncertain.

No –   Continue to the next question.

Am I in a Contentious Environment?

Yes –   Shift responsibility back to management by clarifying and documenting questionable assignments, following instructions, and not suggesting questionable alternative approaches.

No –   Continue to the next question.

Am I in an Antagonistic Environment?

Yes –   Shift responsibility back to management by clarifying and documenting assignments, following instructions with strict precision, and not suggesting alternative approaches.

No –   Continue to the next question.

5. Implement Your Documentation Process

Guiding principle: ***The less supportive the environment, the more I need to document; the more supportive the environment, the less I need to document.***

Is my job comprised of project-related activities?

Yes – Establish a mechanism to document the project description, scope, key personnel, schedule with key milestones; to track progress; and to retain all significant project-related communications.

No – Continue to the next question.

Is my job comprised of cyclical activities?

Yes – Establish a mechanism to retain all relevant communications to document policies and procedures, any deviations from standard practices, and irregular routing of information or materials.

No – Continue to the next question.

Am I in a Supportive Environment?

Yes – Document significant activities and milestones associated with significant assignments so as to have a readily available record of progress for your manager.

No – Continue to the next question.

Am I in a Benign Environment?

Yes – Document your actions, interactions, and milestones associated with all but the most routine activities for any assignments that might be perceived as controversial.

No – Continue to the next question.

Am I in a Contentious Environment?

Yes – Document your actions, interactions, and milestones associated with all but the most routine activities for any assignments that might be perceived as controversial.

No – Continue to the next question.

Am I in an Antagonistic Environment?

Yes – Document your actions, interactions, and milestones associated with all but the most routine activities.

No – Continue to the next question.

6. Recognize Traps and Manipulation Techniques

Guiding principle: ***The less supportive the environment, the more cautious and prepared I need to be to deal with a full range of traps and manipulation techniques.***

Are you familiar with most of the common traps and manipulation techniques used by bosses in non-supportive environments?

Yes – Continue to the next question.

No – Study the techniques and manipulation techniques documented in this text. If necessary, seek the counsel and guidance of a career coach to help you learn how to avoid falling victim to them.

7. Update Your Workplace Survival Plan

Guiding principle: ***The more current my Workplace Survival Plan; the more prepared I am to adapt to the changing demands of my workplace environment.***

> *Has it been more than 6 months since I reviewed and updated my Workplace Survival Plan?*
>
> Yes – Review all elements of your plan and update as necessary. Use the Workplace Survival Plan Checklist as a guide.
>
> No – Continue to monitor the environment for changes that will necessitate a modification to your plan.

My Workplace Survival Plan

1. Workplace Environment

My name is _____ .

My job title is _____ .

I work in the _____ *industry.*

My manager's job title is _____ .

My situation at work is _____

_____

_____ .

Guiding Principle: ***The more I know about my workplace environment, the better I can prepare myself to deal with its demands.***

Type of Environment:

__ *Antagonistic*   __ *Contentious*   __ *Benign*   __ *Supportive*

Key Issues: (map each action in the sections below to one of these issues)

1. _____ .
2. _____ .
3. _____ .
4. _____ .

2. Foundation

Guiding Principle: ***The stronger my foundation, the more resourceful and productive I can be and the more able I am to perform in any environment.***

Actions to Manage **Skills and Knowledge**:

__ *Enhance my skills and knowledge.*   Issue ____

__ _____.   Issue ____

__ _____.   Issue ____

Actions to Manage **Network**:

__ *Expand my network of contacts.*   Issue ____

__ _____.   Issue ____

__ _____.   Issue ____

Actions to Manage **Problem Solving Abilities**:

__ *Improve my problem solving abilities.*   Issue ____

__ _____.   Issue ____

__ _____.   Issue ____

Actions to Manage **Adaptability**:

__ *Become more adaptable to changing environments.*   Issue ____

__ _____.   Issue ____

__ _____.   Issue ____

3. Image

Guiding Principle: ***All of my decisions and activities should be consistent with what I would expect of my employees if I were a manager in a Supportive Environment.***

Actions to Manage **Values, Ethics, and Integrity**:

__ *Enhance my values, ethics, and integrity.*   Issue ____

__ _____.   Issue ____

__ _____.   Issue ____

Actions to Manage **Attitude**:

    __ *Improve my attitude.*   Issue ____

    __ _____.   Issue ____

    __ _____.   Issue ____

Actions to Manage **Productivity**:

    __ *Increase my productivity.*   Issue ____

    __ _____.   Issue ____

    __ _____.   Issue ____

Actions to Manage **Communication**:

    __ *Communicate more clearly and concisely.*   Issue ____

    __ _____.   Issue ____

    __ _____.   Issue ____

Actions to Manage **Self-Management**:

    __ *Take more responsibility for my conduct.*   Issue ____

    __ _____.   Issue ____

    __ _____.   Issue ____

4. Responsibility

Guiding Principle: ***The more supportive the environment, the more responsibility I can safely assume; the less supportive the environment, the less responsibility I should assume.***

Actions to Manage **Responsibility**:

    __ *Ensure expected outcomes are clearly defined.*   Issue ____

__ *Ask for clarification when necessary.*	Issue ____
__ *Learn to assess risk more quickly.*	Issue ____
__ *Learn to shift responsibility back to the boss*	
when your ability to generate the desired	
outcomes are uncertain.	Issue ____
__ _____.	Issue ____
__ _____.	Issue ____

5. Documentation

Guiding Principle: ***The less supportive the environment, the more I need to document; the more supportive the environment, the less I need to document.***

Type of job activities:

__ *Project-based* __ *Cyclic*

Actions to Manage **Documentation**:

__ *Evaluate my need for documentation.*	Issue ____
__ *Establish process for keeping documentation including*	
what to document, where to keep it for easy retrieval,	
and when to use it.	Issue ____
__ _____.	Issue ____
__ _____.	Issue ____

6. Traps and Manipulation Techniques

Guiding Principle: ***The less supportive the environment, the more cautious and prepared I need to be to deal with a full range of traps and manipulation techniques.***

Actions to Recognize and Avoid **Traps and Manipulation Techniques**:

  __ *Learn to recognize and avoid common traps and*
    manipulation techniques.   Issue ____

  __ _____.   Issue ____

  __ _____.   Issue ____

7. Update

Guiding Principle: ***The more current my Workplace Survival Plan; the more prepared I am to adapt to the changing demands of my workplace environment.***

Actions to Update Your **Workplace Survival Plan**:

  __ *Keep my Workplace Survival Plan updated.*   Issue ____

  __ _____.   Issue ____

  __ _____.   Issue ____

Sample Workplace Survival Plans

The following samples of Workplace Survival Plans were created for our fictitious, representative employees Cal Jones, Jennifer Lakes, Mario Molina, and Twila Fletcher who were kind enough to grace these pages with tales of their workplace experiences. These characters are intended to provide examples of issues employees would encounter in the following workplace environments:

- **Cal Jones works in an Antagonistic Environment**
- **Jennifer Lakes works in a Contentious Environment**
- **Mario Molina works in a Benign Environment**
- **Twila Fletcher works in a Supportive Environment**

This Appendix presents a unique Workplace Survival Plan for each of these individuals based on the conditions of their working environment. Note that in these plans italicized entries indicate actions that the employee intends to take to improve his or her ability to deal with the prevailing environment.

While your Workplace Survival Plan will certainly differ from these samples, it should follow the same pattern with a listing of actions that you will take to improve your ability to deal with the specific challenges of the environment in which you work. The questions contained on the Workplace Survival Plan Checklist will help guide you in determining what actions you should take in each of the areas indicated. Each subsequent review of your Workplace Survival Plan should retire actions that have been completed, refine ones that have not been completed, and add new actions to keep your plan current with the changes that have occurred since our last review.

Workplace Survival Plan for Cal Jones

1. Workplace Environment

My name is <u>Cal Jones</u>.

My job title is <u>Salesman.</u>

I work in the <u>Business Services</u> industry.

I report to the <u>Director of Sales</u> (Arthur Breedlove).

Background:

- *I have been with the company for 15 years and am 5 years from retirement.*
- *My clients appreciate me for the good service I provide them.*
- *A new director of Major Accounts was hired this year.*
- *There are rumors of a buyout and layoffs.*

Guiding Principle: ***The more I know about my workplace environment, the better I can prepare myself to deal with its demands.***

Type of Environment: *Antagonistic*

Key Issues:

1. *The new director seems to be gunning for me.*
2. *He leaves abusive messages/threats.*
3. *He indicates clients are dissatisfied with my service.*
4. *He does not accurately relay messages from them.*

Guiding Principle: ***The less supportive the environment, the more cautious and prepared I need to be to deal with a full range of traps and manipulation techniques.***

2. Foundation

Guiding Principle: ***The stronger my foundation, the more resourceful and productive I can be and the more able I am to perform in any environment.***

> Actions to Manage **Skills and Knowledge**:
>
> - *Order an on-line training course on advanced sales techniques to see if there are any new methods that I might use to be even more effective. (Issue 1)*
> - *Take a course on dealing effectively with difficult people. (Issue 2)*

> Actions to Manage **Network**:
>
> - *Join a professional association of salesmen to expand my network of contacts. (Issue 1)*

> Actions to Manage **Problem Solving Abilities**:
>
> - *Meet with clients to identify problems they are encountering then research how a service Axiom provides might help them solve their problems. (Issue 1)*

> Actions to Manage **Adaptability**:
>
> - *Research new technologies and business aids that can help increase my productivity. (Issue 1)*

3. Image

Guiding Principle: ***All of my decisions and activities should be consistent with what I would expect of my employees if I were a manager in a Supportive Environment.***

Actions to Manage **Values, Ethics, and Integrity**:

- *Review my employee handbook. (Issue 1)*
- *Evaluate each decision I make and each action I plan to take in terms of compliance with policies and procedures before going forward. (Issue 1)*

Actions to Manage **Attitude**:

- *Identity and try 2 stress reduction techniques that I can use anytime. (Issue 1)*
- *Identify and try 2 stretching exercises that I can use at my desk. (Issue 1)*
- *Do not take Breedlove's comments personally. (Issue 2)*

Actions to Manage **Productivity**:

- *Continue to recruit new clients and serve existing clients to the best of my ability. (Issue 1)*

Actions to Manage **Communication**:

- *Verify the accuracy of any messages received from Breedlove before acting upon them. (Issue 4)*
- *Maintain a professional demeanor regardless of abusive/threatening messages from Breedlove. (Issue 2)*

Actions to Manage **Self-Management**:

- *Find ways to solve as many problems as I can before taking them to Breedlove. (Issue 1)*

4. Responsibility

Guiding Principle: ***The more supportive the environment, the more responsibility I can safely assume; the less supportive the environment, the less responsibility I should assume.***

> Actions to Manage **Responsibility**:
> - *Since I already hold full responsibility for client accounts due to my senior status, I will continue to ensure clients are well-served by fulfilling all of my duties to the best of my ability. (Issue 1)*

5. Documentation

Guiding Principle: ***The less supportive the environment, the more I need to document; the more supportive the environment, the less I need to document.***

> Type of Job Activities: *Project-related activities*

> Actions to Manage **Documentation**:
> - *Forward thank you notes received from clients to Breedlove and retain copies in the client files and in my performance review file. (Issue 3 and 4)*
> - *Without soliciting praise, ask clients who wish to express their thanks to send a note to Breedlove and Breedlove's superior. (Issue 3 and 4)*
> - *Document any messages from clients that Breedlove has distorted. Correct distortions with an email to Breedlove. Keep a copy in the client file and in my performance review file. (Issue 4)*

- *Document any abusive/threatening messages from Breedlove and keep for future reference. If this continues, consider forwarding his messages to his superior and HR. (Issue 2)*

6. Traps and Manipulation Techniques

Guiding Principle: ***The less supportive the environment, the more cautious and prepared I need to be to deal with a full range of traps and manipulation techniques.***

    Actions to Recognize and Avoid **Traps and Manipulation Techniques**:
- *Learn to recognize the traps Breedlove uses most often and create a way to respond to each. (Issue 1 and 2)*

7. Update

Guiding Principle: ***The more current my Workplace Survival Plan; the more prepared I am to adapt to the changing demands of my workplace environment.***

    Actions to Update My **Workplace Survival Plan**:
- *Monitor workplace for changes and update my Workplace Survival Plan as necessary. (Issue 1, 2, 3, and 4)*
- *Perform a complete review of my Workplace Survival Plan and determine the need to make any changes in 1 month. (Issue 1, 2, 3, and 4)*

Summary of Workplace Survival Plan for Cal Jones

Cal Jones works in an Antagonistic Environment. He suspects that his boss Arthur Breedlove would like nothing better than to fire him. In any case, something has gone extremely wrong in his working relationship with Breedlove and Cal's job is in jeopardy. The seriousness of his situation is compounded by his age as Cal rapidly approaches retirement.

The fact that Cal's boss seems to be gunning for him is Cal's key problem. While implementing a comprehensive Workplace Survival Plan is an essential step in addressing this problem, a primary focus of attention for Cal must be to make certain he can recognize and avoid falling victim to any traps that Breedlove may set for him.

As a salesman, Cal lacks the opportunity to shift very much responsibility to Breedlove. Cal is responsible for serving the needs of his customers, period. He is fortunate, however, in that he has developed positive relationships with his customers. It is important to continue to cultivate these relationships by delivering the products and services his customers require. Cal needs to cultivate an equally positive image with his co-workers. This, too, will help counter any efforts Breedlove may take to undercut Cal's credibility. This could be more challenging if the company employs a completive culture in the sales department. It is imperative that Cal maintain his productivity and monitor his own communications to ensure that he maintains a professional demeanor at all times.

Positive comments about Cal's excellent service from clients and co-workers may surface with senior members of management and filter down to Breedlove letting him know, indirectly, that he must have a strong logical basis for any effort to remove Cal from his job.

Cal should retain praise from clients and co-workers as well as all communications with Breedlove in his files. This is not just a matter of saving emails. This is a matter of preserving all communications that reveal the antagonistic nature of the environment that Breedlove is responsible for creating and will certainly resonate through most of Breedlove's written and verbal communications with Cal.

Cal could not have achieved his senior status as a member of the sales force without having compiled a significant set of skills and knowledge along the way. Even so, there may be room for improvement and he should investigate what that might entail. Joining a professional association could expand his network outside the workplace and should Breedlove actually fire him, such a network may come to his aid with other job opportunities. Additionally, he should use this situation to exercise his problem-solving skills by seeking ways to moderate the effects of Breedlove's misguided and unprofessional management style.

Cal is in an uncompromising position and he knows it. He must be patient and ever thoughtful in his words and deeds. He can ill afford to ruffle the fur of customers or co-workers. Cal's Workplace Survival Plan should help him ease closer to retirement in his current position, unless a lucrative job offer from a company that recognizes him as the amazingly talented salesman he is allows him to depart from Axiom Business Services on his terms.

Workplace Survival Plan for Jennifer Lakes

Workplace Environment

My name is <u>Jennifer Lakes</u>.

My job title is <u>Production Lead.</u>

I work in the <u>Electronic Controls Manufacturing</u> industry.

I report to the <u>Director of Production</u> (Bren Voltek).

Background:

- *I have a long history with the company after having started out at the bottom.*
- *I am a machine operator and oversee other operators.*

Guiding Principle: ***The more I know about my workplace environment, the better I can prepare myself to deal with its demands.***

Type of Environment: *Contentious*

Key Issues:

1. *The machines are old and prone to breakdown which reduces my team's productivity.*
2. *I don't get any support from my boss to fix this situation.*
3. *I wrote a proposal that Voltek said he would submit to upper management but he lied about presenting my proposal to the executive team. I am concerned that he may be lying about other issues also.*
4. *I am afraid I will be blamed for any problems with meeting production targets.*

Guiding Principle: ***The less supportive the environment, the more cautious and prepared I need to be to deal with a full range of traps and manipulation techniques.***

2. Foundation

Guiding principle: ***The stronger my foundation, the more resourceful and productive I can be and the more able I am to perform in any environment.***

Actions to Manage **Skills and Knowledge**:

- *Find copy of the operator's manual for machines and study them to fully understand how the machines should be operated and serviced. (Issue 1)*

Actions to Manage **Network**:

- *Have lunch with Marcia to find out more about whether the Executive Committee has been apprised of machine breakdown situation. Consider letting Marcia know that I am documenting machine breakdowns if the Executive Committee would like to see that information or my proposal to upgrade the machines. Review the data before making this suggestion. (Issue 1 and 4)*

Actions to Manage **Problem Solving Abilities**:

- *Look for ways to keep operators productive during the time their machines are down. (Issue 1 and 4)*

Actions to Manage **Adaptability**:

- *Continue to be flexible to changes in the work environment. (Issue 1)*
- *Look for ways to counter the damaging effects of Voltek's leadership style. (Issue 3)*

3. Image

Guiding Principle: ***All of my decisions and activities should be consistent with what I would expect of my employees if I were a manager in a Supportive Environment.***

> Actions to Manage **Values, Ethics, and Integrity**:
> - *Read and study my employee handbook. (Issue 2 and 3)*
> - *Review each decision I make and each action I plan to take in terms of compliance with policies and procedures before going forward. (Issue 2 and 3)*

> Actions to Manage **Attitude**:
> - *Continue to maintain a positive attitude regardless of Voltek's behavior. (Issue 2 and 3)*
> - *Find ways to release the stress outside of the workplace. (Issue 1, 2, 3, and 4)*

> Actions to Manage **Productivity**:
> - *Gather suggestions from machine operators and mechanics on ways to keep the machines from breaking down. (Issue 1 and 4)*

> Actions to Manage **Communication**:
> - *Continue to communicate clearly and professionally with Voltek and others. (Issue 3)*

> Actions to Manage **Self-Management**:
> - *Continue to demonstrate professional behavior regardless of how Voltek acts. (Issue 3)*

4. Responsibility

Guiding Principle: ***The more supportive the environment, the more responsibility I can safely assume; the less supportive the environment, the less responsibility I should assume.***

Actions to Manage **Responsibility**:

- *Notify Voltek of every machine breakdown incident and request his instructions on how to address the lost productivity that results. Keep a record of all such contacts with Voltek and his responses or lack of them. (Issue 1, 2, and 4)*

5. Documentation

Guiding Principle: ***The less supportive the environment, the more I need to document; the more supportive the environment, the less I need to document.***

Type of Job Activities: *Cyclical activities*

Actions to Manage **Documentation**:

- *Document all downtime and lost productivity caused by machine breakdowns and report these in writing to Voltek. Keep a copy for my files. (Issue 1, 2, and 4)*
- *Document all verbal discussions with Voltek regarding machine downtime and productivity and follow up with an email to Voltek. Ask him to confirm my recollection of the discussion or redline changes to my version. Keep a copy of my original and his redlines for my files. (Issue 1, 2, and 4)*

6. Traps and Manipulation Techniques

Guiding Principle: ***The less supportive the environment, the more cautious and prepared I need to be to deal with a full range of traps and manipulation techniques.***

Actions to Recognize and Avoid **Traps and Manipulation Techniques**:
- *Develop a continuing record of the impact, in terms of cost and manpower that not upgrading the machines is having on the company. Watch for opportunities, especially invitations to share this information with corporate decision-makers other than Voltek. (Issue 1, 2, and 4)*

7. Update

Guiding Principle: ***The more current my Workplace Survival Plan; the more prepared I am to adapt to the changing demands of my workplace environment.***

Actions to Update My **Workplace Survival Plan**:
- *Monitor workplace for changes and update my Workplace Survival Plan as necessary. (Issue 1, 2, 3, and 4)*
- *Perform a complete review of my Workplace Survival Plan and determine the need to make any changes in 2 months. (Issues 1, 2, 3, and 4)*

Summary of Workplace Survival Plan for Jennifer Lakes

Jennifer Lakes works in a Contentious Environment. Her boss Bren Voltek has tried to block her efforts to surface a proposal for improving productivity to the corporate decision-makers. Since she knows she cannot depend upon Voltek to provide her the support she needs, she should focus her Workplace Survival Plan on strengthening her defenses against any adverse actions Voltek might perpetrate upon her while expanding her access to resources that may help her address the problems she is experiencing with the machines.

Her key problem is the fact that Voltek refuses to address the issue of updating the machines. This directly impacts Jennifer's productivity. She should continue to document the extent of the problem including the financial costs as well as the drain on manpower that this problem perpetuates. While she cannot go over Voltek's head with this information without inviting reprisals, she can prepare the data and wait for an invitation to share it with a decision-maker other than Voltek. When this invitation comes, and there is no guarantee that it will, she can send her report to the requesting party with a copy to Voltek. At that time, he may feel obligated to support it since the problem now exists in the light of day.

Until then, Jennifer is particularly vulnerable to reports of downtime and lost productivity which Voltek surfaces to upper management, even though the temperamental machines are at fault. She should shift responsibility for machine breakdowns to Voltek by informing him in writing every time a breakdown occurs and requesting his advice on how to address the downtime and loss of productivity. This may offer him some incentive to participate in finding a solution to this problem.

Since Voltek is inherently untrustworthy, Jennifer should document all issues that arise and communications with him in regard to downtime and lost productivity. Even if she successfully shifts responsibility for the breakdowns to Voltek, Jennifer should remain in control of the facts associated with the situation by performing her own investigation.

In the face of any obstacles placed in her path by Voltek, Jennifer should continue to follow the rules and maintain her positive attitude. She should refrain from vocalizing her frustrations with Voltek at work and pursue ways to reduce the stress of working with a boss she does not trust.

If she were the boss, she would be responsible for finding a solution to the unreliable machines. Given the limitation that she cannot purchase new machines, she should pursue other remedies that might be available. To the best of her ability, she should become the resident machine "behavioral" specialist by learning as much as possible about what makes the machines breakdown and how that can be avoided.

She already has a solid foundation in terms of skills and knowledge and has clearly adapted to the current situation. Her foundation can only be enhanced by seeking inventive ways to solve the two problems that plagues her: Voltek and the machines.

Workplace Survival Plan for Mario Molina

Workplace Environment

> My name is <u>Mario Molina.</u>
> My job title is <u>Aerospace Engineer.</u>
> I work in the <u>Aerospace</u> industry.
> I report to the <u>Project Lead</u> (Sally Beaujolais).

Background:

- *I was recruited from graduate school to join a team of 25 design engineers.*
- *This is my first real job.*
- *I have been on the job a month now and my boss does not recognize me at team meetings.*
- *Plans have been announced to cut 10% of the workforce.*

Guiding Principle: **The more I know about my workplace environment, the better I can prepare myself to deal with its demands.**

Type of Environment: *Benign*

Key Issues:

1. *I have been unable to get the attention of my boss.*
2. *I am unsure as to what I am supposed to be doing or where I fit on the team.*
3. *I am concerned that I am unable to demonstrate my value.*
4. *I am concerned that I will be laid off.*

2. Foundation

Guiding Principle: ***The stronger my foundation, the more resourceful and productive I can be and the more able I am to perform in any environment.***

Actions to Manage **Skills and Knowledge**:
- *Review my skills and knowledge to identify how best to apply them to the mission of the team. (Issue 2, 3, and 4)*

Actions to Manage **Network**:
- *Participate in any luncheon networking sessions and professional association meetings held on-site. (Issue 2, 3, and 4)*

Actions to Manage **Problem Solving Abilities**:
- *Identify an effective problem solving technique to resolve the issue of how I can best contribute to the mission of the team. (Issue 2)*
- *Develop a strategy for demonstrating my value to the organization and communicating this value to Beaujolais. (Issue 1, 3, and 4)*

Actions to Manage **Adaptability**:
- *Look for opportunities to contribute to the mission of the team and quickly adapt to not having a high level of guidance to direct my activities. (Issue 2, 3, and 4)*

3. Image

Guiding Principle: ***All of my decisions and activities should be consistent with what I would expect of my employees if I were a manager in a Supportive Environment.***

Actions to Manage **Values, Ethics, and Integrity**:

- *Read and study the employee handbook. (Issue 2)*
- *Review each of my decisions and actions in terms of compliance with policies and procedures before going forward. (Issue 2)*

Actions to Manage **Attitude**:

- *Maintain a positive attitude. (Issue 3)*

Actions to Manage **Productivity**:

- *Determine the hierarchy of the team. Move down the line from Beaujolais to find someone who can provide guidance on how best to contribute to the team. (Issue 1, 2, and 3)*

Actions to Manage **Communication**:

- *Continue to communicate in a professional manner. (Issue 3)*

Actions to Manage **Self-Management**:

- *Make it my job to figure out how best to contribute to the team. (Issue 2 and 3)*

4. Responsibility

Guiding Principle: ***The more supportive the environment, the more responsibility you should assume; the less supportive the environment, the less responsibility you should assume.***

Actions to Manage **Responsibility**:

- *Find activities for which I am qualified and can complete successfully. (Issue 2 and 3)*

5. Documentation

Guiding Principle: *The less supportive the environment, the more you need to document; the more supportive the environment, the less you need to document.*

> Type of Job Activities: *Project-related activities*

> Actions to Manage **Documentation**:
> - *Document all areas where I have been able to help other team members and email to Beaujolais with the request for guidance regarding where else to focus my efforts. (Issue 1)*

6. Traps and Manipulation Techniques

Guiding Principle: *The less supportive the environment, the more cautious and prepared I need to be to deal with a full range of traps and manipulation techniques.*

> Actions to Recognize and Avoid **Traps and Manipulation Techniques**:
> - *Not a priority at this time.*

7. Update

Guiding Principle: *Keep my Workplace Survival Plan current with the changing demands of my workplace environment.*

> Actions to Update My **Workplace Survival Plan**:
> - *Monitor workplace for changes and update my Workplace Survival Plan as necessary. (Issue 1, 2, 3, and 4)*

- *Perform a complete review of my Workplace Survival Plan and determine the need to make any changes in 1 month. (Issue 1, 2, 3, and 4)*

Summary of Workplace Survival Plan for Mario Molina

Mario Molina works in a Benign Environment. His key problem is that he and his supervisor Sally Beaujolais have hardly met. She does not recognize him at team meetings and he has had little guidance as to what his job is and what he should be doing. Mario's Workplace Survival Plan needs to focus his efforts on finding a way to quickly position himself as a contributing member of the project team.

While Mario may have an untarnished image, he also has one that lacks luster. School has provided Mario with a solid base of knowledge, now he needs to augment that with practical experience in solving real-world problems. He must figure out how he fits in the organization. Finding his place on the team will require that he take responsibility for whatever he decides to do.

Normally in a non-supportive environment, Mario should be cautious about taking on responsibility but given the situation he is in, he must quickly become a contributing member of the team by taking responsibility for doing something the team needs. He must make it his job to be as useful as possible, so that his boss Beaujolais cannot help but notice him.

Of course, there is some risk involved in taking this approach. However, it is clear if he does not quickly define his role as a contributor, he may be one of the first victims to be outsourced. To do nothing at this point will certainly seal his fate.

He will not find direction in this Benign Environment unless he actively seeks it. Since his boss Beaujolais has made no effort to get to know Mario or to provide him any kind of guidance, he should document how he is contributing to the team and share this information with her preferably in person or by email. Failing to establish communications with her will only serve to keep her in the dark with regard to his value to the organization.

Mario also needs to build a network of friends quickly who can help him access needed resources and, most of all, help him adapt to and compensate for the failings of this environment. Continuing to flounder will only serve to sink his fledgling career.

He has yet to take charge of his professional life and is not well positioned for growth that will lead to his success in this position. In a Benign Environment, such as the one in which he finds himself, it is the external forces that will bring him down more so than his boss. Beaujolais is not a direct threat. The external forces that prompted the corporate executives to call for a reduction in force are the threat and without a strong Workplace Survival Plan to help him weather this storm he may not be around to celebrate his one year anniversary.

Workplace Survival Plan for Twila Fletcher

Workplace Environment

My name is <u>Twila Fletcher</u>.
My job title is <u>Steam Press Operator.</u>
I work in the <u>Industrial Laundry</u> industry.
I report to the <u>Manager</u> (Billy Czarnecki).

Background:

- *Czarnecki has been manager for 3 years.*
- *He has been very supportive of my efforts to improve productivity as well as the comfort level of the steam press operators.*
- *I helped the steam press operators become a smoothly functioning team.*

Guiding Principle: ***The more I know about my workplace environment, the better I can prepare myself to deal with its demands.***

Type of Environment: *Supportive*

Key Issues:

1. *Operating a steam press is a hot and demanding job.*
2. *It is sometimes challenging to keep the other press operators motivated.*
3. *I would like to do the best I can in this job.*

Guiding Principle: ***The less supportive the environment, the more cautious and prepared I need to be to deal with a full range of traps and manipulation techniques.***

2. Foundation

Guiding Principle: ***The stronger my foundation, the more resourceful and productive I can be and the more able I am to perform in any environment.***

Actions to Manage **Skills and Knowledge**:
- *Find and read a book on leadership to give me additional ideas on how to be a good leader. (Issue 3)*

Actions to Manage **Network**:
- *Look for opportunities to meet other employees. (Issue 3)*

Actions to Manage **Problem Solving Abilities**:
- *Investigate new problem solving techniques. (Issue 2)*
- *Continue to identify and find solutions to problems. (Issue 2)*

Actions to Manage **Adaptability**:
- *Continue to be flexible to changes in the workplace. (Issue 3)*

4. Image

Guiding Principle: ***All of my decisions and activities should be consistent with what I would expect of my employees if I were a manager in a Supportive Environment.***

Actions to Manage **Values, Ethics, and Integrity**:
- *Continue to comply with policies and procedures. (Issue 3)*

Actions to Manage **Attitude**:
- *Continue to maintain a positive attitude. (Issue 3)*

- *Identify and try 2 stretching exercises that I and the other operators can use at our presses. (Issue 2 and 3)*

Actions to Manage **Productivity**:
- *Continue to look for ways to improve productivity. (Issue 2 and 3)*

Actions to Manage **Communication**:
- *Continue to communicate in a friendly and professional manner. (Issue 2 and 3)*

Actions to Manage **Self-Management**:
> *Continue to identify and find solutions that I can recommend to Czarnecki for problems the other operators and I encounter. (Issue 2)*

2. Responsibility

Guiding Principle: ***The more supportive the environment, the more responsibility I can safely assume; the less supportive the environment, the less responsibility I should assume.***

Actions to Manage **Responsibility**:
- *Continue to accept responsibility for helping make the job as pleasant as possible for all of the steam press operators. (Issue 1 and 2)*

3. Documentation

Guiding Principle: ***The less supportive the environment, the more I need to document; the more supportive the environment, the less I need to document.***

Type of Job Activities: *Cyclical activities*

Actions to Manage **Documentation**:

- *Document how I and the other steam press operators continue to identify and implement changes to make the job easier and safer. Periodically share this information with Czarnecki. (Issue 3)*

6. Traps and Manipulation Techniques

Guiding Principle: ***The less supportive the environment, the more cautious and prepared I need to be to deal with a full range of traps and manipulation techniques.***

Actions to Recognize and Avoid **Traps and Manipulation Techniques**:

- *Not a priority at this time.*

7. Update

Guiding Principle: ***The more current my Workplace Survival Plan; the more prepared I am to adapt to the changing demands of my workplace environment.***

Actions to Update My **Workplace Survival Plan**:

- *Monitor workplace for changes. (Issue 1, 2, and 3)*
- *Perform a complete review of the plan and determine the need to make any changes in 6 months. (Issue 1, 2, and 3)*

Summary of Workplace Survival Plan for Twila Fletcher

Twila Fletcher works in a Supportive Environment. She and her manager Billy Czarnecki work as a team in their combined efforts to achieve the goals of the organization. Czarnecki recognizes Twila's commitment to her job and to her co-workers and respects her contribution. Therefore, Twila's Workplace Survival Plan need not focus on defending her position. She can devote nearly all of her energy to addressing and solving problems related to the productivity of the steam press operators while continuing to pursue her own professional growth.

She need not worry about evaluating how much responsibility she should or should not assume. She knows the boundaries with which Czarnecki is comfortable and has no problem communicating with him to ensure that he is on-board with whatever she decides to tackle.

Likewise, she can document any changes to policies and procedures not as a defensive measure but rather to ensure that she and her co-workers are up to speed with any changes. Other documentation can serve her efforts to increase productivity or keep Czarnecki informed of significant accomplishments.

Twila already presents an admirable image. She is aware of and complies with company policies and procedures. She has a very positive attitude. She monitors her own productivity as well as that of the other press operators and continually seeks ways to improve their performance. She maintains a positive, professional working relationship with Czarnecki and communicates freely with him.

She brings to the job a solid foundation of skills and knowledge. She knows how to operate the equipment safely and has shown a propensity to lead. Even so, this seems an area that she can pursue further, not to correct any apparent deficiency but rather to enhance what she already knows about leadership.

Twila can also look for ways to meet more people in the company and to grow her network, again, not for purposes of remediation but rather to expand her network of contacts. She seems to have a natural ability and desire to solve problems which could only be enhanced by familiarizing herself with additional problem solving techniques.

She has demonstrated an innate ability to adapt to the environment. In fact, she has implemented positive steps to alter the environment so as to produce better working conditions for her and her co-workers.

Twila has taken charge of her professional life and is well positioned for continued growth. Her key problem is not a problem in the traditional sense. She simply needs to keep working on enhancing her self-management skills as that will improve her ability to assume more responsibility and allow her to manage others more effectively than she does already.

As is common with most individuals in a Supportive Environment, her Workplace Survival Plan is less about survival and more about keeping her professional development efforts progressing in the right direction.

Traps and Manipulation Techniques

Deliver a Gift Before Dropping the Bomb

Watch out for a boss who will soften up his prey with a nice gesture, comment or gift before letting loose with a bomb.

It is frequently assumed that bosses in Antagonistic or Contentious Environments are not aware of the environment that they have created. Not true. While this is sometimes the case, just as frequently, they are not only aware of the environment they created but actually are quite proud of it.

One particularly cantankerous boss, with whom I am familiar on both a personal and professional level, has a philosophy of control that includes never being predictable. As a consequence, when he senses that his staff is about at the end of its rope, he is quite capable of doing some very decent things for them. This is always, of course, followed by the bomb intended to knock them off balance once again.

Avoid falling victim to this technique by recognizing that a boss in a non-supportive environment will rarely offer a nice gesture, comment or gift without strings attached. When she does, make certain you have your survival gear tested and ready for service.

Keep 'Em Off Balance

Some bosses will forego the nice gesture, comment or gift and simply implement a strategy to keep you and your co-workers off balance. This makes it just as hard to plan for success as it is to plan an insurrection which is what these bosses fear most.

While a manager in a Supportive Environment encourages and fosters teamwork, some bosses in non-supportive environments see employees working together as a threat. Instinctively, they know they will never be a part of that team. A boss who views employees in this manner sees a high turnover rate as working to their advantage because it inhibits the formation of teams.

Early on in my career, I was exposed to a boss who would state often and loudly his theory that, "Firing someone every so often keeps the rest of the troops on their toes." Cross him on the wrong day and you left the office with your walking papers in hand. As a result, people were always coming and going. Relationship building among co-workers was virtually impossible. No one was there long enough to develop the sense of trust and camaraderie that fosters true teamwork. The environment was similar to that seen in war movies when the seasoned vets refuse to learn the name of the new guy because it makes it easier to cope when he gets killed.

The best you can do under these circumstances is to take a risk and introduce yourself to the new guy. Even though he may be gone tomorrow, he may turn out to be the ally you need today.

Divide and Conquer

Some bosses who feel threatened by your skills or willingness to excel will try to separate you from your co-workers or coerce you to segregate yourself by pitting you against your peers. She may try to embarrass you in front of co-workers by hinting that you may not have been straightforward with them. She may also try to elicit some comment or action from you that would be viewed by your co-workers as condescending toward them. She may try the silent treatment in an effort to isolate you from information vital to your ability to perform. She will do anything to drive a wedge between you and your co-workers.

Don't fall for this ploy. It is simply a technique to weaken your voice in the organization by separating you from a source of support. Alone, you are less capable, more susceptible to manipulation, and much more vulnerable. Always be on the watch for efforts by bosses in non-supportive environments to destroy a sense of teamwork.

Your willingness to continue to collaborate with co-workers can help you avoid being isolated by your boss. Plus, your co-workers offer you a source of feedback, in regard to your performance, that may counteract whatever your boss might suggest in an effort to shake your self-confidence.

Create Internal Competition

The internal competition tactic is closely related to divide and conquer in that its purpose is to pit employees against each other.

The movie *Glengarry Glenross* offers a raw vignette of internal competition. In one memorable scene, sobering to those of us who have been there and seen it firsthand, the "Big Gun" comes down from corporate to explain the plan: a monthly contest for the sales staff.

"The winner gets a new car," the Big Gun explains. "Second place takes home a set of steak knives."

A long dramatic pause lets his words soak in.

"Third place? What does third place get?" one of the salesmen asks.

"There is no third place. Everyone finishing below second will be terminated!"

The Big Gun slaps his portfolio closed and walks out.

Several years ago, a good number of major corporations fell in love with this system, only they skipped the contest. As part of the performance review, they implemented the "Rank and Yank" system. All employees ranked above a certain percentile received a raise and bonus. Those who ranked below that percentile were terminated.

Such systems work well to cull the dead wood in the first couple years. After that, they foster development of a cut-throat environment. Teamwork is non-existent while setting co-workers up for failure is viewed by some as the best means to ensure their own survival. Workers quickly tire of this high stress environment.

Unfortunately, if your boss, or the entire company, opts for such a pernicious system, there is little you can do but continue to perform at your best without sinking to the practice of tarnishing someone else's efforts to make yourself look shiny.

Fake Urgency

It is two o'clock in the afternoon and the boss rushes into your office. She slaps a folder down on your desk.

"Drop what you're doing. This report has to be done by C.O.B., today!" she exclaims.

So, you drop what you are doing and spend the rest of the day working on the report knowing you will have to spend several extra hours of your time finishing up your regular work. On your way out, you drop by the boss's office to deliver the report only to find that she has already gone for the day. So, you leave it with her secretary.

"Here's the urgent report the boss wanted done today."

The secretary responds with a puzzled look. "Oh, you didn't need to rush. This report isn't due till next month."

You suddenly realize that your boss fabricated an arbitrary sense of urgency to get you to interrupt your regular work.

310

Most professionals have a pretty good grasp of the priorities necessary to reach organizational goals. If your boss asks you to focus your attention elsewhere, you might ask, *when do you need to submit this report?* She may not have a satisfactory answer for that question. If, however, she creates a sense of urgency, either real or arbitrary, around her request then you may get caught up in that urgency. You might not think to involve her in reprioritizing your work by asking how this fits with your other priorities. Even if you maintain the presence of mind to ask, she might let it suffice with *I need it done right away.* The result is she has successfully enticed you to alter your focus to suit her agenda which may have nothing to do with organizational priorities and everything to do with disrupting your work.

The catch phrase you will hear the boss use is, *drop what you are doing; I need you to do this right away!* Old timers recognize the boss's accelerated gate as she approaches with another "urgent" assignment and quickly slip out for a break or bury themselves in their work just in time to keep the footsteps from stopping at their desks. It is the new guy, eager to help, who is ripe for the picking. It is not till the next day that he sees the fruits of his labor gathering dust on the boss's desk that he begins to realize what the old timers know; that report is not due until next month. It was simply time for the boss to remind the troops who runs the ship.

Control Access to Resources

This is one of the "Old Darlings" of bosses in non-supportive environments. Give the team a task to do, then tie their hands by withholding access to the support needed to guarantee a successful outcome. It could mean not giving them a budget, not giving them security clearances, not giving them data or not giving them the time needed to successfully complete the task. It is not that the budget, security clearances, data or time are not available. It is that the boss does not want a successful outcome from the team.

Bosses who employ this technique, generally, oppose employees working in teams as an invasion of their territory. Too much team work or sharing of information, especially with employees from other departments, could expose the boss's vulnerabilities. As a consequence, employees are expected to produce project plans without input from accounting on the budget or help from production planners as to the schedule. Then, when your project experiences cost over-runs or cannot be completed on time, you can guess whose fault it will be.

A common variation on this technique is for the boss to limit access to him. Employees willing to trumpet the boss's line will get the open door policy and red carpet treatment. Employees, who do not *toe the line*, even though they may be dealing with mission-critical information, will have no access whatsoever.

The best time to ensure access to the resources you need is before you assume responsibility for a particular outcome. That is the time to make it clear to your boss what resources you need to ensure successful results. Be as specific as you can what resources you will need to access. If such access is not guaranteed then you must reflect responsibility for the results back to the boss.

You Go First

Most of us remember when we were kids at the Saturday matinee movie, the boy next door who offered to pay us back a quarter if we would loan him a nickel for some candy. Admittedly, candy was not as expensive back then as it is now. Ever see that quarter? Of course, not! You never saw your nickel again, either. I did but it was not until I reminded the kid, more than thirty years later at a high school reunion, that he owed me a nickel.

In a non-supportive environment, your boss might pull the same trick by making a promise she has no intention of keeping. It might go something like this.

"Hey, I know you are already overloaded and I wouldn't ask if there were anybody else with your attention to detail," your boss tells you. "Maybe we could work something out to let you take some time off next week."

You finish the work for your boss. Next week, you drop by her office to arrange for the time off.

"I'm sorry," she laments. "Jerry already had time scheduled for his daughter's wedding. I can't afford to have two people gone at the same time."

The bargain could be for time off, a bonus, a raise, a promotion, a larger office, your choice of assignments or any number of perks, small or large.

What can you do? Undo the work you've already done? Not likely.

When she firsts asks for your help, you say, "Let's go put those days off on the schedule, then I can get to work on this assignment for you."

That is not to say that she might remove you from the schedule with a swift stroke of her eraser as soon as you return to your desk but, at least, she knows you saw her put it on the schedule. You might be able to reopen the negotiations once you find out she has reneged on the deal.

If the boss is reluctant to put your days off on the schedule then you know up front that you are being set up and you could respond, "I'm really busy. If you actually need this done right now, then I won't have that project you wanted for your meeting with the execs next week finished on time."

With a boss in a non-supportive environment, what bargaining power you have is on the front end of the deal.

Call a Meeting

Any boss who has been a boss long enough knows that if you want to delay or postpone action on an issue surfaced by one of the employees, call a meeting. Better yet, call a meeting and filibuster. As everyone in the meeting reaches a point of dazed stupor, you can slip out with reasonable certainty that no one will ever bring up the subject again.

The next time the boss calls a meeting "to discuss how to resolve an important issue," more people may take the advice of noted consultant T. Frank Hardesty as reported by colleague Jack Pachuta in an article entitled "We've Got To Stop Meeting Like This!" Hardesty advises, "Be sick when meetings are called. Never attend them." You may not be able to pull this off but you certainly can be aware that some meetings which are called to discuss what to do about an important issue are intended to make certain that whatever is done, if anything, will in no way serve to resolve the issue.

Study It to Death

When there is a problem that has visibility beyond the organization and something obviously needs to be done but the boss does not want to act on the problem, a common stalling technique is to study the problem to death. A committee will be established, a chairperson selected, decision-making processes defined, and a report produced. All this takes time, sometimes weeks, months or even years. During the time the committee studies the problem, the boss can smugly respond to inquiries about why nothing has been done to correct the problem with a simple comment. *We're waiting on the committee report before we act.* Meanwhile, the problem still exists.

When the committee finally releases its report, you may not be any closer to a solution then before. Additionally, the boss might reject the report outright and instruct the group to go back and review their findings until they can get it "right." This gives the boss an additional window of time before taking action.

Your best defense against such a tactic is to lobby for a less formal process that focuses on resolving the problem, not studying it. Once the committee has been empanelled, the boss has her stall technique in place. Participating on a committee established for the purpose of delaying action can be an extremely frustrating experience.

Unless you are up for that challenge, it may be better to disconnect from the process and figure out how to minimize the impact of the problem on your work.

Now Is Not the Right Time

Often after an incident happens that attracts attention to the fact that the current situation is not working, there will be a loud call for change. To forestall any immediate action, a boss may announce that this is not the right time. And, while will everyone may agree that the immediate priority should be to serve the needs of those negatively impacted by the situation and to return things to normal, the bosses statement is really intended to prevent any action, now or later, that would create change.

Wait and See

Another technique to delay action is to wait and see. Take some minor action to placate critics, then wait and see what happens. The boss knows that these actions will not produce significant results but the wait-and-see technique offers her the luxury of stalling any moves proposed by the opposition.

In an article for *The Financial Times*, Jeremy Grant writes, "Public pension funds and unions have urged advisory votes as a way of allowing shareholders a way of expressing their views on whether CEO pay is commensurate with performance." The opposition wants to allow shareholders to vote on CEO pay packages.

Grant continues, "Critics of moves to install new mechanisms for controlling executive pay argue that shareholders should wait and see how executive pay disclosure rules issued last year by the Securities and Exchange Commission work out." While the measures implemented by the Securities and Exchange Commission bring increased visibility to the issue of CEO compensation, they still prevent the issue from being voted on by shareholders at annual meetings. The longer critics of these measures can block significant action through a *wait-and-see* strategy, the longer they can preserve the status quo which is their real agenda.

Opponents of reform will implement small incremental changes, each followed by a request for all interested parties to *wait and see*, with the hope that detractors will tire of the game before real reform must be implemented. Here, patience is not a virtue. The longer you wait, the longer you will be denied the satisfaction of seeing the change you desire.

Run Out the Clock

Another delaying technique is to run out the clock with meaningless action. Opponents are kept busy thinking progress is being made until some deadline is reached that prevents further action on the subject.

Kyle Sampson, chief of staff to embattled United States Attorney General Alberto Gonzales, described this technique in an email to an unnamed White House aide, "Ask the senators to give Tim [Griffin] a chance ... then we can tell them we'll look for other candidates, ask them for recommendations, evaluate the recommendations, interview their candidates, and otherwise run out the clock. All this should be done in 'good faith,' of course." Tim Griffin was the Karl Rove protégé appointed to replace the U.S. Attorney that had been recently asked to resign. Sampson's email was made public during Congressional hearings on the untimely removal of federal prosecutors by the Attorney General and quoted by Richard L. Fricker in an article for *Consortium News*.

The deadline Sampson sought was the end of the Bush presidency. An incoming administration following the 2008 election would certainly appoint its own slate of federal prosecutors and Griffin would be out. The aim seemed to be to keep Griffin in the post until then.

You can avoid falling victim to this technique by carefully evaluating the actions your boss suggests taking when you know a deadline that will prevent further action looms ahead. When a boss that has never empowered you to do anything of consequence suddenly suggests that you *take the lead in evaluating new methods for producing widgets that might be implemented in next year's budget*, watch out, especially when you've been pushing for new procedures all year and he has resisted your every effort.

Process Perfect

Bosses have a wide range of techniques at their disposal to stall forward motion. When all else fails they can be sticklers for a detailed process. Any other time, the process be damned, full speed ahead. But when a detailed, convoluted, ritualistic process can effectively delay something your boss has no desire to implement, the process is everything. This is one of the only times that every "t" must be crossed and every "i" dotted, checked, and double checked. You may actually see an individual who has no concept of perfection argue that everything has to be *perfect*. She will use your eagerness to bring the project to fruition against you by arguing that "you want it to be done right, don't you?"

Your best defense to combat this stalling tactic is to line up all your ducks at the start with their little running shoes laced up and ready to go. You had better be able to cruise your way through the bureaucratic mire before your boss cans the project because of the slightest little misstep.

Ask Everyone Who Doesn't Know

Some years ago a machine operator shared a personal story with me that left me aghast. This fellow was a manufacturing engineer who operated a machine in a plant that did very high precision work. On the morning he returned from a weeklong vacation, he found a high-level group meeting on the shop floor around his machine. Everyone from the plant manager to the engineering manager and on down was there.

The subject being discussed was whether to replace the machine in question. This was a serious matter as the replacement would have had to come from Germany at a cost of over a million dollars. The operator listened intently as the managers discussed the fact that for the past week everything run on this machine was out of tolerance. The managers went around the room asking everyone to comment on the matter except the machine operator.

Finally, as the discussion ran out of gas, the operator took a matchbook out of his pocket, folded it a certain way, and shimmed it under the machine. He fired up the machine and turned out a new product. He handed it to the engineering manager who checked and found it perfectly within tolerance. The operator, and only the operator, knew this machine well enough to know that the machine was not the problem; the unleveled floor on which machine rested was the problem. The operator saved the company one million dollars. He could have just as easily kept quiet.

Some bosses in non-supportive environments may try to isolate you by avoiding your input to important decisions and, instead, asking everyone else. If they do, they run the risk that you are the one who really has the solution to their problem.

Create Confusion

For some bosses, creating confusion comes naturally. Others use it as a well-practiced technique. Have you ever heard a boss lament that she never has time for anything else because she is always too busy, *putting out fires?* That is the clue. This tactic provides her a way to look busy as she scurries around trying to solve the problems she helped cause. It works to her advantage by keeping employees confused and provides her a handy excuse when upper management wonders why the unit is not performing up to par. "If I didn't have to fix all these problems, maybe I'd have time to get more work done!"

The sad fact is that many bosses in non-supportive environments start "fires" to create a smoke screen of activity intended to disguise their incompetence. Bosses have a variety of tools at their disposal to create such confusion in the workplace: undocumented procedures, unclear instructions, obstructed access to resources, and disrupted schedules are just a few. Were the smoke screen not there, the boss's inability to lead would become immediately apparent. Just watch how much more smoothly the organization runs when the boss takes a vacation.

Just because your boss runs around with her hair on fire, does not mean that your curly locks must also be ablaze. Knee jerk reactions and a blind flurry of activity are not in your best interests as a professional. Your Workplace Survival Plan will provide you a solid operational foundation to help you remain productive within whatever tumultuous environment your boss may have created.

Fight It Till You Take Credit

Sometimes, no matter how hard the boss fights their efforts at constructive change employees do actually make real progress. After ignoring employee suggestions, appointing a task force to study employee proposals, kicking their ideas upstairs, kicking employees down stairs, and pulling out every other stall tactic known to bosses, an employee idea is so representative of common sense that it cannot be resisted any longer. At that point, there is only one thing left the boss can do, write a position paper and take ownership of the idea. Of course, she must give the idea a new name, change the words around, and package it a little differently but that is easy. If the program fails, the boss can always dust off the original employee proposal and lay blame at their feet.

I was once a member of a team chartered to move our department from paper-based workstation manuals to on-line electronic documents. During our first few weeks, every idea the team generated was shot down by the boss. We finally got smart and shifted our focus from coming up with ideas on how to implement the electronic manuals to figuring out how to make the boss believe that these were her ideas. From that point on, the project moved forward quite nicely.

Omit Key Information

Ever start work on an assignment that appeared simple and routine, only to find out that significant pieces of the picture your boss gave you were missing? This is a set up for failure, so the boss can leave you high and dry or step in at the last minute to save the day. Either way, you end up looking incompetent, ridiculous or both.

You benefit yourself when you research your assignments up front. Bring any questions you have to your boss in writing. Email works well to document this process. If your boss hedges on the answers to your questions, at least, you have a clue that there is more to the story than you have been given. Do your best to obtain the whole picture, before you accept responsibility for the results. Your boss almost always wants full responsibility to reside in your lap. You should accept responsibility only for the outcomes over which you have control.

Distort Reality

Whether you believe that perception is reality, a boss with the desire to do so can certainly skew your perception of reality. There are literally hundreds of variations on this theme. One of the most common is, "Look, I'm on your side. If it were up to me, we'd walk this project right on through to completion but the corporate office says, 'No can do!'"

As a result, your perception is that corporate nixed the project. The reality may very well be that corporate neither knows about the project nor cares about it. Your boss nixed the project and blamed it on corporate. He could say that rules which he instituted when casting about for new ways to irritate you were handed down from high especially if they prove to be overly unpopular. Are you going to march into the corporate offices and demand an explanation? Not likely, and your boss knows it.

A particularly devastating version of this technique is the creation of fictitious enemies. As long as you have little or no contact with the so-called enemy, "those guys" can be blamed for almost anything. *They don't care whether things actually work as long as they get a paycheck.* Anyone who questions this reality is severely ostracized, first by the boss then by other employees who buy into the myth.

If the boss can place a wall between you and the source of valid information on a particular issue, then she can control you. Reality becomes whatever she tells you it is. Without going into detail, the Nazis under Hitler mastered this technique. Unfortunately, unscrupulous bosses in government and business still use it as a means to convince people to endorse policies that they would not otherwise support.

Sometimes an entire corporation will try to sway public opinion in their favor rather than change the way they do business. Robert Greenwald, director of the documentary *Wal-Mart: The High Cost of Low Prices*, is quoted on the Workplace Fairness web site as saying, "If only Wal-Mart would spend as much money trying to improve the working conditions for employees ... as they do on self-congratulatory P.R. advisers."

Distortion of reality means creating a different *reality*, one that can be used to manipulate your thoughts and decisions. In the classic film *Wizard of Oz*, Dorothy and her companions were instructed not to look behind the curtain. The desire was for them to see only the illusion of the all-powerful wizard. When Toto directed Dorothy's attention to the man behind the curtain who was actually running the show, the truth was revealed.

APPENDIX C: TRAPS AND MANIPULATION TECHNIQUES

Truth is the strongest counterbalance to this technique. A strong network of contacts can help you break down the wall of ignorance by providing you access to other points of view which may be more aligned with true reality.

Offer False Choices

Either you work late to finish the project or you have to come in this weekend. Have you ever been coerced into having a choice between two bad options? Other choices such as assigning another person to the project, fixing a flawed process or delaying the delivery date are not mentioned. As long as the boss can limit the options, he can guide your selection. He probably does not care if you work late or work on the weekend as long as you are an exempt employee and it does not impact his budget.

You can have that raise but then I'll have to lay off two people. Select the option you prefer and something bad will happen. *You don't want that, do you?* As soon as you say, *of course, not,* the boss has you right where he wants you. He can shut down your request for a raise knowing you do not want the responsibility of causing two people to be laid off.

You could reject your bosses contrived options out of hand. *I can't work late tonight or this weekend. It's my wife's birthday. I'm taking her to Emeril's in New Orleans for dinner. Our flight leaves right after work.* Try that and you may win the battle but be assured the boss will find a way to make you pay later for your obstinacy.

You could engage your boss in a game of *What About This Option* or *What About That Option*? That would be a futile exercise because your boss can easily shoot down as many options as you can toss out unless you have foolproof logic supporting them. If the boss does relent and accept your option, you had better be able to make it work no matter what because you have inherently accepted full responsibility for the outcome while your boss can co-opt any support or actively work to undermine your success.

Intimidate

Intimidation is a common technique employed by a boss. In fact, when we first used the word *boss*, you will recall that we highlighted corrupt politicians Boss Tweed and Boss Tom as examples.

Webster's New Universal Unabridged Dictionary indicates that **intimidate** means "to make timid; fill with fear." In other words, it implies a threat of some kind. While Boss Tweed and Boss Tom did not earn their reputations by making idle threats, laws have changed and prosecutors are much more inclined to enforce the law than when corruption saturated the political culture. While some bosses certainly do back up intimidation by breaking bones and bodies, the practice is no longer as widely accepted in the workplace as it might have been a hundred years ago. Even so, it still exists. Blackmail with its threat of public embarrassment through the release of incriminating information is a specialized form of intimidation.

Bosses only use intimidation if they think it will work. Whether it does work depends to some degree upon you. In the case of blackmail, the best remedy is to avoid placing yourself in the position of being blackmailed. A rational assessment of whether the boss can actually carry out the threat that underlies his effort to intimidate you may lead to the conclusion that the threat is little more than bluster and you can let it roll off your back like rain off a duck's feathers. Even if the boss could carry out the threat, would he? Remember mutually assured destruction? It works both ways and your boss knows it.

Micromanage

Micromanagement can be a useful management technique, a bad management technique or a delay tactic. When used with employees who have not developed the skills to manage their own affairs, micromanagement may be necessary to keep them productively headed in the right direction. As the employee develops the necessary skills to keep things on track himself, a supportive manager will back off.

Micromanagement becomes a bad management technique when the boss uses it with employees who are already able to manage their time and work effectively. A boss who constantly looks over the shoulder of a veteran employee, constantly redlines her work, and continually requires her to obtain the boss's approval before taking a step is micromanaging inappropriately. Some bosses will do this purposefully in an effort to impede progress or frustrate the employee to the point of making a mistake. On the other side of the coin, a boss who micromanages your work inherently retains responsibility for the eventual outcome of the work.

The bottom line is that your job is to operate as effectively as possible given the circumstances of the environment. If you are in a non-supportive environment then you may very well have a boss who micromanages inappropriately.

One approach that sometimes dissuades a boss from micromanaging is to pre-empt her overbearing oversight by bringing every minute decision you make to her for review throughout your day. She may become so tired of making all your decisions for you that she actually instructs you to make the decisions yourself.

My Poop Doesn't Stink

Bosses who are so convinced that they were chosen for their positions as bosses by a celestial tap on the shoulder may have a tendency to act condescendingly toward subordinates. This can be a specialized form of intimidation or an effort to cover up inadequacies. When the boss conveys the impression that his and only his opinion is correct no matter what, who is going to argue with him?

It does not take long to see that such a blindly stubborn boss quickly buries the organization in one disastrous decision after another. An effectively executed Workplace Survival Plan may help you sequester yourself from the fallout.

Creative Bureaucracy

A certain amount of bureaucracy may be necessary in any organized effort that involves more than a handful of people. Certain policies and procedures can serve a useful purpose in communicating common expectations throughout the group.

Bosses who desire to retard your progress, for whatever unsavory reason, may take bureaucracy to the extreme where even hot syrup flows at a snail's pace. Any efforts you undertake at streamlining the process may be effectively rebutted by the boss as long as it is perceived that her creative bureaucracy applies equally across the board. Convoluted policies and procedures that weigh inequitably on your work may offer you room to question. It would behoove you to select the most effective time and place to voice your questions, and to have a chorus of friendly voices to join you.

Call to a False Crusade

The boss who crusades for clear policies and procedures may have the most convoluted policies and procedures in the department. The boss who rails at company meetings for better communications may be the last person in the company to communicate information to his employees.

This is a well-known technique for distracting attention from a weakness. It may be effective with those who do not work with the boss that uses this technique but certainly those who know him know all too well that his crusade is little more than a charade.

Some bosses take the crusade a step further and start pointing fingers. The boss may target for blame the employee who is working to clarify the policies and procedures or the one who has ideas for new, more effective channels of communication. The point is the boss does not want these things. Obscure policies and procedures and miscommunication provide cover for a boss lacking in management skills.

Know that any effort you take to remedy the problems a misguided boss crusades against may place you squarely in his crosshairs. A thorough assessment of the environment combined with a good measure of caution is advised. As long as you have adequately addressed through your Workplace Survival Plan any direct impacts on your performance that the subject of your bosses crusade may have, then you may not need to take any further action and it may not be wise to do so.

Kill the Messenger

This technique is so commonly known that if it were not still so commonly employed, we would not need to mention it. Unfortunately, it is widely used by bosses in non-supportive environments.

Recently I had the opportunity to observe it once again when a healthcare company retained a new manager for one of their clinical labs. She was suitably qualified having earned a graduate degree and several certifications. Shortly after she started, she discovered that her immediate superior was a high school graduate with no certifications but some long-term political relationships with powerful influences within the organization.

Upon taking over the clinical lab, the new manager noted a number of long standing practices that were not in compliance with existing state regulations. She moved quickly to correct these practices and reported them, as required, to the institution's compliance officer. On her fiftieth day on the job, she was notified by her boss that she did not fit the culture of the organization and her services would no longer be required. *May another messenger rest in peace!*

This lady had little choice but to report the infractions she noticed at the clinic since to not report them would have made her potentially liable for non-compliance with state regulations and could have posed a safety issue for clients. If you find yourself in similar circumstances, we recommend the same course of action. On other occasions where the implications of the message are not life threatening or illegal, you may want to evaluate the risk of being the one to deliver the message. Should you decide that it is important to deliver the message and that it is your responsibility to do so, then you would be wise to phrase it in the most benevolent manner and select the most palatable time and place for delivery.

Persuasion with Penalties

"Persuasion involves both incentives and penalties," Henry Kissinger once remarked in response to a question about international affairs explaining that "there is an element of implied coercion." This reported by Niall Ferguson of *The Los Angeles Times*.

Coercion sounds so polite. But have no misgivings, the implications of coercion can be quite severe. John Perkins, author of *Confessions of an Economic Hit Man*, explains how this game is played out on the international stage in an interview with Amy Goodman, host of the daily radio and television news program *Democracy Now!*

"We use many techniques, but probably the most common is that we'll go to a country that has resources that our corporations covet, like oil, and we'll arrange a huge loan to that country from an organization like the World Bank or one of its sisters, but almost all of the money goes to the U.S. corporations, not to the country itself, corporations like Bechtel and Halliburton, General Motors, General Electric, these types of organizations, and they build huge infrastructure projects in that country: power plants, highways, ports, industrial parks, things that serve the very rich and seldom even reach the poor," Perkins explains. "In fact, the poor suffer, because the loans have to be repaid, and they're huge loans, and the repayment of them means that the poor won't get education, health, and other social services, and the country is left holding a huge debt, by intention."

Perkins, recruited to this role by the National Security Agency, first offers an incentive to invite concessions. "We go back, we economic hit men, to this country and say, 'Look, you owe us a lot of money. You can't repay your debts, so give us a pound of flesh. Sell our oil companies your oil real cheap or vote with us at the next U.N. vote or send troops in support of ours to some place in the world such as Iraq.'"

If that does not work, he offers the foreign leader an incentive backed by a penalty. "We have several hundred million dollars in this pocket if you play the game our way. If you decide not to, over in this pocket, I've got a gun with a bullet with your name on it, in case you decide to keep your campaign promises and throw us out.'"

Perkins does not actually carry a gun in his pocket. The figurative gun, Perkins mentions, is embodied by the fact that the interests that recruited him "will send in the people to try to overthrow him, as, in fact, we recently did with the President of Ecuador [Jaime Roldós Aguilera], or if we don't overthrow him, we'll assassinate him. And these people all know the history. They know that this has happened many, many, many times in the past."

In the workplace, your boss may imply: *Do what I ask and I will give you a window office; don't do it and you will never see another raise, ever!* In one pocket the incentive. In the other pocket the penalty. Both working to achieve the result the boss desires. Of course, the level of sophistication and finesse with which the message is delivered depends on how experienced your boss is with this technique.

Ready, Set, Retaliate

Some bosses in non-supportive environments are not at all adverse to the idea of retaliation. They may withhold promotions, make it difficult to schedule time off or vacations, assign the worst projects or no projects, give bad references to the next prospective employer, start a whispering campaign to damage your reputation or worse.

Attorney Rita Risser, founder of Fair Measures which provides legal training for managers, writes in *Fair Measures eNews*, "A woman property manager was sexually harassed and ultimately raped by her manager. She told him she was going to report him to the company, but before she could make her report, he called her supervisor and the Regional Human Resource Director and convinced the two men that he and she had an affair that had gone wrong, and that she was making the complaint because of her poor performance. The three men began documenting the alleged performance problems." The woman escalated the issue and was fired the next day. She took the company to court and eventually won with "the Court of Appeals excoriated the company for having a policy that prohibited retaliation, but no procedures for reporting retaliation." Still, she had to seek relief outside the company.

An old friend of mine, himself an attorney, has prodded me to refer clients to him who may have grounds for some actionable offense perpetrated against them by their boss. Rarely have I done so, on the simple premise that the risk of retaliation is usually too great.

Whistleblowers are particularly vulnerable to retaliation. Often, they have embarrassed the boss in public and the boss wants a pound of flesh or at the very least to discredit the whistleblower. While whistleblower protections do exist, they have been substantially weakened or ignored in recent years. National Public Radio reporter Ari Shapiro writes about U.S. Special Counsel Scott J. Bloch, who oversaw protection for federal whistleblowers under the second Bush Administration, "One of Bloch's first official actions was to refuse to investigate any claims of discrimination based on sexual orientation. When the news of his refusal was leaked to the press, career employees in his office say, Bloch blamed them for the leak. He retaliated, the employees said, by creating a new field office in Detroit and forcing them either to accept assignments there or resign."

Why set yourself up for disappointment? Be realistic about the type of environment in which you work. Employees in non-supportive environments often face a constant barrage of retaliatory tactics from the boss. Be ready for them. Do not expect a boss in such an environment to play fair. Act accordingly and defend yourself as best you can. If you know your boss is prone to use retaliation then be particularly careful which battles you chose to fight. You may win the battle, today, and fall victim to a retaliatory ambush, tomorrow. Therefore, any efforts to lessen conflict between you and your boss may minimize any reasons he could use to justify retaliating against you.

Oops!

From time to time, even a boss skilled in the art of manipulation will get sloppy and get caught red handed. All bosses know that the ultimate defense is the mea culpa.

"Sorry; it was just an oversight," she will claim. "I meant to sit down with you and explain that the new employee, my husband's cousin, would be taking on most of your job responsibilities and you would be left with only the parts you hate. We really need to work on your ability to communicate. I think HR has a class on communication skills. Why don't you register for the next session?"

If you genuinely believe this was an oversight and, furthermore, that the boss will not blame you for it, all we can do is offer you our condolences.

Quick Reference Charts

The following charts serve as a quick reference tools in support of developing and implementing your Workplace Survival Plan.

- **Performance Chart** – recommended approaches for responding to the key challenges in each of the four workplace environments.

- **Guiding Principles Chart** – guiding principles for successful self-management.

Performance Chart

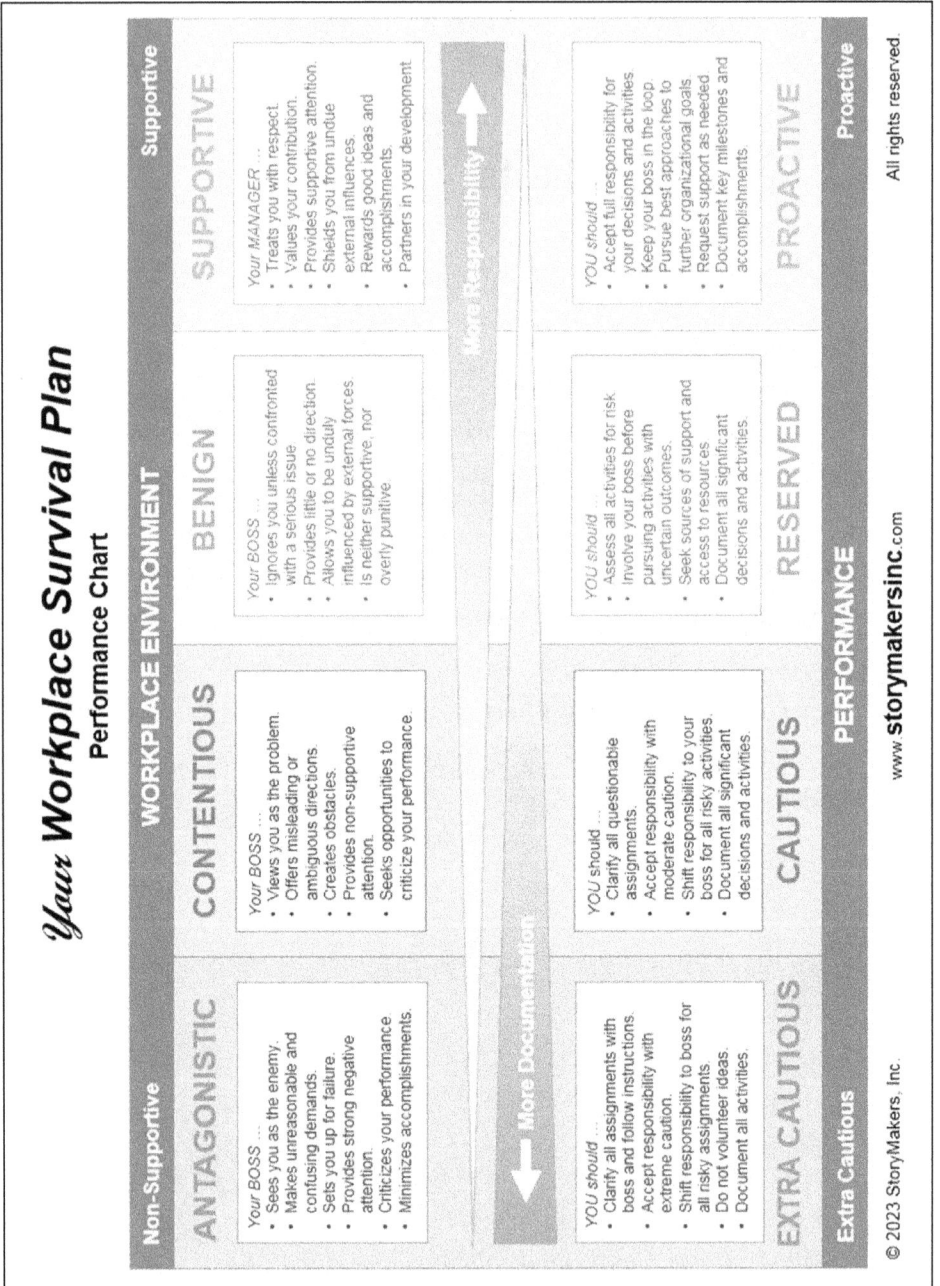

Your Workplace Survival Plan
Performance Chart

WORKPLACE ENVIRONMENT

Non-Supportive → Supportive

ANTAGONISTIC

Your BOSS ...
- Sees you as the enemy.
- Makes unreasonable and confusing demands.
- Sets you up for failure.
- Provides strong negative attention.
- Criticizes your performance.
- Minimizes accomplishments.

CONTENTIOUS

Your BOSS ...
- Views you as the problem.
- Offers misleading or ambiguous directions.
- Creates obstacles.
- Provides non-supportive attention.
- Seeks opportunities to criticize your performance.

BENIGN

Your BOSS ...
- Ignores you unless confronted with a serious issue
- Provides little or no direction.
- Allows you to be unduly influenced by external forces.
- Is neither supportive, nor overly punitive.

SUPPORTIVE

Your MANAGER ...
- Treats you with respect.
- Values your contribution.
- Provides supportive attention.
- Shields you from undue external influences.
- Rewards good ideas and accomplishments.
- Partners in your development.

↑ More Responsibility
↓ More Documentation

EXTRA CAUTIOUS

YOU should ...
- Clarify all assignments with boss and follow instructions.
- Accept responsibility with extreme caution.
- Shift responsibility to boss for all risky assignments.
- Do not volunteer ideas.
- Document all activities.

CAUTIOUS

YOU should ...
- Clarify all questionable assignments.
- Accept responsibility with moderate caution.
- Shift responsibility to your boss for all risky activities.
- Document all significant decisions and activities.

RESERVED

YOU should ...
- Assess all activities for risk.
- Involve your boss before pursuing activities with uncertain outcomes.
- Seek sources of support and access to resources.
- Document all significant decisions and activities.

PROACTIVE

YOU should ...
- Accept full responsibility for your decisions and activities.
- Keep your boss in the loop.
- Pursue best approaches to further organizational goals.
- Request support as needed.
- Document key milestones and accomplishments.

PERFORMANCE

Extra Cautious → Proactive

Guiding Principles Chart

Your **Workplace Survival Plan**
Guiding Principals

ENVIRONMENT — The more I know about my workplace environment, the better I can prepare myself to deal with its demands.

FOUNDATION — The stronger my foundation, the more resourceful and productive I can be and the more able I am to perform in any environment.

IMAGE — All of my decisions and activities should be consistent with what I would expect of my employees if I were a manager in a Supportive Environment

RESPONSIBILITY — The more supportive the environment, the more responsibility I can safely assume, the less supportive the environment, the less responsibility I should assume.

DOCUMENTATION — The less supportive the environment, the more I need to document; the more supportive the environment, the less I need to document.

TRAPS — The less supportive the environment, the more cautious and prepared I need to be to deal with a full range of traps and control techniques.

PLAN — The more current My Workplace Survival Plan, the more prepared I am to adapt to the changing demands of my workplace environment.

About the Author

Fred Stawitz

Fred Stawitz—an award-winning author and international speaker—researches, writes, speaks, and consults on creating high-performing organizations with workplace environments that inspire high-levels of employee engagement; avoid layering disruption over dysfunction; and adapt to emergent technologies while shaping a corporate culture that promotes safe, productive, and sustainably profitable operations. He provides science-based, logical, easily usable, and effective guidance

A Leadership 500 LEAD Award recipient and popular international speaker, he has been featured on CNN Headline News, a PBS affiliate special program, TV news/talk shows, and nationally syndicated radio programs. He has chaired and spoken at major HR, safety, and educational conferences around the world and was quoted in a Special Congressional Quarterly Report.

As an experienced program development manager, he has more than fifteen years of expertise in successfully designing, implementing, and managing programs that maximize safety and productivity while ensuring regulatory compliance. He was recruited to develop the first technical training program for the American Space Shuttle Program (United Space Alliance) flight design engineers in the wake of the Challenger explosion and created desktop simulations to train the astronauts. He developed, implemented, and managed a technical training program for a Royal Dutch Shell energy venture with Bechtel (InterGen) that maximized safety and productivity while ensuring regulatory compliance. Additionally, he established the in-house ability to create computer-based training, produced live interactive video streams from remote locations, and created a portable video production studio for the largest natural gas pipeline company in America (El Paso Natural Gas Pipeline).

He is a recipient of the National Education Association A+ for Excellence in Education Award, NASA and the National Science Teachers Association National Honors Teaching Award, and judge of Diversity Value Index Benchmark & Awards Program. He coauthored the award-winning book *Homeboy's Soul: Pride, Terror & Street Justice in America*, a harrowing true account of life and death in a violent street gang and exposé on the destruction gangs perpetrate upon communities. He penned and produced the award-winning stage play *Soldier Mom* and is currently the President of Storymakers, Inc., a creative arts enterprise and publisher guiding writers through the process of creating marketable books with global distribution.

Stawitz graduated from Washburn University with dual degrees in mathematics and computer science backed by a minor in foreign languages and served as an assistant professor of mathematics after graduation.

He achieved the following accomplishments while fully experiencing life and developing a better understanding the world and its inhabitants:

- Created the first training CD to blowup in space.
- Piloted the USS Topeka (LA Class fast attack submarine) in the Atlantic Ocean off Cape Canaveral, Florida.
- Attended a briefing at The White House with spouse hosted by the G.W. Bush Administration.
- Originated the "Reach for the Stars" aerospace education program that impacted nearly one million K-12 students throughout the U.S.
- Navigated inland passage from Vancouver, British Columbia, Canada, to Petersburg, Alaska on a 34-foot fishing boat with two dogs, seven pups, and four nautical novices.

- Took a friend with spina bifida and his wheel chair on a 3500-mile, cross-country motorcycle adventure to the Pacific Ocean.
- Hitchhiked more than 17,000 miles across America experiencing lots of weird and wonderful people and places.
- Certified as a NAUI Sport Diver.